KOREAN YEARBOOK OF INTERNATIONAL LAW

KOREAN YEARBOOK OF INTERNATIONAL LAW

Edited by LEE Jang-Hie

Volume 3
2015

ILCHOKAK

THE KOREAN BRANCH OF THE INTERNATIONAL LAW ASSOCIATION

KOREAN YEARBOOK OF INTERNATIONAL LAW

Copyright © The Korean Branch of the International Law Association 2016
Published by ILCHOKAK

ILCHOKAK Publishing Co., Ltd.
39, Gyeonghuigung-gil, Jongno-gu, Seoul, 03176, Korea
Tel 82-2-733-5430
Fax 82-2-738-5857

First published 2016
Printed in Seoul, Korea
ISBN 978-89-337-0721-0 93360

For subscriptions to this Yearbook, please contact the sole distributor, ILCHOKAK Publishing Co., Ltd.
39, Gyeonghuigung-gil, Jongno-gu, Seoul, 03176, Korea
Tel 82-2-733-5430 Fax 82-2-738-5857 E-mail: ilchokak@hanmail.net

KOREA KF
FOUNDATION
한국국제교류재단

The Korea Foundation has provided financial assistance
for the undertaking of this publication project.

A CIP catalogue record of the National Library of Korea for this book
is available at the homepage of CIP(http://seoji.nl.go.kr)
and Korean Library Information System Network(http://www.nl.go.kr/kolisnet).
(CIP2016026713)

MEMBERS OF EXECUTIVE COUNCIL

DOH See-Hwan

LEE Chang-Youl

LEE Chang-Wee

LEE Gyooho

LEE Keun-Gwan

LEE Hwan-Gyu

LEE Kil-Won

LEE Seryon

PARK Young-Kil

SUNG Jae-Ho

YANG Hee-Cheol

YOO Joon-Koo

SUPPORTING MEMBERS

Northeast Asian History Foundation

Korea Maritime Institute

Korea Institute of Ocean Science & Technology

BAE, KIM & LEE, LLC

SHIN & KIM

YULCHON, LLC

Law Firm J & C

KH Research Center for International Security and Trade

SKKU BK21+ Research Group
on Educational Reform for Cultivating Law Professional
in ICT Global Legal Standards

Views or opinions expressed herein are to be attributed to their authors and
not to this publication, its editors nor to the Korean Branch of the International Law Association.

CONTENTS

RECENT DEVELOPMENTS

CONTEMPORARY PRACTICE AND JUDICIAL DECISIONS

EDITOR'S NOTE

As KYIL Vol. 3 is being published, the year 2016 is a critical moment where peace on the Korean Peninsula is being threatened by North Korea's nuclear weapons testing. On March 2, 2016, the Security Council of the UN issued its harshest sanctions against North Korea for its fourth nuclear weapons test conducted on January 6th and for a long range rocket launched on February 7th. Following the UN Security Council sanctions, South Korea decided to shut down the Gaesung Industrial Complex in terms of national sanctions and cut off all channels of dialogue between South Korea and North Korea. The military tensions on the Korean Peninsula are at its highest point since the Korean War in the 1950s. On the other hand, national public opinion is very confusing due to the General Elections held on April 13th and its political disputes.

There was also the 12.28 Verbal Agreement between Korea and Japan over Japan's sexual enslavement of Korean women as comfort women for its military. The 12.28 Agreement failed to admit to the state-led war crimes and refused to recognize the 1 billion yen ($8.5 million) fund as legal compensation. Japan does not accept legal responsibility for its conduct during the war. To make matters worse, after the conservative regime of Prime Minister Shinzo Abe came back into power in 2012, the Japanese government went back on its past promises with international society and denied legal responsibility of the Pacific War and sophisticated the "Colonial Modernization" theory. In February 2014, Japan's Chief Cabinet Secretary Yoshihida Suga said in the Japanese Parliament that the Japanese government was considering re-examining the testimony given by 16 former sex slaves (a.k.a Korean comfort women), which was used to draw up the "Kono Statement."

We should protect the territorial sovereignty and historical justice of the Korean nation and keep independent diplomacy from foreign nations. Thus, international law should play a key role in supporting the legality and logic of territorial sovereignty, historical justice, and maintaining independent diplomacy of Korea. This implies the importance of research and study in the area of international law in resolving the current legal issues surrounding the Korean Peninsula.

In considering the conflicts within the Korean Peninsula, and to increase understanding of the issues about international laws regarding Korea, the editing policy for KYIL Vol. 3 prioritized "International Law and Korea & Its State Practice" from the beginning of KYIL Vol. 1.

On January 12, 2016, Professor Sung Jae-Ho, Sungkyunkwan University, was elected as the new President of the Korean Branch of International Law (ILA). All members of the Editorial Board of the Korean Branch of ILA wholeheartedly welcome the new president's inauguration and extend our sincere appreciation for his contribution and sacrifice in publishing Volume 3 of KYIL.

KYIL Volume 3 would like to extend our deepest appreciation to Professor Lee Seryon for editing Volume 3, KYIL in a very detailed and sincere manner. She devoted her time in reviewing the last manuscripts.

Lastly, from the publication of KYIL Volume 1 to Volume 2, warm gratitude is extended to Professor Choi Seung-Hwan, the former president of the Korean Branch of ILA, Kim Si-Yeon who worked tirelessly on editing despite their busy schedules, and the authors who sent us their precious research. Also, I would like to commend the hard work, effort, and sacrifice put into editing KYIL Volume 3 by Mr. Seo Jin-Woong, the Secretary of the Korean Branch of the ILA.

Lee Jang-Hie
Editor-in-Chief
Professor Emeritus, Hankuk University of Foreign Studies

ARTICLES

Legal Principles and Policy Proposals for the Creation of the East Asian Economic Community (EAEC): In Search of Peace and Prosperity Based on Human Dignity*

CHOI Seung-Hwan
Professor
Kyung Hee University Law School, Seoul, Korea

Abstract

As of 1 February 2016, there is no economic integration covering most of the East Asian countries, with the exception of the ASEAN Economic Community (AEC), which was officially established on 31 December 2015. This article proposes effective legal principles, policy objectives and proposals for the establishment of the East Asian Economic Community (EAEC), which can contribute to the maintenance of sustainable peace and prosperity in East Asia. The author advocates that economic integration based on four policy objectives (high living standards through the expansion of free trade and investment, sustainable development and prosperity, effective and fair resolution of disputes, harmonization of economic and social integration) and six basic legal principles (human dignity ensuring social and economic human rights, comprehensive liberalization of trade and

* This article is a modified version of my paper ("Policy Proposals for the Creation of the East Asian Economic Community (EAEC): In Search of Peace and Prosperity Based on Human Dignity") which was presented at the 4th International Conference on 'Contemporary Legal Problems: The New Haven School of Thought from a Comparative Perspective' held at the City University of Hong Kong, 5-6 Ocotober 2012. I appreciate thoughtful comments made by distinguished participants, especially Professor Michael Reisman and Dean Guiguo Wang. Any errors remain, of course, entirely mine. The author may be contacted at: tomichoi@khu.ac.kr.

investment, progressive liberalization of trade and investment, non-discrimination with substantial fairness, transparency, public participation) may contribute to the maintenance of sustainable peace and prosperity by increasing economic interdependence and solidarity among the countries in East Asia.

In consideration of the goal of maintaining sustainable peace and prosperity in East Asia, this article will also make some policy proposals for the creation of EAEC, based on a policy-oriented approach developed by the New Haven School. It should be noted that a high level of economic development is not in itself a goal of economic integration, but merely a means for ensuring human dignity. Human dignity may, therefore, serve as an indispensable requirement for successful regional economic integration, considering the different political systems, religions and cultures in East Asia. Since economic integration cannot guarantee peace and prosperity without taking serious account of human dignity for the people of member States, the key goal of EAEC should be sustainable prosperity that ensures human dignity.

Key Words

East Asian Economic Community (EAEC), regional economic community, economic integration, free trade agreements (FTAs), regional trade agreements (RTAs), ASEAN Economic Community (AEC), Regional Comprehensive Economic Partnership (RCEP), human dignity, New Haven School

1. INTRODUCTION

There is deep concern over the possibility that recent developments in the political relationship between the United States (US) and the People's Republic of China (China) might cause a second cold war. Moreover, recent territorial controversies surrounding certain islands (Kuril Islands,[1] Dokdo Islands,[2] Senkaku Islands,[3] Paracel Islands,[4] Spratly Islands,[5] etc.) in East Asia[6] might also harm political relationships among the East Asian countries,[7] and prohibit the closer economic and political cooperation necessary for sustainable development and prosperity in East Asia. Is it possible to maintain sustainable peace and prosperity in East Asia without resolving these pending conflicts, such as the territorial disputes among the East Asian countries?

With a view to maintaining sustainable peace and prosperity in East Asia, this article will make some policy proposals for the creation of the East Asian Economic Community (EAEC), based on a policy-oriented approach developed by the "New Haven School."[8] Since any and every person is entitled to participate in the processes of decision-making that affect their lives, the New Haven School, among others, "undertakes to improve the performance of the decision processes themselves and enhance their capacity to achieve outcomes more consonant with human dignity."[9] This article will argue that the expansion of a Free Trade Area is not enough to ensure sustainable prosperity, and that economic integration cannot guarantee peace and prosperity without taking serious account of human dignity for the people of its Member States.

In this context, Section 2 of this article will articulate the necessity of creating the EAEC, while Section 3 will propose the vision and policy objectives of the EAEC for successful economic integration in East Asia and Section 4 will suggest basic legal principles to govern the EAEC. Section 5 will review preconditions for the creation of the EAEC and make policy proposals to remove obstacles to the creation of EAEC, and Section 6 will draw conclusions.

2. THE NECESSITY OF THE EAEC

Since the early 1990s, regional trade agreements (RTAs) have become increasingly prevalent. As of 1 February 2016, some 625 notifications of RTAs (counting goods, services and accessions separately) had been received by the General Agreement on Tariffs and Trade (GATT) and the World Trade Organization (WTO). Of these, 267 (counting goods, services and accessions together) were in force.[10] What all RTAs in the WTO have in common is that they are reciprocal free trade agreements between two or more member States.

Regional economic integration in East Asia has been carried out mainly through the conclusion of free trade agreements (FTAs). Recently China, Japan, the Republic of Korea (Korea), the Association of South-East Asian Nations (ASEAN), India, Pakistan, Australia, New Zealand, and Singapore have concluded their own FTAs,[11] most of which are in force, while some FTAs initiated by East Asian countries are under negotiation. Since May 2012, a Trilateral FTA has been under negotiation among China, Japan and Korea. The ten member States of ASEAN officially established the ASEAN Economic Community (AEC) on 31 December 2015[12] in order to achieve a single market and production base, a highly competitive economic region, equitable economic development and a complete integration into the global economy.[13] The ASEAN is currently negotiating the Regional Comprehensive Economic Partnership (RCEP) with its six FTA partners (China, Korea, Japan, India, Australia and New Zealand).[14] As of 1 February 2016, there is, however, no FTA or economic integration covering most of the East Asian countries.

Recently, a regional economic community for East Asia has been proposed and discussed by some scholars. It should be noted that, unlike an FTA, a regional economic community, in accordance with the agreement establishing the economic community, is delegated comprehensive authority on sensitive sectors of all members' public policy, including on the environment, culture, labor and employment, social security and policy, etc. The necessity for the creation of the EAEC, as a regional economic community rather than a Free Trade Area, can be summarized as follows:

Firstly, members of the EAEC can increase economic development and efficiency by realizing economies of scale and expanding trade and investment in a larger common market than before. Secondly, the expansion of economic cooperation through economic integration can intensify solidarity among members in East Asia by increasing inter-dependency. Thirdly, an increase in economic interdependency and community solidarity can provide an incentive for members to co-operate with each other to address pending problems related to terror, environmental pollution, climate change, energy, financial crisis, ocean development, etc., and to peacefully solve long-standing disputes such as territorial and maritime conflicts. Fourthly, members may be able to enhance their negotiating power in international negotiations, including the DDA round. It should be noted that Luxembourg, as a member of the European Union (EU), was able to have strong negotiation leverage comparable to that of US at the Uruguay Round. Finally, economic cooperation and interdependency may also facilitate international cooperation in other fields, such as security, the environment and energy. European countries were able to successfully maintain sustainable peace and prosperity by concluding the European Economic Community (EEC). In view of the fact that most armed conflicts and wars are the result of economic disputes, it is expected that coordination of economic and monetary policies among members will prevent a trade war, and contribute to the maintenance of international peace and security.

3. VISION AND POLICY OBJECTIVES OF EAEC

3-1. THE VISION OF EAEC

In general, economic integration including FTAs pursues the expansion of free trade and investment among their members in order to maximize mutual economic benefits. The expansion of free trade and investment by removing obstacles to trade and investment is, however, not in itself a goal, but a tool for sustainable prosperity among members.

Sustainable prosperity cannot be maintained without sustainable peace. The incident of September 11, 2001 in US shows us that "prosperity without peace" cannot guarantee sustainable prosperity. "Peace without prosperity" is not sustainable. "Sustainable prosperity" should be, therefore, a key goal of economic integration.

However, "sustainable prosperity" should not be in itself a goal of economic integration, but a means for ensuring human dignity. As such, economic integration should serve not only to maintain sustainable prosperity but also to ensure and maximize human dignity. "A public order of human dignity," according to the New Haven School, "is defined as one which approximates the optimum access by all human beings to all things they cherish: power, wealth, enlightenment, skill, well-being, affection, respect, and rectitude."[15] Since economic integration that ignores human dignity cannot be a goal for EAEC, the vision of EAEC should be "sustainable prosperity that ensures human dignity." The "vision" here means an ultimate goal or final purpose to be shared and pursued together among the members.[16]

The EAEC should, therefore, pursue economic integration ensuring human dignity, and not undermine human dignity for the sake of economic benefits. "Sustainable prosperity that ensures human dignity," as a vision and guiding principle, is critical in interpreting the policy objectives and basic principles of EAEC.[17]

3-2. POLICY OBJECTIVES FOR THE CREATION OF EAEC

3-2-1. HIGH LIVING STANDARDS THROUGH THE EXPANSION OF FREE TRADE AND INVESTMENT

The first policy objective of EAEC is to accomplish high living standards through the expansion of free trade and investment. The central aims of the Treaty Establishing the EEC were "by establishing a common market and progressively approximating the economic policies of Member States, to promote throughout the community a harmonious development of economic activities, a continuous and balanced expansion, an increase in stability, an accelerated raising of the standard of living and closer relations between the States belonging to it."[18] The preamble of the Free Trade Agreement between Korea and US (KOR-US FTA) articulates as policy objectives "to raise living standards, promote economic growth and stability, create new employment opportunities, and improve the general welfare in their territories by liberalizing and expanding trade and investment between their territories."

With a view to maximizing the synergistic effects of economic integration, the scope of trade liberalization and market access should be comprehensive, covering trade in goods and services, agriculture, intellectual property, finance and investment, e-commerce, competition policy, labor, environment, energy, etc.

3-2-2. Sustainable Development and Prosperity

The objective of sustainable development and prosperity involves a comprehensive and integrated approach to economic, social and political processes, which aims for the sustainable use of natural resources and the protection of the environment and which seeks to realize the right of all human beings to an adequate living standard, with due regard to the needs and interests of future generations. In the climate change regime, the obligation to develop in a sustainable way is framed not just as an obligation but also as a right.[19] The Preamble to the WTO Agreement includes direct references to the objective of sustainable development and to the need to protect and preserve the environment. The 2001 Doha Ministerial Declaration, which launched the Doha Development Agenda (DDA) negotiations, also reaffirmed this mandate (see Paragraph 6), and it is an objective running through all subjects in current DDA negotiations. A number of international judicial decisions by the International Court of Justice (ICJ), International Tribunal for the Law of the Sea (ITLOS), the WTO Panel and Appellate Body, and the European Court of Justice, have explicitly referred to sustainable development as a legal principle.[20]

With a view to facilitating sustainable development for members participating in EAEC, the progressive and gradual liberalization of trade and investment should be allowed, taking properly into account their respective needs and concerns at different levels of economic development. As the radical expansion of trade liberalization and investment might destroy the fundamentals of the national economy, policy should be flexible in order to activate domestic industry and assist the structural adjustment for sustainable development. For example, all domestic support taken to maintain a certain degree of domestic production of basic food security crops should be exempted from any form of domestic support reduction commitments, and not subject to countervailing duties.[21]

3-2-3. EFFECTIVE AND FAIR RESOLUTION OF DISPUTES

The objective of the effective and fair resolution of disputes is to peacefully settle trade disputes through a rule-oriented dispute settlement mechanism. The effective and fair resolution of disputes might not only mitigate international tension but also contribute to the maintenance of international peace and security by providing a cooling-off period for the peaceful settlement of disputes. Economic integration cannot be carried out successfully and consistently unless disputes and controversies among members are solved fairly and effectively. In view of the fact that most armed conflicts and wars have been caused by economic disputes, the peaceful, effective and fair resolution of disputes might be indispensable for the successful operation of the EAEC. For this purpose, the EAEC may establish an East Asian Court of Justice, like the European Court of Justice.

Since the establishment of the European Court of Justice in 1952, through its case-law, the Court has identified an obligation of administrations and national courts to apply EU law in full within their sphere of competence and to protect the rights conferred on citizens by that law (direct application and effect of EU law), and not to apply any conflicting national provision, whether prior or subsequent to the EU provision (primacy of EU law over national law).[22] It should be noted that the European Court of Justice, based on a rule-oriented dispute settlement mechanism, has contributed to the successful development of economic and social integration through the peaceful, effective and fair resolution of disputes among EU Member States.

3-2-4. HARMONIZATION OF ECONOMIC AND SOCIAL INTEGRATION

In general, the primary goal of FTAs is to maximize economic benefits by expanding trade liberalization and investment. Too much emphasis on economic interests might, however, cause conflicts among domestic groups and undermine the social solidarity or social integration necessary for sustainable development by neglecting the public interests of domestic industries or groups damaged by economic integration. Economic integration that fails to take into account the public interests of groups damaged and disadvantaged by trade liberalization can fail if it damages people's livelihoods and undermines social integration.

In this context, economic integration that adequately takes social integration into account is indispensable for sustainable economic integration. The harmonization of economic and social integration might function as a policy objective to induce a consensus on the need for the creation of the EAEC, ensure the successful operation of the EAEC and maintain sustainable prosperity by protecting damaged industries and disadvantaged groups.

4. BASIC LEGAL PRINCIPLES OF THE EAEC

With a view to successfully establishing the EAEC, it is necessary for participating members to agree on the basic legal principles governing the Agreement Establishing the EAEC for the purpose of effective negotiation. This Section will propose six basic legal principles of the Agreement, which can effectively accomplish the vision and policy proposals made in Section 3.

4-1. The Principle of Human Dignity Ensuring Social and Economic Human Rights

In this article, "sustainable prosperity ensuring human dignity" was proposed as a primary goal of EAEC, because economic integration that infringes on human dignity cannot ensure sustainable prosperity for EAEC. To ensure social and economic human rights, the principle of human dignity should be the most important of the basic legal principles of the Agreement that establishes the EAEC, simply because basic human rights cannot be sacrificed for the economic benefits received from economic integration. The ultimate goal of legal control as conceived by Lasswell and McDougal is "a world community in which ⋯⋯ the protection of human dignity is regarded as a paramount objective of social policy."[23]

Therefore, the policy objectives of economic integration should be modified, should basic human rights or human dignity be infringed upon by the expansion of free trade and investment. Without proper social and economic human rights, people cannot adequately enjoy human dignity and the eight values (power, wealth, enlightenment, skill, well-being, affection, respect, and rectitude) upheld by the New Haven School.[24] In this context, the value of human dignity should prevail over that of free trade, and the principle of human dignity ensuring social and economic human rights should be a key principle to govern the Agreement Establishing the EAEC.[25]

4-2. The Principle of Comprehensive Liberalization of Trade and Investment

With a view to attaining a high level of living standards and maximizing the economic benefits of economic integration, the scope of trade liberalization and market access should be comprehensive, covering the trade in goods and service, agriculture, intellectual property, finance and investment, e-commerce, competition policy, labor, environment, energy, etc. Limited liberalization of special sectors cannot maximize the synergistic effects of economic integration through the effective allocation of resources.

In order to effectively enforce common trade policies for the comprehensive liberalization of trade and investment, they should be incorporated into national regulations and applied uniformly by the member States. To achieve the uniform application of common trade policies, different trade rules of members should be harmonized. This "harmonization"[26] of different trade rules may expand free trade and investment by removing the trade-distorting effects caused by different trade rules, facilitate fair trade by ensuring free competition, realize economies of scale by reducing production and information costs, enhance transparency by prohibiting trade regulations that protect domestic industries, and contribute to the development of trade rules for free and fair trade.

4-3. THE PRINCIPLE OF PROGRESSIVE LIBERALIZATION OF TRADE AND INVESTMENT

The principle of progressive liberalization of trade and investment allows members to open their markets gradually, taking into account their different levels of economic development. When the expansion of trade liberalization is too rapid, it might cause fatal and irreversible effects on domestic industry and the economic development of some members. The principle of progressive liberalization of trade and investment may play a role in mitigating adverse effects on the national economy and providing appropriate periods for structural adjustment. The principle of progressive liberalization of trade and investment might induce the participation of developing countries in the creation of EAEC.

For example, the General Agreement on Trade in Services (GATS) is based on the principle that trade in services may be liberalized progressively in accordance with each member's different level of economic development. The GATS adopts an 'opt-in' or positive approach, whereby members are bound to open their markets only with respect to specific commitments by sector or subsector. This positive approach may be also adopted in the EAEC, as a principle of progressive liberalization.

If members agree to the establishment of EAEC in ten years, members may remove tariff and non-tariff barriers among members, step by step, for up to ten years, taking into consideration the different level of each member's economic development. An agreement among members should be made to set up common external tariffs to be enforced after 10 years against non-members of the EAEC.

4-4. THE PRINCIPLE OF NON-DISCRIMINATION WITH SUBSTANTIAL FAIRNESS

The principle of non-discrimination, as expressed in Most Favoured Nation (MFN) treatment and national treatment principles, is one of the most important legal principles under GATT and WTO Agreement. The MFN and national treatment principles are the core of most other international economic agreements, such as bilateral investment treaties, intellectual property agreements, etc. However, the uniform application of a 'level playing-field' based on the principle of non-discrimination might result in unfair and inequitable results and cause a problem of unfairness and injustice, because it fails to adequately consider the economic situations of developing countries.

With a view to rectifying this problem, the principle of non-discrimination embodying substantial fairness should be adopted as a legal principle justifying trade regulations among members of the EAEC.[27] From the viewpoint of developing countries, the formal and mechanical application of the principle of non-discrimination without considering different levels of economic development may result in unfair or unjust results in terms of equity. Since trade regulations based on substantial fairness take into account the different levels of economic development, the principle of non-discrimination embodying substantial fairness might contribute to harmonious and sustainable development among the members of the EAEC. In this context, special and differential (S&D) treatment may be properly applied for developing countries. On 14 November 2001, members of the WTO adopted a Ministerial Declaration agreeing that "special and differential treatment for developing countries shall be an integral part of all elements of the negotiations, and shall be embodied in the schedules of concessions and commitments and as appropriate in the rules and disciplines to be negotiated, so as to be operationally effective and to enable developing countries to effectively take account of their development needs, including food security and rural development."[28]

4-5. THE PRINCIPLE OF TRANSPARENCY

The principle of transparency allows the public or stakeholders to get accurate information on the trade rules in which they have an interest. So long as trade rules affect the daily lives of people, they have a right to know. Transparency here means the degree to which trade policies and practices, and the process by which they are established, are open and predictable. For the purpose of transparency, trade rules must be as "clear and public" as possible.

Many WTO Agreements require governments to disclose their policies and practices publicly within the country or by notifying the WTO. For example, the transparency obligation in GATS operates on three levels: Firstly, WTO Members have to publish all relevant measures of general application "which pertain to or affect the operation of this Agreement." Secondly, WTO Members must periodically inform the GATS Council of "any new, or any changes to existing, laws, regulations or administrative guidelines which significantly affect trade in services covered by its specific commitments under this Agreement." Finally, WTO

Members must respond promptly to all requests by any other Member for specific information on any of its measures of general application.

4-6. THE PRINCIPLE OF PUBLIC PARTICIPATION

Since economic integration has a great impact not only on the national economy, public policy and social sectors, but also on people's daily lives, the public is entitled to participate directly or indirectly in the process of concluding and implementing trade agreements, in a democratic way. Indeed, "[e]quipped with an appropriate jurisdictional frame, each and every person can now participate, whether directly or through the mediation of groups, in the process of decision that affects their lives."[29] Public participation in trade policy and trade rule-making might contribute to ensuring the legitimacy of government policy by enhancing the credibility of government policy with the public.

Under the principle of public participation, private parties should be given a right to make a claim to the East Asian Court of Justice, and to make a petition before the EAEC Council or the East Asia Free Trade Commission. The participation of the public in the process of dispute settlement may also contribute to the effective resolution of trade disputes and the rule of law by facilitating the implementation of trade rules.

The Aarhus Convention on Access to Information, Public Participation in Decision-making and Access to Justice in Environmental Matters (Aarhus Convention) in 1988 established a milestone in linking environmental protection with sustainable development and human rights in international law.[30] The principle of public participation has been applied by WTO Panel/Appellate Body, the North American Free Trade Agreement (NAFTA) Tribunals and the International Centre for Settlement of Investment Disputes (ICSID) Tribunals.

In the *US-Shrimp*, the WTO Appellate Body affirmed Members' right to attach *amicus curiae* briefs to their own submissions.[31] As far as separate *amicus curiae* briefs are concerned, the Appellate Body considered that the panel had the discretion either to accept or to reject the briefs submitted to it, whether requested by a panel or not.[32]

The Appellate Body in the *EC-Sardines* reaffirmed its authority to receive an *amicus curiae* brief from a private individual or an organization. The Appellate Body further stressed that acceptance of any *amicus curiae* brief is a matter of discretion to be decided on a case-by-case basis, and that it could exercise its discretion to reject an *amicus curiae* brief if accepting it would interfere with the "fair, prompt and effective resolution of trade disputes."[33]

Amicus curiae briefs have been filed and admitted in the NAFTA and ICSID arbitral tribunals as well. Neither the United Nations Commission on International Trade Law (UNCITRAL) Arbitration Rules nor Chapter 11 of the NAFTA contain express provision on non-disputing party participation. The NAFTA arbitral tribunal in the *Methanex* decided that it had the power to accept *amicus* briefs, and allowed the petitioners to submit *amicus* briefs. In this case, the Tribunal accepted the Petitioners' argument that there was an increased urgency warranting amicus participation in light of the award dated 30th August 2000 in *Metaclad Corporation v. United Mexican States* and an alleged failure to consider environmental and sustainable development goals in that NAFTA arbitration.[34] It further emphasized that the case concerned a matter of public interest "not merely because one of the Disputing Parties is a State" but also because its subject matter concerns the public interest.[35]

5. PRECONDITIONS AND POLICY PROPOSALS FOR THE CREATION OF THE EAEC

5-1. PRECONDITIONS FOR THE CREATION OF THE EAEC

Since the countries in East Asia lack community solidarity because of their different political systems, religions and cultures, there might be more obstacles to the creation of a regional economic community.[36] The obstacles on the road leading to the EAEC can be summarized as follows:

Firstly, territorial disputes among East Asian countries have generated inter-country tensions in East Asia. Deep-rooted distortions of historical events (such as Japanese occupation by force, forced labor, sex slavery of women, etc.) by Japan also make it hard to establish the EAEC for sustainable peace and prosperity in East Asia. Recently, a territorial dispute between Japan and China regarding ownership of the Senkaku Islands (Diaoyudao in Chinese) led to armed demonstrations by both sides and a boycott of Japanese products in China. The increase of tensions and hostilities between countries and people in East Asia have caused distrust and antagonism among relevant countries, presenting a major obstacle to the formation of community solidarity and the creation of a regional economic community, like EEC.

Secondly, energy disputes among East Asian countries also make it hard for East Asian countries to establish a regional economic community like the EAEC. Territorial and maritime disputes may stem from conflicting claims on energy. Judging from the importance of energy and natural resources for economic development, the peaceful administration of energy in East Asia might contribute to the maintenance not only of sustainable economic development but also of sustainable peace and security. It should be noted that the peaceful development and administration of atomic energy under the Treaty Establishing the European Atomic Energy Community (Euratom) was considered to be of great importance, in terms of sustainable peace and security in Europe.[37]

Finally, the maintenance of sustainable peace and security are also indispensable for the creation of the EAEC, because it can provide members with an external environment facilitating international economic transactions and investment. In Europe, the maintenance of a regional collective security regime by the North Atlantic Treaty Organization (NATO) played a decisive role in the establishment of the European Economic Community, European Community and European Union.

As of February 2016, in East Asia, there is no regional collective security regime similar to NATO.

5-2. Policy Proposals for the Creation of the EAEC

With a view to establishing the EAEC, community solidarity among the East Asian countries must first be fostered. With different and diverse cultural backgrounds based on different religions and social customs, it might be difficult for the East Asian countries to establish the EAEC.[38] However, as we can see by the example of US, community solidarity is not limited to areas with a single culture and religion. So long as there is an open and mature cultural sense that respects diverse and different cultures, multi-cultural community solidarity may be developed. The need for international cooperation to solve global problems including climate change, terror and energy has already called upon countries to recognize and establish a multi-cultural community. In order to strengthen community solidarity, social and cultural solidarity should be improved through education and cultural exchange among the people in East Asia. Not unilateral introduction, but open and two-sided cultural exchange may be an important means to strengthen community solidarity, by broadening the mutual understanding of different cultures and facilitating mutual respect for diverse cultures.

For the success of the EAEC, it is indispensable for the East Asian countries to restore and maintain political credibility, especially among China, Japan and Korea. The recent increase of tension and conflicts between China and Japan over the Senkaku Islands has cast a cloud over the prospect of the development of a regional economic community in East Asia. It is true that this political hostility and historical discord have engendered a pessimistic view regarding the creation of the EAEC.

However, as was pointed out by Frederich Holderlin, the German poet, as a crisis approaches, a solution to overcome the crisis may also be discovered. In order to construct and maintain sustainable peace and prosperity in East Asia, an area with a long history of discord, various pending conflicts can be used as a chance for political leaders to resolve them peacefully, and eliminate the disagreements and antagonism.

If we do not first empty the dish full of discord and antagonism, peace and prosperity cannot be poured in. Hands that are filled with distrust and hegemony will not be able to catch peace and prosperity. The author proposes a 100-year freeze on all of the almost-intractable disputes on territories and maritime boundaries to seek a mutually satisfactory solution, and then share, among the East Asian countries, the benefits resulting from the exploitation of resources, after concluding agreements of joint development for peaceful use.[39] Political leaders in East Asia may meet together to discuss the project of creating the EAEC, design road maps leading to the EAEC, and develop working plans for the successful creation of the EAEC.

6. CONCLUSION

Contrary to the general understanding, sustainable prosperity or a high level of economic development is not in itself a goal of economic integration, but merely a means for ensuring human dignity. Economic integration should serve not only to maintain sustainable prosperity but also to maximize human dignity. Since economic integration that neglects human dignity cannot be a goal for a regional economic community, the key goal of the EAEC or FTAs should be "sustainable prosperity that ensures human dignity." The maintenance of peace and security is also indispensable for continued sustainable prosperity, because sustainable prosperity cannot be maintained without peace and security.

The EAEC should not impair or undermine but must improve and enhance the rights of private parties, according to the principle of human dignity embodying social and economic human rights. Thus, the EAEC, with the key goal of sustainable prosperity that ensures human dignity, may contribute to the maintenance of sustainable peace and prosperity by facilitating public participation.

With a view to achieving the policy goal of sustainable prosperity that ensures human dignity, the value of human dignity should prevail over free trade, and the principle of human dignity ensuring social and economic human rights should be a key principle to govern the Agreement Establishing the EAEC. The increased economic interdependency that is developed through the EAEC can also contribute to the peaceful resolution of other pending conflicts, including territorial disputes, energy and environment disputes among the East Asian countries, and facilitate sustainable peace and prosperity in East Asia.

Notes

1 The Kuril Islands (composed of 56 islands) are known as Northern Territories in Japan, and Kurilskiye Ostrova in Russia. All of the islands are occupied effectively by Russia, but Japan claims the two southernmost large islands (Iturup and Kunashir) as part of its territory, as well as Shikotan and the Habomai islets.

2 The Dokdo Islands (occupied effectively by the Republic of Korea) are known as Dakeshima in Japan.

3 The Senkaku Islands (occupied effectively by Japan) are known as Diaoyudao in China.

4 The Paracel Islands (occupied effectively by China), also called Xishaqundao in Chinese, and Hoàng Sa Islands (Quần đảo Hoàng Sa) in Vietnamese. Taiwan and Vietnam also claim sovereignty of these islands.

5 The Spratly Islands, also called Nanshaqundao in Chinese. China, Taiwan, Philippines, Vietnam, Malasysia and Brunei claim sovereignty of these islands.

6 On 16 September, 2012, US Defense Secretary Leon Panetta warned that a worsening territorial spat between Japan and China could draw East Asia into a war. http://pentagon-chief-calls-calm-japan-china-spat [Visited on 17 September 2012]

7 China and the Philippines have both claimed conflicting jurisdictions over the South China Sea, including Scarborough, known as Huangyan Islands in China. Historically China has maintained effective control, but in the 1990s the Philippines began to claim authority. When Philippine ships occupied positions near Scarborough, the conflict has become a crisis. Most of territorial and maritime disputes in East Asia resulted from imperial powers' decolonization process following World War II, during which they neglected clear demarcation for their past colonies.

8 The New Haven School developed by Professors Myres S. McDougal and Harold D. Lasswell defines "law as a process of decision that is both authoritative and controlling." W. Michael Reisman, *The New Haven School: A Brief Introduction*, 32 Yale Journal of International Law 575 (2007), p. 576.

9 *Ibid.*, p. 577. "Starting from the premise that law should serve human beings, the New Haven School anchors its policy-oriented search for a world public order of human dignity." *Ibid.*, p. 380.

10 Information on RTAs notified to the WTO is available in the RTA Database. Available at: http://rtais.wto.org/UI/PublicMaintainRTAHome.aspx. [Last visited on 22 February 2016]

11 China concluded the Closer Economic Partnership Arrangement (CEPA) with Hong Kong and Macau, in June, 2003 and in October, 2003, respectively. China

also concluded the CEFA with Taiwan in June, 2010.

12 As to the roadmap to the completion of AEC by 2025, see ASEAN Secretariat, *ASEAN Economic Community Blue Print 2025*, 2015. [Last visited on 22 February 2016]

13 ASEAN Secretariat, *ASEAN Economic Community 2015: Progress and Achievements*, 2015. [Last visited on 22 February 2016] Although ASEAN has very little in common with the EU, the ultimate goal of maintaining peace and prosperity in the region is similar. P. Demaret, J.F. Bellis and G.G. Jimenez, *Regionalism and Multilateralism after the Uruguay Round* (European Interuniversity Press, 1997), p. 200.

14 On 4 February 2016, The Trans-Pacific Partnership (TPP) Agreement was signed by 12 Asia-pacific countries (Australia, Brunei Darussalam, Canada, Chile, Japan, Malaysia, Mexico, New Zealand, Peru, Singapore, US, and Vietnam) at Auckland, New Zealand.

15 W. Michael Reisman (note 8 above), p. 576.

16 The meaning of "vision" in dictionary is "the ability to make plans for the future with a clear purpose." *Dictionary of American English* (Longman, 1997), p. 891.

17 As to the concept of human dignity, see Seung Hwan Choi, *'Human Dignity' as Indispensable Requirement for sustainable Regional Economic Integration*, 6 Journal of East Asia and International Law 81 (Spring 2013), pp. 84-87.

18 Article 2. The Treaty Establishing the European Economic Community (Rome Treaty) was signed on 25 March 1957, and entered into force on 1 January 1958.

19 The United Nations Framework Convention on Climate Change: A Commentary, art. 3(4).

20 C.J. Joerges and E-U. Petersmann (eds.), *Constitutionalism, Multilevel Trade Governance and International Economic Law* (Hart Publishing, 2011), p. 27. Also see, International Law on Sustainable Development, Final Report, adopted at Sophia Conference (2012), ILA, pp. 8-13.

21 Seung Hwan Choi, *Food Security and the Doha Development Agenda Negotiations on Agriculture: A Korean Perspective*, in *WTO and East Asia: New Perspectives*, edited by M. Matsushita and Dukgeun Ahn (Cameron May, 2004), p. 183.

22 The European Court of Justice, founded in 1952, is the judicial institution of EU and of the European Atomic Energy Community (Euratom). Its primary task is to examine the legality of EU measures and ensure Member States to comply with obligations under the Treaties through the uniform interpretation and application of EU law.

23 Edgar Bodenheimer, *Jurisprudence: The Philosophy and Method of the Law*, Revised Edition (Harvard University Press), p. 150.

24 For a detailed introduction of these eight values, See Harold D. Lasswell and Myres S. McDougal, *Jurisprudence for a Free Society*, Volume I (New Haven Press, 1992), pp. 399-590.

25 Professor John Shijian Mo also contend that "human dignity and the eight values endorsing it must be the basic values for assessing and guiding the negotiation and operation of China's FTAs" under the "human dignity compliance principle." Thus, he argues that "[u]nder this principle, the government should stipulate the private rights in as detailed a manner as possible to ensure the realization of these values." John Shijian Mo, *A 'New Haven' Solution to the Protection of Private Rights in China's FTAs*, 19 Asia Pacific Law Review 135 (2011), p. 151.

26 In general, "harmonization" involves the adoption of an international standard that adjusts the regulatory trade rules or procedures of two or more countries until they are the same. Sidney A. Shapiro, *International Trade Agreements, Regulatory Protection, and Public Accountability*, 54 Administrative Law Review 435 (2002), at 436.

27 Fairness may refer to justice, equity or social justice (equality and solidarity in a society), distributive justice (equal allocation of goods in a society). According to Professor Franck, legitimacy (procedural fairness) and distributive justice (substantive fairness) are two aspects of the concept of fairness. From the viewpoint of legitimacy, a rule is fair if it was made and is applied in accordance with "right process." In terms of substantive fairness, any analysis of fairness must consider, however, the consequential effects of the rule: distributive justice. Thomas M. Franck, *Fairness in International Law and Institutions* (Oxford University Press, 1995), pp. 7-9, 26.

28 Doha Ministerial Declaration, para. 13.

29 W. Michael Reisman (note 8 above), pp. 576-577.

30 The Aarhus Convention forged a new process for public participation in the negotiation and implementation of international agreements.

31 "We consider that the attaching of a brief or other material to the submission of either appellant or appellee, no matter how or where such material may have originated, renders that material at least *prima facie* an integral part of the participant's submission." *United States— Import Prohibition of Certain Shrimp and Shrimp Products*, WT/DS58/AB/R, 12 October 1998, para. 89.

32 For example, the *EC-Biotech* case (*European Communities— Measures Affecting the Approval and Marketing of Biotech Products*, WT/DS291/R, WT/DS292/R, WT/DS293/R, 29 September 2006, paras 7.10 and 7.11) and the *US-Zeroing* case (*United States— Laws, Regulations and Methodology for Calculating Dumping Margins ("Zeroing")*, WT/DS294/R, 31 October 2005, para. 1.7).

33 *European Communities— Trade Description of Sardines*, WT/DS231/AB/R, 26

September 2002, paras. 164 & 167.

34 *Methanex Corpoaration v. United States of America*, NAFTA, Decision of the Tribunal on Petitions from Third Persons to Intervene as *Amici Curiae*, 2001, para. 6.

35 *Ibid.*, para. 49.

36 According to Professor Daniel Drache, six requirements are necessary for a successful operation of a regional economic community: ① There must be roughly equivalent levels of per capita; ② members must share a common geographic regionally-based economy which can minimize information and transportation costs; ③ there must be compatible trading practices and norms with trade liberalization practices; ④ there must be a political commitment to the regional organization of trade; ⑤ there must be the active support of a world economic power with a leading international currency; ⑥ there must a real potential for growth through economic integration. D. Drache, *Dreaming Trade or Trading Dreams : The Limits of Trade Blocs*, in W. Bratton, J. McCahery, S. Picciotto & C. Scott (eds.), *International Regulatory Competition and Coordination* (Clarendon Press, 1996), pp. 421-423.

37 The Treaty Establishing the Euratom was signed on 25 March 1957, and entered into force on 1 January 1958. Paul Craig and Grainne de Burca, *EC Law: Texts, Cases, and Materials* (Oxford University Press, 1995), p. 8.

38 As to an argument that FTA is more appropriate than Regional Community for the East Asian countries, because there are no common values such as democracy, transparency, rule of law, and respect for human right, see Hatakeyama Noboro, *Why a Community Rather Than an FTA?*, CEAS Commentary (2006. 3. 7).

39 The President Ma Ying-jeou, the Republic of China, proposed the South China Sea Peace Initiative May 26 in Taipei at the 2015 International Law Association-American Society of International Law Asia-Pacific Research Forum. The Peace Initiative called upon all parties concerned to exercise restraint in the South China Sea, observe relevant international law, settle disputes peacefully, *shelve sovereignty disputes and cooperate on the development of resources*, and work together on such nontraditional security issues as scientific research, environmental protection, humanitarian assistance and disaster relief [Emphasis added]. Press Release, President Ma proposes South China Sea Peace Initiative, Press Release, 26 May 2015, <http://www.mofa.gov.tw/en/News_Content.aspx?n=8157691CA2AA32F8&sms=4F8ED5 441E33EA7B&s=F71CA7963F189938> [Last visited on 19 February 2016].

Principles and Relevant Circumstances in Maritime Delimitation between Northeast Asian States*

LEE Seok-Yong
Professor
Hannam University, Daejeon, Korea

Abstract

Northeast Asian countries are expected to resume negotiations to reach definitive maritime boundary agreements in the near future. In 2015, Korea and China agreed to make greater efforts to conclude maritime delimitation agreement. As the Korea-Japan Continental Shelf Agreement will be expired in 2028, two countries are expected to begin a new negotiation for a permanent maritime delimitation in the East China Sea. In spite of the dispute over the sovereignty of Senkaku(Diaoyu) island, China and Japan will choose to resume talks over maritime issues to make the East China Sea the Sea of Peace. Northeast Asian countries, maintaining respective traditional positions on maritime delimitation principle, keep different stances on relevant circumstances which will be considered for equitable results.

This paper will look into the issues of maritime delimitation in the Northeast Asia comprehensively. Considering the changes in international law on maritime delimitation and analyzing the positions of Northeast Asian countries, principles and methods of maritime delimitation will be examined. Relevant circumstances such as previous agreements, baselines, islands, and geology will be analyzed to decide the effects on maritime boundary lines.

---

* A draft of this paper was used as a basis for a presentation at the Seminar entitled "China-Korea Round Table on the Law of the Sea 2015." The Seminar was held in Wuhan (China) in November 2015.

1. INTRODUCTION

As national maritime jurisdictions has been expanding beyond territorial sea through EEZ (Exclusive Economic Zone) and the continental shelf, conflicts between countries over maritime delimitation have been intensified. Especially in the late twentieth century, there was a substantial growth in bilateral and multilateral treaties and relevant state practices regarding maritime boundary delimitation. The jurisprudence in this field has developed relatively well and there are many cases which maritime boundaries has been resolved by agreements between the coastal states and decisions by international courts or tribunals. However, there still are cases where opposite or adjacent states have difficulties settling their maritime boundaries.[1] In spite of the controversy and efforts to devise principles and methods for equitable maritime delimitation, setting a mechanism that embraces numerous elements and leads to equitable results is still incomplete.

The seas in Northeast Asia such as the Yellow Sea, East China Sea, and East Sea (Sea of Japan in Japan) are very complex and complicated from various perspectives. Geographic situation in this area is complicated because of the deeply indented coasts and scattered insular formations and peninsulas. Also, due to the shallow water, large continental shelf, and the Okinawa Trough, underwater topography of this area is not simple. What makes the circumstances more complicated is the unresolved conflicts over the ownership of some islands and historical issues still left unsettled.

In spite of the complexities, Northeast Asian countries have resolved urgent maritime issues by concluding bilateral agreements such as fishery agreements and mineral resources development agreements. Bilateral fisheries agreements concluded among Korea, China, and Japan belong to the former, and the 1974 Korea-Japan Continental Shelf Agreement is an example of the latter. However, since those agreements are provisional in character and do not ultimately determine permanent boundary lines, final maritime delimitation is necessary. In light of the acrimonious arguments between coastal states over maritime territory issues, stability in the Northeast Asia would be fragile without clear maritime delimitations.[2]

Northeast Asian countries are expected to accelerate negotiations to reach definitive agreements on maritime delimitation. At a summit meeting held in July 2015, the Republic of Korea (hereinafter, 'Korea') and China agreed to make greater efforts to reach maritime delimitation agreement between themselves and a high-level talk was held subsequently in December of the same year to discuss future negotiation.[3] As the Korea-Japan Continental Shelf Agreement will be expired in 2028, two countries are expected to begin a new negotiation for a permanent maritime delimitation. In spite of the dispute over the sovereignty of Senkaku (Diaoyu) island, China and Japan have reasons to resume talks over maritime delimitation. Maintaining traditional positions on maritime delimitation principle respectively, Northeast Asian countries keep different stances on relevant circumstances which will be considered for equitable results. However, as maritime delimitation is determining ultimate ocean boundary where there is little definite historical trace, an agreement on delimitation line is very hard to reach.

This paper will look into the issues of maritime delimitation in the Northeast Asia comprehensively. Considering the changes in international law on maritime delimitation and analyzing the positions of Northeast Asian countries, principles and methods of maritime delimitation will be examined. Relevant circumstances such as previous agreements, islands, geology, and baselines will be analyzed to decide the effects on maritime boundary lines.

2. DELIMITATION SITUATION IN NORTHEAST ASIA

In 1966, the Committee for Coordination of Joint Prospecting for Mineral Resources in East Asian Offshore Areas (CCOP) was organized for a geophysical survey in the Yellow Sea and the East China Sea under the auspices of the United Nations Economic Commission for Asia and the Far East (ECAFE). The survey report released in 1969 said that the continental shelves of the East China Sea and the Yellow Sea had a high probability to be one of the most prolific oil reservoirs in the world.[4] This report caused a competition for maritime jurisdiction among Northeast Asian countries. They hastily claimed jurisdiction over the continental shelf as wide as possible and established development zones. By late September 1970, seventeen zones were established by Korea, Japan and Taiwan, resulting in overlapping maritime zones.[5]

What made the situation surrounding the Yellow and the East China Seas more tough was the different positions of the coastal states regarding maritime delimitation principle. Japan insisted delimitation by the equidistance rule, but China maintained that maritime boundaries should be established by the equitable principle taking into account the circumstances like natural prolongation. Korea claimed the equidistance rule to delimit the continental shelf toward China, but it insisted the natural prolongation theory toward Japan on the ground that Okinawa Trough is a deep rift disconnecting the continental shelf between both countries. In January 1974, Korea and Japan concluded the Agreement Concerning Joint Development of the Southern Part of Continental Shelf Adjacent to the Two Countries (Joint Development Agreement) to establish a Joint Development Zone (JDZ) of the size of 82,000km^2. This Agreement will be expired in 2028.

The East Sea is bound by Korea, Japan, Russia, and North Korea, thus four maritime delimitation agreements can be concluded. Since its coastline is relatively simple and the continental shelf is narrow, maritime delimitations between coastal states are expected to be relatively easy. In 1985, North Korea and the USSR (Russia) concluded the Agreement of the Economic Zone and Continental Shelf Boundary to delimit boundary lines following the equidistance line.[6] However, the unresolved sovereignty issue over Dokdo prevents Korea and Japan from a sincere negotiation on maritime boundaries in the East Sea. Once the sovereignty issue over

Dokdo is resolved, Korea and Japan could reach maritime boundaries between them with ease maybe in accordance with median line.

Changes in the perception of states on maritime space is aggravating the disputes between states over maritime zones. According to Professor Oxman, although the history of international law of the sea used to be characterized by the triumph of Grotius's freedom of the sea theory, since the mid-twentieth century the territorial temptation have thrust seaward with a speed and geographic scope.[7] Nowadays coastal states are increasingly strengthening their maritime jurisdiction quantitatively and qualitatively through national maritime zones. It is the same in Northeast Asia. The countries in this area have asserted maritime delimitation principles, baselines, and relevant circumstances which are most favorable to their national interests. However, if the ocean space beyond territorial sea is perceived as a maritime zone subject to a powerful jurisdiction as sovereignty of a coastal state, maritime disputes will be too heavy to be dealt with.

3. MARITIME DELIMITATION PRINCIPLE AND METHOD

The 1945 Truman Proclamation by the United States was the first systematic claim over the continental shelf and its resources beyond the territorial sea. The Proclamation made it clear that the United States regards the natural resources of the subsoil and seabed of the continental shelf as appertaining to the United States.[8] However, the United States did not provide any criterion indicating the outer limits of its continental shelf. In fact, the outer limit of the continental shelf was not seemed important in the early stage of the development of this jurisdiction.[9] However, with the rapid development in marine science and the widening scope of human activities at sea, defining the outer limits of the continental shelf became necessary. Article 1 of the 1958 Convention on the Continental Shelf provides that the term 'continental shelf' refers to the seabed and subsoil of the submarine areas to a depth of 200 meters or to where the depth of the superjacent waters admits the exploitation of the natural resources of the seabed. With respect to maritime delimitation, the Convention adopted equidistant or median line principle, which was researched before by some scholars like Boggs.[10] Article 6 of the Convention provides:

> Where the same continental shelf is adjacent to the territories of two or more states whose coasts are opposite or adjacent, the boundary of the continental shelf shall be determined by agreement between them. In the absence of agreement, and unless another boundary line is justified by special circumstances, the boundary line is median line or equidistant line.

In spite of this provision, ICJ recognized an equitable solution to be the principle and purpose of maritime delimitation in its historical judgment on the North Sea Continental Shelf cases in 1969. The World Court said that delimitation is to be effected by agreement in accordance with equitable principles taking account of all the relevant circumstances, in such a way as to leave as much as possible to each Party all those parts of the continental shelf that constitute a natural prolongation of its land territory into and under the sea.[11] Subsequent decisions on the continental shelf delimitation cases by international courts and arbitral tribunals followed the points rendered by ICJ in this judgment. Decisions on Anglo-French Continental Shelf case (1977), Tunisia/Libya Continental Shelf case (1982), and Gulf of Maine case (1984) stressed the equitable principle in maritime delimitation. In Tunisia/Libya case, ICJ was called upon to take account of the new trends in the Third United Nations Conference on the Law of the Sea (UNCLOS III) as well as equitable principles and relevant circumstances. In its judgement, the Court led the equitable principle to an extreme, and the decision was regarded as a typical expression of the idea of *Unicum*.[12] The Court made clear its result-oriented approach by saying that "the result of the application of equitable principles must be equitable" and "the equitableness of a principle must be assessed in the light of its usefulness for the purpose of arriving at an equitable result."[13]

ICJ judgment in Libya/Malta case has a special importance in observing the overall maritime delimitation trend. In its judgment, ICJ declared that the principles and rules of international law applicable to the delimitation are (i) the delimitation is to be effected in accordance with equitable principles and taking account of all relevant circumstances, so as to arrive at an equitable result, and (ii) where the area of continental shelf to be found to appertain to either Party not extending more than 200 miles from the coast of the Party concerned, no criterion for delimitation of shelf areas can be derived from the principle of natural prolongation in the physical sense.[14] The Court followed the equitable principles established by the previous judgements in theory, but it kept balance between the equitable principle and the equidistance principle in practice.

The Convention on the Law of the Sea has articles dealing with maritime delimitations of territorial sea (Art. 15), EEZ (Art. 74), and the continental shelf (Art. 83). While Article 15 envisages the use of the equidistance principle, Articles 74 and 83 enjoin agreement on the basis of international law with the aim of achieving an equitable solution.[15] Articles 74 and 83 of the Convention stipulate as follows:

> The delimitation of EEZ (continental shelf) between States with opposite or adjacent coasts shall be effected by agreement on the basis of international law, as referred to in Article 38 of the Statute of the International Court of Justice, in order to achieve an equitable solution.

The Equitable Principle Group welcomed this provision since they referred to an equitable solution as the purpose of maritime delimitation. The Equidistance Group entertained this provision too because of the reference to 'international law' which they wanted to insert in delimitation provision. Since the clauses of the LOS Convention on delimitation of

EEZ and the continental shelf are not definite, international courts and tribunals are anticipated to take important roles again in formulating relevant international customary law.

The international courts and tribunals have been subject to criticism for decades, because the decisions have swung between the two rules on maritime delimitation. Since the 1969 North Sea cases, the applicability of the equidistance rule was diminished and the equity doctrine gained strength the most at the Tunisia/Libya and Gulf of Maine cases. However, the equidistance rule returned to the middle ground at the Libya/Malta case partially due to the emergence of EEZ.[16]

Given the infinite diversity of the ocean environment, the equidistance rule holds flaws to be a general principle. Considering the relevant customary law and the provisions of the LOS Convention, equitable principles could be recognized as the main principle in maritime delimitation.[17] However, in practice, only few maritime delimitation followed the equitable principle while most of the cases were determined by the equidistance or median line rule. According to Antunes, a comprehensive analysis on maritime delimitation practices by states shows that reference to equitable principles are found in 10% of the cases analyzed, which was later cut to 2%. In fact, equitable principle has been rarely mentioned in the cases of EEZ delimitation and two-thirds of unilateral declarations by states have regarded the equidistant line as provisional boundary line.[18] Recently, majority of maritime delimitations have been effected by application of equidistance or median rule for equitable result, if there are no factors which make the application of the rules inappropriate.[19]

To be sure, there are cases where it is impossible to achieve an equitable result with minor modification of the provisional equidistance or median lines. Where adjacent states have only one or two basepoints each on long coasts, a perpendicular line to a line representing general direction of the coast of the two adjacent states could be an alternative.[20] For a similar purpose, ICJ, in Nicaragua v. Honduras case, recognized the equidistance to be the general rule in territorial sea delimitation, but presented its position that special circumstances required the use of a different method of delimitation, the bisector method.[21]

With regard to the maritime delimitation in the Yellow and the East China Seas, the positions of the Northeast Asian states are markedly different. According to China, the continental shelf off its coast which is a natural prolongation of its land to the sea should be under its jurisdiction. Thus China has maintained the position that continental shelf and EEZ delimitation line should be established by equitable principle taking into account the natural prolongation of the land territory. This especially means that the Okinawa Trough just west of Ryukyu Islands should be considered as the maritime delimitation line in the East China Sea.[22]

Japan's jurisdictional claim over marine living and non-living resources in water column and the continental shelf has mainly based on equidistance line principle which was reinforced recently by the emergence of EEZ. Although Korea and China have emphasized the application of natural prolongation doctrine for the maritime delimitation in the East China Sea, Japan argues that Okinawa Trough is not a disconnection in the continental shelf but an incidental sinking. For Japan, geomorphology is not a consideration for maritime delimitation in the East China Sea, because the distance between the coasts of Japan and China (or Korea) is less than 400 miles.

Korea insists that maritime delimitation between itself and China in the Yellow Sea and the East China Sea should be effected in accordance with median line method. Korea suggests that continental shelf between them is connected as one without discontinuity. However, Korea has insisted that maritime delimitation with Japan in the East China sea should consider the geological rupture by the Okinawa Trough.

Korea, China, and Japan ratified the LOS Convention respectively in late 1990s. Therefore, the three countries would compromise on delimiting the maritime boundaries based on international law for equitable results as stipulated in Articles 74 and 83 of the Convention.

However, the provisions on maritime delimitation of the Convention are not specific and parties tend to interpret them to their advantages. Positions of the Northeast Asian countries on maritime delimitation principle are somewhat clearly reflected in their national laws and regulations. Article 3 of the EEZ and Continental Shelf Act of China clearly provides that if there is a jurisdiction overlapping area between China and its adjacent or opposite state, the boundary should be effected by agreement based on international law for an equitable result. The EEZ and Continental Shelf Act of Japan, on the other hand, clearly adopted median line as the principle for maritime delimitation. Korea's legislation on maritime delimitation is very similar to the relevant provisions of the LOS Convention. Article 2 Paragraph 2 of Korea's Exclusive Economic Zone Act of 1996 provides that EEZ boundary between Korea and the other opposite or adjacent state should be delimited through agreement based on international law.[23]

Nowadays maritime delimitation usually proceeds step by step following the three stage method which was explained earlier by ICJ in the judgement on Libya/Malta case.[24] This three stage method has been entertained by those insisting delimitation based on equidistance line.[25] In the Black Sea case between Romania and Ukraine, ICJ had another opportunity to restate its jurisprudence regarding the methodology for maritime delimitation.[26] At the first stage, provisional delimitation lines are established using methods that are geometrically objective and appropriate for the geography of the delimitation area. Equidistance or median lines will be drawn between adjacent or opposite coasts respectively, unless there are compelling reasons that make this unfeasible.[27] At the second stage, relevant factors calling for adjustment of the provisional lines are considered. The Court will consider whether there are factors calling for adjustment or shifting of the provisional lines for an equitable result.[28] As Roach noted, the relevant factors considered by the ICJ in the second step are disproportionate coastal length, geographic context such as concavity of coasts, outlying islands of little significance, but population, socioeconomic factors, conduct of parties in other negotiations, size of landmass, and lack of natural resources are considered not relevant.[29] At the third stage, equitableness of the boundary lines will be examined. Considering balance between the ratio of the respective coastal lengths and the ratio between the relevant maritime areas of the coastal states, the Court will verify whether the delimitation lines produce an inequitable result to be corrected.[30] In the Bay of Bengal case between Bangladesh and Myanmar, the International Tribunal for the Law of the Sea (ITLOS) also applied this three stage method.[31]

Northeast Asian countries have different positions on methods for maritime delimitation. China, a supporter for the equitable principles and natural prolongation theory, might insist reaching an equitable boundary lines at once through a comprehensive consideration of the relevant circumstances. As an advocate of the median line principle, Japan might have in mind the general delimitation process which use equidistance or median lines as provisional lines at the first stage. Korea prefers median line principle in the Yellow Sea and the East Sea, and thus, it will welcome the establishment of provisional lines at the first stage of maritime delimitation. However, Korea insists that southern part of the East China Sea between Korea and Japan should be delimited in accordance with the equitable principle considering natural prolongation of land territory. As there are no factors requiring for the use of another method except for the southern part of the East China Sea, it will be preferable to use the equidistance or median lines as provisional boundaries for final equitable results. If China argues for deciding on the final boundaries without drawing provisional lines, then reaching an agreement on maritime boundaries might be a laborious work due to the complexities in the process.[32]

4. PREVIOUS AGREEMENTS

If a maritime delimitation is achieved by an agreement between opposite or adjacent states, it could be the most efficient and idealistic one from jurisdictional perspectives. This is why international conventions such as the LOS Convention have emphasized maritime delimitation by agreement. In this vein, if there are previous agreements concluded between the coastal states, which are directly or indirectly related to the area under consideration, they can be treated as relevant circumstances.[33] An implied agreement can also have an important bearing on maritime delimitation lines, if it is recognized to have relevance to maritime boundary. However, if the parties have different views regarding the existence or legal character of an agreement, international judicial organs or the third party would not readily recognize it relevant to the new boundary line. In Nicaragua v. Honduras case, ICJ, having reviewed the evidences and practices produced by Honduras, concluded that there was no tacit agreement in effect between them of a nature to establish a legally binding maritime boundary.[34]

The effect of a previous agreement on a new boundary agreement, or the effect of a continental shelf agreement concluded before on EEZ boundary or single boundary agreement, should be analyzed in terms of its contents and scope of application. Coastal states' jurisdictions over the continental shelf and EEZ are closely related to each other. The former was introduced for the development of resources of seabed and subsoil while the latter is a more comprehensive jurisdiction that was introduced to secure resources jurisdiction of seabed, subsoil, and superjacent waters. Given the similar scope of these economic jurisdictions and the same delimitation provision of the LOS Convention, drawing a single boundary for EEZ and continental shelf is desirable. But, in case there is a large gap between each equitable solution for the continental shelf and EEZ respectively, then introducing separate boundaries can be considered.[35]

The existing agreements that should be considered for maritime delimitation in the Northeast Asia are agreements relating to continental shelf and fisheries. In 1974, Korea and Japan concluded the Continental Shelf Agreement to draw continental shelf boundaries between them and establish a Joint Development Zone (JDZ) in the area where the two countries' claims overlap.[36] As this agreement is a result of a definite arguments and lengthy negotiations on continental shelf boundary, the points of the agreement should not be lightly treated. Although the contents and the legal characteristic of the agreement are not clear, the China-Japan Agreement on a Joint Development in the East China Sea concluded in June 2008 might be considered as relevant as well.[37] Meanwhile, fishery agreements which were concluded between Korea, China, and Japan in late 1990s and early 2000s will have somewhat strictly limited effect on maritime delimitation lines.[38] As fishery agreements are provisional in character and usually have definite provisions limiting the scope of application only to fisheries matters, the effect that these agreements might have on final maritime delimitation boundaries will be marginal.

In maritime boundary delimitation in the Yellow Sea and the East China Sea, predicting the possible effect of the previous agreements on the new boundaries is not simple considering different positions of the coastal states. However, it is important that natural prolongation along with the distance was recognized relevant in the 1974 Korea-Japan Continental Shelf Agreement. It is also notable that Korea and China agreed to divide relevant waters equally between them in Korea-China Fishery Agreement. Positions of China and Japan shown in the 2008 Consensus on the East China Sea can be guidelines in the future negotiations between them.[39]

5. BASELINE

As a state's entitlement to maritime jurisdiction is defined by reference to its coastline, it is necessary to determine the coastline of each party that generates overlapping claims. Relevant coasts mean the coasts that give rise to claims on overlapping jurisdiction by coastal states.[40] International courts and tribunals have mentioned that the title of a state to the continental shelf and EEZ is based on the principle that the land dominates the sea through the projection of the coasts. ICJ, in the Black Sea case, observed that it is important to determine the coasts of Romania and Ukraine, which would generate the rights of the countries to the continental shelf and EEZ where the projections of those coasts overlap.[41]

Once the relevant coasts are determined, baselines for maritime delimitation can be drawn if equidistance or median line rules are applicable for maritime delimitation. Baselines are originally drawn to define the scope of maritime zones of coastal states.[42] In spite of the relatively detailed provisions on baselines in the LOS Convention, some states have established too long straight baselines on the coasts where the conditions were not met.

East Asian States have established excessive straight baselines. China established 49 basepoints on the continental coast and 28 basepoints around Paracel Islands by the 1992 Territorial Sea and Contiguous Zone Act. Some of the straight baselines connect the basepoints situated on tiny features. Among the basepoints, those on Macaiheng, Waikejiao, Haijiao, and Dongnanjiao are set on features which are too tiny and situated far away from the mainland coast. They could affect maritime boundaries between Korea and China, if equidistant or median line rule is employed for maritime delimitation. In spite of the rule that baselines should not be departed too much from the general direction of the coast, Haijiao and Dongnanjiao are too far from the coast.[43] Japan had maintained three mile territorial sea until it extended territorial sea to twelve miles by the 1977 Territorial Sea Act. Japan ratified the LOS Convention in 1996 and revised the Act to apply straight baseline system over the whole coast. Japan established 194 basepoints and 165 straight baselines, but some of them caused controversies in terms of relevant international norms. Straight baseline system was applied on coasts that are not deeply indented or have no fringe of islands in the vicinity, and some straight baselines are departed too far from the general direction of the coast.[44] Korea established a baseline system as it enacted the Territorial Sea Act in 1977 and promulgated enforcement ordinance in 1978. The country has drawn normal baselines in the east coast while drawing straight baselines in the west and the south coast of the peninsula. Given the indented and complicated geography of the coasts, straight baselines around Korean Peninsula are justified. Some of the straight baselines reach 60 miles, but they are not too long compared to the baselines of other countries in Northeast Asia.[45]

As Professor Weil mentioned, the function of a baseline system as the starting point for the measurement of maritime zones can be quite different from its role in delimiting maritime zones between opposite or adjacent states. In the Black Sea case, ICJ also observed that identifying basepoints to draw an equidistance or median line for the purpose of delimiting the continental shelf and EEZ between adjacent or opposite states is different from determining baselines for the purpose of measuring the breadth of the continental shelf and EEZ.[46] If the coastal states of Northeast Asian countries agree on maritime delimitation by median or equidistant line, the baseline for delimitation can be drawn considering relevant circumstances of the waters, regardless of the baselines that each country has arbitrarily set for national maritime jurisdiction.

International Courts and Tribunals have been selective in establishing appropriate basepoints for the construction of provisional equidistant or median boundaries. ICJ and ITLOS have not established strict equidistance lines, but discounted certain island basepoints to draw the provisional equidistant lines.[47] Such a practice for the adoption of flexible approach in maritime delimitation was reflected in the Black Sea case. ICJ identified 'the most appropriate points' on the parties' relevant coasts which mark a significant change in the direction of the coast.[48] A new way of choosing basepoints, which is clearly displayed in the determination of 'the most appropriate basepoints' in this case, can lead to somewhat revolutionary changes in the maritime delimitation system. There may be conflicts between negotiators with different views on what is appropriate. However, If 'the most appropriate points' is considered at the first stage of drawing provisional lines, questions on equitableness will arise from the initial stage.[49]

6. ISLANDS

From the perspective of international law of the sea, legal regime of islands is examined from two viewpoints: the legal entitlement of islands to maritime zones and the effect of islands on maritime delimitation lines.[50] During the UNCLOS III, there were conflicting positions over the issue of maritime zones of insular formations. States including most island states asserted that all islands should be allowed to have maritime zones like other land territories, but the other states opposed permitting tiny islands generate EEZs and the continental shelves around them. Article 121 of the LOS Convention defines an island as naturally formed, surrounded by water, and emerging above water at high tide (para. 1), and stipulates that it is entitled to territorial sea, EEZ, and continental shelf (para. 2). However, paragraph 3 of the article states that "rocks which cannot sustain human habitation or economic life of its own shall have no exclusive economic zone or continental shelf." Basically, this provision was introduced to prevent a tiny feature from generating excessively vast maritime zones around it.[51] The criterion which distinguishes the islands entitled to EEZ and the continental shelf from rocks entitled only to territorial sea is the feature's capacity to sustain human habitation or economic life of its own. Since the meaning of the conditions 'human habitation' and 'economic life of its own' is not clear, it is disputable whether the conditions can be met if a lighthouse or a laboratory is built on a tiny feature.[52] There are diverse interpretations about the provision on 'rock'. It should also be noted that the Convention refers to uninhabitable rocks, not uninhabited rocks.

As there is no specific provision as to which features meet the criteria of an island, most states have claimed EEZs and continental shelves from tiny insular formations which could be classified as rocks. The only exceptions are Rockall (UK) and Alijos Rocks (Mexico).[53] Given the decentralized state of the international community, if a state takes an action without protests from other countries, a *fait accompli* could be established. An example is the Japanese position over Okinotorishima.

Korea and China protested against Japan's claim to an extended continental shelf surrounding the feature by arguing that Okinotorishima is a rock that cannot sustain human habitation and economic life of its own.[54] They also raised the issue at the Meeting of States Parties and the International Seabed Authority (ISBA) without achieving desired results.[55] Meanwhile, China is also attempting to claim maritime jurisdiction over the waters surrounding tiny features in the South China Sea. Even the United States has given full effect to all territories. According to Roach, United States has not applied LOS Convention Article 121(3) to maritime features that might be considered as rocks.[56] States are taking advantage of the ambiguity to expand their national jurisdiction by using a small rock as a basepoint for EEZ and continental shelf.[57]

In maritime delimitation, the effect of an island on boundary lines varies depending mainly on the area of the island, population size, and the distance from the mainland coast. However, various other factors should be considered to decide exact roles of an island in maritime delimitation. In the Bay of Bengal case, ITLOS considered geographic realities and other circumstances to decide whether St. Martin's Island is a relevant circumstance requiring adjustment of the provisional equidistance lines. The Tribunal said that each case is unique and requires specific treatment for an equitable solution.[58] International courts and tribunals usually have hesitated to grant full effects on small islands in maritime delimitation. In 1968 Iran/Saudi Arabia Agreement (Kharg Island of Iran), Libya/Tunisia case (Kerkenna Islands of Tunisia), and Anglo-French case (Scilly Isles of UK), the islands were given half or partial effects. In Black Sea case between Romania and Ukraine, Serpents' Island which is located 20 miles east of the Danube delta was only allowed to generate territorial sea.[59]

Dokdo in the East Sea has an area of 180,920m². This island is 217 km away from the mainland of Korea, 87km away from Ulleung-do, and 158km away from Oki Island of Japan. Dokdo is large enough to generate EEZ and continental shelf. It is larger than a 'rock' by any standard. The effect of Dokdo on maritime delimitation line will be determined considering its area, location, and economic importance. In Korea, there was a lot of debate on the effect of the Korea-Japan Fishery Agreement on sovereignty over Dokdo and maritime delimitation boundaries with Japan in the East Sea. Those who were against the agreement were concerned that Korea's position on Dokdo might be weakened as the island is situated in the 'Intermediate Zone (or Provisionally Arranged Zone)' established by the new fishery agreement. Thus, once the sovereignty issue over Dokdo is resolved in favor of Korea, Korea and Japan could reach an agreement on EEZ boundary or a single boundary of EEZ and continental shelf relatively smoothly. However, as witnessed in the Nicaragua v. Honduras case, islands can have reduced effect on boundary line if maritime delimitation is determined at the same time when the sovereignty issue is resolved.[60] The Japanese islands that can be considered in maritime delimitation in the East China Sea are Torishima and Danjo-gunto. Located in the west of Kyushu, Torishima has an area of $50m^2$ and has been regarded as a rock. Danjo-gunto is located in the southeast of Torishima Island and has an area of $4.75km^2$. In the past, lighthouse guards lived there, but now there is no inhabitant. Japan claimed that Danjo-gunto held effect in negotiation with Korea on maritime delimitation, but Korea has opposed the Japanese claim on the ground that it is only a rock.[61]

7. GEOLOGY AND GEOMORPHOLOGY

The concept of continental shelf is inseparable from the idea of natural prolongation of land territory. International courts and tribunals clearly recognized the relevance of the geophysical characteristics of the disputed area in maritime delimitation. In the North Sea cases, ICJ said that delimitation is to be effected by agreement in accordance with equitable principles in such a way as to leave as much as possible to each party with all those parts of the continental shelf that constitute a natural prolongation of its land territory into and under the sea.[62] In the Tunisia/

Libya case, the Court went to the extreme by noting that a marked disruption or discontinuance of the seabed may constitute an indisputable indication of the limits of two separate natural prolongations or two separate continental shelves.[63]

Since the 1969 North Sea case, international courts have repeatedly confirmed the equitable principle in maritime delimitation, but were not so enthusiastic in applying the principle in practice.[64] Though natural prolongation was regarded as a key component of equitable delimitation principle for some time, it has become one of the factors to be considered for equitable boundary making. The advent of EEZ was a reason for the decline in importance of natural prolongation in maritime delimitation, as it allowed the coastal states to assert jurisdiction up to 200 nautical miles from baselines, regardless of geology and geomorphology of the area. The growing importance of EEZ meant that distance has become more important than natural prolongation in maritime delimitation.[65]

In an area where the distance between the coasts of the coastal states is less than 400 miles, the effect of natural prolongation or geology on maritime delimitation has been a point of argument. In Libya/Malta case, Libya contended that the 'rift zone' between two countries indicated the boundary zone.[66] However, the World Court said that there is no reason to ascribe any role to geological or geophysical factors within 200 miles from the coasts either in verifying the legal title of the States concerned and in proceeding to a delimitation.[67] ICJ's decision shows that even in continental shelf delimitation the role of geology has been rapidly diminishing.

Korea basically does not agree on determining maritime delimitation in accordance with the principle of natural prolongation, but it insists that the principle is applicable to a continental shelf with marked geologic discontinuity. Korea supports maritime delimitation following the median line rule with Japan in the East Sea and with China in the Yellow Sea. However, Korea prefers natural prolongation principle in delimitation with Japan in southern part of the East China Sea, because Okinawa Trough is certainly a geological discontinuity.[68] Almost three-fourths of the East

China Sea is less than 200 meters in depth, and its average depth is only 350 meters. The Okinawa Trough is the deeper part of the Sea with a large section being more than 1,000 meters deep while the maximum depth is 2,716 meters.

China and Taiwan also argue that this Okinawa Trough terminates the natural prolongation of the Japanese territory and constitutes natural boundary between Japan and other countries. China have asserted the equitable principle emphasizing natural prolongation of land territory in delimiting the East China Sea.[69] Taking account of the surrounding geology and geomorphology, China has considered the natural prolongation doctrine meet its national interest. There have been claims that its continental shelf in the Yellow and the East China Seas extends to silt line which is formed by accumulation of deposits flowing in from Yellow River and Yangze River.[70] However, it is doubtful whether the silt line is clearly identifiable. Even some Chinese scholars raise a question of whether the silt line is significant enough to overshadow the fact that a considerable part of the Yellow Sea and the East China Sea is connected with a single continental shelf.[71] For China, it will be tricky to overcome the widespread perception that geology cannot be a consideration in areas where the distance between opposite states is less than 400 miles. Though there is an expectation that China would rather utilize the principle of proportionality, it would never give up insisting on natural prolongation theory which best benefits the country.[72] Delimiting nonidentical boundaries for the continental shelf and EEZ could be an alternative.[73]

8. OBSERVATIONS

Northeast Asian countries have maintained their traditional positions to maritime delimitation. Japan adheres to the equidistance principle, but China asserts that maritime boundaries should be established following the equitable principles taking into account the natural prolongation of land territory. Korea prefers the equidistance principle for maritime delimitation in the East Sea and the Yellow Sea, but it insists application of the natural prolongation doctrine toward Japan in the East China Sea.

Articles 74 and 83 of the LOS Convention stipulate that delimitation of EEZ and the continental shelf between states with opposite or adjacent coasts should be effected by agreement on the basis of international law in order to achieve an equitable solution. Korea, China, and Japan are parties to the Convention. Therefore, these countries would compromise on delimiting the maritime boundaries based on international law for equitable results. However, as the provisions on maritime delimitation of the Convention only specify the purpose but no method, the parties tend to interpret them to their advantages.

Northeast Asian countries have also maintained different stances on the methods of maritime delimitation. Japan is likely to prefer establishing provisional lines at the first stage following the three stage method, while China would insist on setting an equitable boundary at once through a comprehensive consideration of the relevant circumstances. Korea may accept the establishment of the provisional median lines at the outset in general, but would take a different position in the East China Sea due to the presence of Okinawa Trough.

Maritime delimitation can be effected not only by the third party dispute settlement system such as arbitration or adjudication but also by bilateral agreement between coastal states. In general, if the states with opposite or adjacent coasts try to settle their maritime boundaries by negotiation, various relevant circumstances could be considered in more affirmative ways.[74]

The following is a summary of some relevant circumstances that can be considered in maritime delimitation between Northeast Asian countries.

Previous agreements such as joint development agreement of continental shelf and fishery agreement are rarely considered to be relevant in establishing a new or single boundary. However, if there were some points agreed or negotiated that are related to maritime delimitation, they could have limited bearings on maritime boundary lines. Baseline system could lead to a distorted maritime boundaries, if coastal states decide to use their somewhat excessively established straight baseline system for maritime delimitation. However, the baselines drawn for measuring the breadth of maritime zones such as the continental shelf and EEZ are different from the baselines for the purpose of delimiting the maritime jurisdiction between adjacent or opposite states.

In spite of the Article 121 of the LOS Convention on island system and heated discussion on the criteria which distinguishes the islands entitled to EEZ and the continental shelf from rocks entitled only to territorial sea, some ambiguities still remain about the legal status of islands in international law of the sea. The effect of an island on delimitation line varies mainly depending on the area of the feature, size of the population, and distance from the coast. However, it is necessary to consider other elements from a variety of perspectives in order to decide appropriate values of the islands on maritime boundary lines.

In the past, international courts and tribunals clearly recognized the relevance of the geophysical characteristics of the disputed area to maritime delimitation. They regarded natural prolongation of land territory one of the most important factor to be reflected in maritime delimitation, but recent decisions and state practices have greatly diminished the role of it. China insists on maritime delimitation in accordance with equitable principle reflecting natural prolongation of land territory, but it is not easy to overcome the general perception of international community that geology cannot be a consideration in areas where the distance between opposite states is less than 400 miles. However, the definite discontinuity of the continental shelf by the Okinawa Trough should be considered as a relevant circumstance in the East China Sea maritime delimitation.

NOTES

1 Donald R. Rothwell and Tim Stephens, The International Law of the Sea, Hart Publishing, 2010, pp. 383-384.

2 Changes in the perception of states on maritime space also affect maritime boundary delimitation. As the so-called 'territorialization of the oceans' is under way, coastal states try to expand its maritime zones and strengthen the national jurisdiction in the zones. States are exploiting the more or less ambiguous provisions in the United Nations Convention Law of the Sea (LOS Convention) on baselines, insular formations, scopes of national maritime zones, and maritime delimitation. EEZ, for example, is considered the most important national maritime jurisdiction under the LOS Convention, but the Convention did not clearly provide the legal character of this jurisdiction. Powerful maritime states including the U.S. regard EEZ as a part of high sea, but other states like China insist that EEZ is a part of jurisdictional waters of the coastal states. Louis B. Sohn and John E. Noyes, Cases and Materials on the Law of the Sea, Transnational Publishers, 2004, p. 552.

3 The Korea Ministry of Foreign Affairs, 2015. 12. 23. (http://mofakr.blog.me/220576314455)

4 CCOP/ECAFE, "Geological Structure and Some Water Characteristics of the East China Sea and the Yellow Sea," Technical Bulletin, No. 2, 1969, pp. 39-40.

5 The Republic of Korea established 7 development zones by the Submarine Mineral Resources Development Act which was enacted in January 1970 and subsequent Presidential Decree which was proclaimed in May 1970. Choon-Ho Park, East Asia and The Law of the Sea, Seoul National University Press, 1985, pp. 6-13.

6 Jonathan I. Charney and Lewis M. Alexander (eds.), International Maritime Boundaries, Vol. 1, Martinus Nijhoff Publishers, 1993, pp. 1135-1138.

7 Professor Oxman said that the mid-twentieth century was a watershed for the development of international law of the sea. Before then, the history of international law starting from the Peace of Westphalia was a description of the territorial temptation, but the sea showed a different history. While the history of the international law of land can be characterized by the progressive triumph of the territorial temptation, the history of international law of the sea can be characterized by the triumph of Grotius's freedom of the sea theory. Bernard B. Oxman, "The Territorial Temptation: A Siren Song at Sea," American Journal of International Law, Vol. 100, 2006, pp. 830-832.

8 Policy of the United States with Respect to the Natural Resources of the Subsoil and Sea Bed of the Continental Shelf, United States Presidential Proclamation 2667, 28

September 1945.

9 R. R. Churchill and A. V. Lowe, The Law of the Sea, Manchester University Press, 1988, p. 144. The claims followed by other states, especially by the Latin American states, were different so much in the limit of application and in character. Then the continental shelf could not be treated to have definitive status in international law.

10 Whittemore Boggs was a Geographer of the United States Department of State. He, as member of the United States delegation to the 1930 Hague Conference, also led its submissions on the methods to be adopted as the rule for territorial sea delimitation. Later he developed and expanded median line method. Rothwell and Stephens, *op.cit.*, pp. 385-386. In his book published in 1940, Boggs said boundaries in waters like lakes, straits, and rivers generally follow the median line, the navigable channel or Thalweg, or an arbitrary geometrical line such as a parallel of latitude or azimuth line. According to him, of these four types, the median line was least clearly defined back then. Boggs tried to explain four types of median lines. Among them, he highly regarded the median line which is every point of which is equidistant from nearest point or points on opposite shores of the lake, river or strait. S. Whittemore Boggs, International Boundaries: A Study of Boundary Functions and Problems, Columbia University Press, 1940, pp. 178-183.

11 North Sea Continental Shelf, Judgement, ICJ Reports, 1969, para. 101.

12 L. D. M. Nelson, "The Roles of Equity in the Delimitation of Maritime Boundaries," American Journal of International Law, Vol. 84, 1990, pp. 837-838.

13 Continental Shelf (Tunisia/Libyan Arab Jamahiriya), Judgment, ICJ Reports, 1982, para. 70.

14 Continental Shelf (Libyan Arab Jamahiriya/Malta), Judgment, ICJ Reports, 1985, para. 79.

15 E. D. Brown, The International Law of the Sea, Vol. 1, Dartmouth Publishing Co., 1994, p. 157. During the UNCLOS III, the provisions contained in Articles 74 and 83 were subject to a lengthy negotiation between the Equidistance Group and the Equitable Principle Group. Tommy Koh, the president of the conference, proposed a compromise to be accepted by the conference at the final stage.

16 Prosper Weil, The Law of Maritime Delimitation-Reflections, Grotius Publications, 1989, pp. 169-177.

17 In Nicaragua v. Honduras case, ICJ explained the recent trend in maritime delimitation. The Court recalled it has made it clear on various occasions that where a line covering several zones of overlapping jurisdictions is to be determined, the equitable principle and relevant circumstances method may be effective. Equidistance method has certain intrinsic value in its scientific character and the relative ease with which it can be applied. However, the equidistance method does

not automatically have priority over other methods of delimitation and, in particular circumstances, there may be factors which make the application of the equidistance method inappropriate. Territorial and Maritime Dispute between Nicaragua and Honduras in the Caribbean Sea (Nicaragua v. Honduras), Judgment, ICJ Reports, 2007, para. 271.

18 Nuno Marques Antunes, Towards the Conceptualization of Maritime Delimitation: Legal and Technical Aspects of a Political Process, Martinus Nijhoff Publishers, 2003, pp. 96-97. Explaining U.S. maritime boundary practice, Roach said that the country have established single boundary employing equidistance approach which is most favorable to it. A Maritime boundary agreement where special circumstances were present was the 1990 Agreement with former Soviet Union. J. Ashley Roach, "Maritime Boundary Delimitation: United States Practice," Ocean Development and International Law, Vol. 44, 2013, p. 4.

19 Today the equitable principle and the equidistance principle are considered to be in a complementary relationship. In Qatar v. Bahrain case, ICJ noted that the equitable principle-relevant circumstances rule which was developed in case law and the equidistance-special circumstances rule were closely interrelated.

20 David H. Anderson, "Maritime Delimitation in the Black Sea Case (Romania v. Ukraine)," The Law and Practice of International Courts and Tribunals, Vol. 8, 2009, p. 326.

21 Shi Jiuyong, "Maritime Delimitation in the Jurisprudence of the International Court of Justice," Chinese Journal of International Law, Vol. 9, 2010, p. 281.

22 Peter Dutton, "Carving Up the East China Sea," Naval War College Review, Vol. 60, No. 2, 2007, pp. 51-52. The LOS Convention provided that coastal state's right over EEZ or the continental shelf is not sovereignty but sovereign right. However, some scholars contend that Chinese tend to consider sovereign right similar to sovereignty. Sohn and Noyes, *op.cit.*, p. 552.

23 Korea Law of the Sea Forum, Commentary on the Law of the Sea Convention, Vol. 1, 2009, pp. 269-277.

24 Libya/Malta case, *op.cit.*, para. 60.

25 ICJ, in the Jan Mayen case, admitted that the equitable principle is an international customary law. But, the Court ruled that taking into consideration the special circumstances to review the need for arrangement or shift of the provisional equidistant or median lines conforms to precedents. Maritime Delimitation in the Area between Greenland and Jan Mayen (Denmark v. Norway), Judgment, ICJ Reports, 1993, para. 51.

26 Anderson, *op.cit.*, p. 306.

27 Maritime Delimitation in the Black Sea (Romania v. Ukraine), Judgment, ICJ

Reports, 2009, para. 116.

28 *Ibid.*, para. 120.

29 Roach, *op.cit.*, p. 2.

30 Romania v. Ukraine, *op.cit.*, para. 122.

31 Dispute concerning Delimitation of the Maritime Boundary between Bangladesh and Myanmar in the Bay of Bengal (Bay of Bengal case), Judgment, ITLOS, 2012, paras. 239-240.

32 Seokyong Lee, "Maritime Delimitation between Korea and China," Korean Journal of International Law, Vol. 52, No. 2, 2007, p. 267.

33 Robert W. Smith, "Maritime Delimitation in the South China Sea: Potentiality and Challenges," Ocean Development and International Law, Vol. 41, 2010, p. 217.

34 In the Nicaragua v. Honduras case, Honduras insisted that the existence of a de facto boundary along the 15th Parallel based on tacit agreement of the parties was confirmed by various evidences. Although there was no formal and written treaty governing the delimitation, it asserted that countries and international organizations had consistently recognized the line. Territorial and Maritime Dispute between Nicaragua and Honduras in the Caribbean Sea (Nicaragua v. Honduras), Judgment, ICJ Reports, 2007, paras. 237-258.

35 Australia-Papua New Guinea Border Treaty concluded in 1978 is a good example. They agreed to introduce four types of boundaries between them.

36 In 1974 Korea and Japan concluded 2 continental shelf agreements. They are "The Agreement between the Republic of Korea and Japan concerning the Establishment of Boundary in the Northern Part of the Continental Shelf" and "Agreement between the Republic of Korea and Japan concerning the Joint Development of the Southern Part of the Continental Shelf."

37 China and Japan had 11 rounds of consultations from October 2004 to November 2007. After that the two countries had exchange of visits of leaders and issued a joint statement calling for cooperation in making the East China Sea a 'sea of peace, cooperation, and friendship.' On 18 June 2008, foreign ministers of China and Japan released the Principled Consensus on the East China Sea Issue. Xinjun Zhang, "Why the 2008 Sino-Japanese Consensus on the East China Sea has Stalled: Good Faith and Reciprocity Considerations in Interim Measures Pending a maritime Boundary Delimitation," Ocean Development and International Law, Vol. 42, 2011, pp. 56-57. The first step of joint development was expected to happen in Shirakaba on the Chinese side of the median line. To be noted, a new treaty is needed to implement the joint development. Michael Sheng-ti Gau, "Problems and practices in Maritime Delimitation in East Asia: With Special Reference to Taiwan," Journal of East Asia and International Law, Vol. 2, 2011, pp. 393-394.

38 Korea-Japan Fishery Agreement and Korea-China Fishery Agreement were concluded in 1998 and 2001 respectively. China-Japan Fishery Agreement was signed in 1997.

39 There were some estimates that gas and oil deposits in the East China Sea could be a catalyst for negotiation as Chunxiao joint development agreement shows. However, recent confrontation between China and Japan over Diaoyu(Senkaku) Islands demonstrates that economic, historic, emotional, and national confrontation between them can be barriers to a more cooperative and peaceful future for the East Asia. Dutton, *op.cit.*, pp. 49-50.

40 Shi, *op.cit.*, p.275.

41 Black Sea case, *op.cit.*, para. 77. 'Relevant coasts' are also helpful in checking whether any disproportionality exists in the ratios of the coastal length of the states parties and maritime areas which will be vested on them respectively. *Ibid.*, para. 78.

42 Whereas a normal baseline is the low-water line along the coast, a straight baseline is applicable in localities where the coastline is deeply indented and cut into or where there is a fringe of islands along the coast. A straight baseline must not depart too far from the general direction of the coast. See LOS Convention, Art. 7.

43 United States Department of State, "Straight Baselines and Territorial Sea Claims: China," Limits in the Seas, No.117, 1996, pp. 2-5; Yang Heecheol," Research on the Factors to Consider in the Yellow Sea Maritime Delimitation between Korea and China and Countermeasures to It," Korean Journal of International Law, Vol. 57, No. 3, 2012, pp. 115-125.

44 United States Department of State, "Straight Baselines and Territorial Sea Claims: Japan," Limits in the Seas, No. 120, 1998, pp. 5-6; Korea Law of the Sea Forum, Commentary on the Law of the Sea Convention, Vol. 1, 2009, pp. 64-65; Changryol Lee, Choi Jihyun, Chang Jinhee, and Kim Donguk, A Study on the Practices of Straight Baselines in East Asia, KMI, 2011, pp. 65-78.

45 United States Department of State, "Straight Baselines and Territorial Sea Claims: South Korea," Limits in the Seas, No. 121, 1998, pp. 3-5.

46 ICJ need not to base itself on the basepoints designated by the coastal states to delimit the maritime areas involving two or more states. The Court said that when delimiting the continental shelf and EEZ, it must select basepoints considering the physical geography of the relevant coasts. Black Sea case, *op.cit.*, para. 137.

47 Clive Schofield, "Departures from the Coast: Trends in the Application of Territorial Sea Baselines under the Law of the Sea Convention," The International Journal of Marine and Coastal Law, Vol. 27, 2012, pp. 730-731.

48 Black Sea case, *op.cit.*, para. 127.

49 Anderson, *op.cit.*, pp. 326-327.

50 Jon M. Van Dyke, "The Role of Islands in Delimiting Maritime Zones: The Case of the Agean Sea," Ocean Yearbook, Vol. 8, 1989, p. 65.

51 A mere point of a feature above water at high tide could produce an EEZ of 430,796km^2 in size, if there is no competing claim. Smith, *op.cit.*, pp. 220-221.

52 *Ibid.*, p. 221.

53 Roach, *op.cit.*, p. 6.

54 See China Note Verbal to the UN Secretary General dated February 2, 2009; Korea Note Verbal to the UN Secretary General dated February 27, 2009.

55 Roach, *op.cit.*, pp. 7-8.

56 *Ibid.*, p. 4.

57 Judge Vukas of the ITLOS pointed out in his declaration that international courts and tribunals had disregarded the application of the rules regarding limited entitlement of tiny islands to maritime zones. Vukas voted in favour of the Tribunal's findings since he agreed with the findings with regard to the release of the Volga. But he expressed serious doubts as to the establishment of EEZ off the shores of the 'uninhabitable and uninhabited' islands such as Heard and Mcdonald. The Volga Case, Judgement, ITLOS, 2002, Declaration of Judge Vukas.

58 Dispute concerning Delimitation of the Maritime Boundary between Bangladesh and Myanmar in the Bay of Bengal (Bay of Bengal case), Judgment, ITLOS, 2012, para. 317.

59 Rothwell and Stephens, *op.cit.*, pp. 405-406. Ukraine contended that Serpents' Island has vegetation and sufficient supply of fresh water, so this is an 'island' under Article 121, paragraph 2 of the LOS Convention. Black Sea case, *op.cit.*, para. 184; Anderson, *op.cit.*, p. 323.

60 *Ibid* (Anderson)., para. 300.

61 Changwi Lee, Korean Journal of International Law, Vol. 54, 2009, pp. 215-217.

62 North Sea case, *op.cit.*, para. 101.

63 Tunisia/Libya case, *op.cit.*, para. 66.

64 Stuart Kaye, "Lessons Learned from the Gulf of Maine Case: The Development of Maritime Boundary Delimitation Jurisprudence since UNCLOS III," Ocean and Coastal Law Journal, Vol. 14, 2008, p. 73.

65 Smith, *op.cit.*, pp. 75-76.

66 Libya/Malta, *op.cit.*, para. 38.

67 *Ibid.*, para. 39. ICJ said that it is especially clear that where verification of the validity of title is concerned, at least in so far as those areas are situated at a distance of under 200 miles from the coasts, title depends solely on the distance from the coasts of the claimant States of any areas of sea-bed claimed by way of continental shelf, and the geological or geomorphological characteristics of those areas are

completely immaterial.

68 On 11 May 2009, South Korea submitted Preliminary Information indicating the outer limits of Korea's continental shelf beyond 200 nautical miles from the baselines in the East China Sea. According to the document, the outer limits of its continental shelf in the East China Sea are located in the Okinawa Trough. Japan filed a communication with the Secretariat of the United Nations in relation to Preliminary Information submitted by Korea, indicating that the distance between Korea and Japan is less than 400 nautical miles. Republic of Korea, Preliminary Information Regarding the Outer Limits of the Continental Shelf, 11 May 2009. Considering that Paragraph 3 of Article 76 of the LOS Convention defines the continental shelf as the submerged prolongation of the landmass of the coastal state, however, some scholars indicated that there is no reference to the precedence between continental margin and the 200mile distance. Bernard H. Oxman, Memorandum, 2008, pp. 2-3.

69 Gau, *op.cit.*, pp. 388-389.

70 Jeanette Greenfield, China's Practice in the Law of the Sea, Clarendon Press, 1992, pp. 125-127.

71 Yang, *op.cit.*, pp. 126-131.

72 Zou Keyuan, "China's Exclusive Economic Zone and Continental Shelf: Developments, Problems, and Prospects," Marine Policy, Vol. 25, 2001, pp. 77-78.

73 The 1978 Australia-Papua New Guinea Border Treaty is a good precedent. Australia and Papua New Guinea agreed to introduce four types of boundaries between them. The boundaries are sovereign boundaries between territorial waters, seabed boundary, fisheries boundary, and a special reservation area for aboriginal peoples. Dutton, *op.cit.*, p. 58.

74 Rothwell and Stephens, *op.cit.*, pp. 408-409.

References

Antunes, Nuno Marques, *Towards the Conceptualization of Maritime Delimitation: Legal and Technical Aspects of a Political Process*, Martinus Nijhoff Publishers, 2003.

Boggs, S. Whittemore, *International Boundaries: A Study of Boundary Functions and Problems*, Columbia University Press, 1940.

Brown, E. D., *The International Law of the Sea*, Vol. 1, Dartmouth Publishing Co., 1994.

Charney, Jonathan I. and Lewis M. Alexander (eds.), *International Maritime Boundaries*, Vol. 1, Martinus Nijhoff Publishers, 1993.

Churchill, R. R. and A. V. Lowe, *The Law of the Sea*, Manchester University Press, 1999.

Greenfield, Jeanette, *China's Practice in the Law of the Sea*, Clarendon Press, 1992.

Lee, Changryol, Choi Jihyun, Chang Jinhee, and Kim Donguk, *A Study on the Practices of Straight Baselines in East Asia*, KMI, 2011.

Park, Choon-Ho, *East Asia and The Law of the Sea*, Seoul National University Press, 1985.

Rothwell, Donald R. and Tim Stephens, *The International Law of the Sea*, Hart Publishing, 2010.

Sohn, Louis B. and John E. Noyes, *Cases and Materials on the Law of the Sea*, Transnational Publishers, 2004.

Weil, Prosper, *The Law of Maritime Delimitation-Reflections*, Grotius Publications, 1989.

Anderson, David H., "Maritime Delimitation in the Black Sea Case (Romania v. Ukraine)," *The Law and Practice of International Courts and Tribunals*, Vol. 8, 2009.

Gau, Michael Sheng-ti, "Problems and Practices in Maritime Delimitation in East Asia: With Special Reference to Taiwan," *Journal of East Asia and International Law*, Vol. 2, 2011.

Dutton, Peter, "Carving Up the East China Sea," *Naval War College Review*, Vol. 60, No. 2, 2007.

Lee, Seokyong, "Maritime Delimitation between Korea and China," *Korean Journal of International Law*, Vol. 52, No. 2, 2007.

Schofield, Clive, "Departures from the Coast: Trends in the Application of Territorial Sea Baselines under the Law of the Sea Convention," *The International Journal of Marine and Coastal Law*, Vol. 27, 2012.

Kaye, Stuart, "Lessons Learned from the Gulf of Maine Case: The Development of Maritime Boundary Delimitation Jurisprudence since UNCLOS III," *Ocean and Coastal Law Journal*, Vol. 14, 2008.

Smith, Robert W., "Maritime Delimitation in the South China Sea: Potentiality and Challenges," *Ocean Development and International Law*, Vol. 41, 2010.

Nelson, L. D. M., "The Roles of Equity in the Delimitation of Maritime Boundaries," *American Journal of International Law*, Vol. 84, 1990.

Oxman, Bernard B., "The Territorial Temptation: A Siren Song at Sea," *American Journal of International Law*, Vol. 100, 2006.

Roach, J. Ashley, "Maritime Boundary Delimitation: United States Practice," *Ocean Development and International Law*, Vol. 44, 2013.

Shi, Jiuyong, "Maritime Delimitation in the Jurisprudence of the International Court of Justice," *Chinese Journal of International Law*, Vol. 9, 2010.

Van Dyke, Jon M., "The Role of Islands in Delimiting Maritime Zones: The Case of the Agean Sea," *Ocean Yearbook*, Vol. 8, 1989.

Zhang, Xinjun, "Why the 2008 Sino-Japanese Consensus on the East China Sea has Stalled: Good Faith and Reciprocity Considerations in Interim Measures Pending a maritime Boundary Delimitation," *Ocean Development and International Law*, Vol. 42, 2011.

Zou, Keyuan, "China's Exclusive Economic Zone and Continental Shelf: Developments, Problems and Prospects," *Marine Policy*, Vol. 25, 2001.

A Study on the Relevant Circumstances and Countermeasures Associated with the Maritime Boundary Delimitation in the Yellow Sea between the Republic of Korea and China

YANG Hee-Cheol
Senior Researcher
Korea Institute of Ocean Science & Technology, Ansan, Korea

Abstract

The most conflicting elements associated with the maritime boundary delimitation in the Yellow Sea between the Republic of Korea (hereinafter, 'Korea') and China would be basepoints, resources, proportionality as a verification factor depending on the length of coastlines, etc. Out of the basepoints declared by China, those that would have the biggest impact on the boundary delimitation are points 9, 10, 12, and 13. Points 9 and 10 situated about 80 km off the coastline are doubted to be on low-tide elevations, or submerged sandbars. The UNCLOS stated, "where a low-tide elevation is situated wholly or partly at a distance not exceeding the breadth of the territorial sea, the low-water line on that elevation may be used as the baseline for measuring the breadth of the territorial sea." In this respect, the basepoints declared by China are against the convention. It is nearly impossible, with any interpretation method, to interpret that the basepoints meet the condition, "the sea areas lying within the lines must be sufficiently closely linked to the land domain to be subject to the regime of internal waters."

The principle of proportionality in delimiting maritime boundaries is used to draw the boundaries that are governed by two states with a proper ratio of the length of coastlines and the area of waters. China claims that the ratio of the coastlines between China and Korea is approximately 1:0.8, but, given precedents ruled by the International Court and bilateral agreement cases, it is doubtful that this is substantial enough for adjusting the median line between the two states.

In conclusion, China's stance toward the maritime boundary delimitation in the Yellow Sea secures neither any legal ground nor transparency, except its arbitrary interpretation on the ambiguous methods of drawing boundaries set forth by the UNCLOS. In particular, unless it is viewed that there is no specific circumstance to be considered other than disputes between the two states over basepoints in the Yellow Sea, an approach of considering and quantifying all relevant circumstances to be raised by each country would rather become a cause to make directions and solutions for the maritime boundary delimitation between the two states more complicated.

Key Words

Yellow Sea, Maritime Boundary Delimitation, Relevant circumstance, Baselines(Basepoint), Low-tide elevations, Proportionality

1. INTRODUCTION

Relevant legal circumstances in the maritime boundary delimitation in the Yellow Sea between Korea and China could be relatively simple, but they can be more complicated when political or security concerns are taken into account together. As prof. Oxman pointed out, starting to handle maritime boundaries as issues itself, and the entire process of boundary delimitation could be indeed all about political decisions.[1] Given that the maritime boundaries of the neighboring states of the Korean Peninsula are mostly associated with historical, geographical and political environments, the argument of prof. Oxman is quite persuasive. Still, if the two states started to negotiate the boundary delimitation in the

Yellow Sea, the negotiation is highly likely to begin focusing on certain relevant circumstances to be considered in the waters even under political circumstances. It is because the Yellow Sea does not involve issues like the sovereignty of islands or does not have complex topographical structures unlike other waters, and because the circumstances of the maritime boundary delimitation in the Yellow Sea argued by the two states can be also adjusted within the frame of legal interpretation.

This study aims to discuss the maritime boundary delimitation in the Yellow Sea focusing on relevant circumstances that may result in legal and academic arguments from the perspective of Korea (especially its counter-argument), excluding political factors that cannot be quantified. Meanwhile, detailed discussions on circumstances such as EEZ; approaches to the single line of a continental shelf that should be considered and analyzed on the basis of general understanding; and economic circumstances are excluded from the body of this study. This study also aims to provide a theoretical foundation to be used by Korea in the process of relevant negotiations by reviewing international or bilateral discussions on boundary delimitation; a series of the policies of the expansion of maritime jurisdiction executed by China; and problems in China's domestic laws. In particular, there is indeed considerable gap between China's domestic laws and basepoints claimed by China associated with the maritime boundary delimitation between Korea and China, which is expected to have a significant implication for Korea to set a strategic direction for the maritime boundary delimitation in the Yellow Sea going forward.

2. APPROACHES FOR KOREA-CHINA MARITIME BOUNDARY DELIMITATION AND RELEVANT CIRCUMSTANCES

2-1. APPROACHES FOR KOREA-CHINA MARITIME BOUNDARY DELIMITATION IN YELLOW SEA

2-1-1. GEOGRAPHICAL STATUS OF YELLOW SEA AND RESOURCE DEVELOPMENT

The Yellow Sea extends by about 470 nautical miles from north to south, and about 360 nautical miles from east to west. Its depth is about 44 m on average with a maximum of about 140m. It has an area of about 380,000km.[2] The sea bottom is slowly decreasing from the north, east and west sides toward the middle and southeastern parts of the Yellow Sea. The depth reaches about 90-100m near Jeju Island.[3]

The Yellow Sea is situated on the same continental shelf. Basins near the southern and northern parts of the sea as well as those near the Korean Peninsula are reported to have large amounts of oil and gas deposits, but as the boundaries between South Korea and China, and between China and North Korea have not been clearly established, conflicts over the issue have been continuously raised.[4] South Korea and China already tried to establish the boundaries for the development of resources in the Yellow Sea, but they only mutually exchanged diplomatic complaints.[5] When the Korea National Oil Corporation tried to explore oil at Block 2, located within the EEZ of the Yellow Sea 250 km off the coast of Gunsan, China sent complaints to Korea six times,[6] claiming that "crude oil under the Penglai oil field on the offshore of the Shandong Peninsula, 400 km away from Block 2, can be flown toward Korea if Block 2 starts to produce crude oil." The Chinese National Offshore Oil Corporation signed a production sharing contract, including drilling exploratory wells, with Devon Energy Corporation (U.S.) in 2006 at Block 11/34, which is highly likely to be overlapped with the second seabed mining area established by Korea,[7,8] and the Korean government sent a complaint to its counterpart.[9] Even in the midst of such conflicts between the two, a series of efforts for bilateral cooperation regarding issues of the Yellow Sea have been witnessed. Korea and China signed a fisheries agreement in 2000 to maintain order in fishing operations before establishing the maritime boundary delimitation in the Yellow Sea, and officially enacted the agreement in 2001. China and North Korea also signed a joint oil and gas development agreement in Bohai and West Korea Bay Basins.[10]

2-1-2. PRINCIPLES AND STANCES OF KOREA AND CHINA ON
MARITIME BOUNDARIES

Conflicts between Korea and China over maritime jurisdiction started
back in the 1970s, but their will to delimit maritime boundaries was not
strong enough to bear political burdens until an exclusive economic zone
(EEZ) of 200 nautical miles was first adopted in the UNCLOS. Upon the
enactment of the UNCLOS, however, the two states declared their EEZ
of 200 nautical miles (Korea and China declared the EEZ Act, and the EEZ and
Continental Shelf Act respectively in 1996 and 1998.), and, thus, they could no
longer delay the establishment of the maritime boundary delimitation.

Korea took a very passive stand on an exclusive economic zone in
the 3rd United Nations Law of the Sea Conference started in 1973. It was
because Korea had to take into consideration its industrial structure highly
dependent on the deep-sea fishing, but upon the ratification of the United
Nations Convention on the Law of the Sea in 1996, Korea shifted its
policy direction toward the exclusive economic zone of 200 nautical miles.
The Exclusive Economic Zone Act declared in 1996 states that Korea
shall not exercise its rights in the area beyond the median line between
Korea and relevant states unless agreed separately with the relevant states
(Article 5), and that the delimitation of the exclusive economic zone shall
be "established by agreement with the relevant states on the basis of
international laws (Article 2)." Meanwhile, its stance toward a continental
shelf was specified in the Submarine Mineral Resources Development Act
in 1970.[11] The mining areas near the maritime boundary with China in
the Yellow Sea were established using the method of drawing a median
line from the outermost islands. Korea also claimed to Japan its maritime
boundary up to the Okinawa Trench based on the principle of the natural
extension of land, while China and Japan claimed the continental shelf
boundary based on the principle of natural extension, and of the median
line respectively.

China started to express its concrete argument over its maritime
jurisdiction and boundary delimitation in the 3rd United Nations Law

of the Sea Conference, and it also showed its support for the declaration of South American countries on the jurisdiction of 200 nautical miles in the 1970s.[12] However, China's stance toward the maritime jurisdiction scope was reflected in its domestic acts after Korea and Japan declared their EEZ and Continental shelf act in 1996. China officially declared the EEZ and Continental Shelf Act in 1998. Under the act, when its claim over the EEZ and continental shelf conflicts with that of the relevant states, the delimitation of the EEZ and continental shelf shall be "established by agreement with the relevant states based on the principle of equity on the basis of international laws (Article 2)." China's principle and approaches toward maritime boundary delimitation have often become controversial due to the selection of basepoints for straight baselines as well as ambiguous meanings.

Given the stances of the two states on the maritime boundary delimitation in the Yellow Sea, Korea's method of drawing a median line and China's principle of equity seem to be in conflict with each other, but, considering that China has not officially suggested the principle of equity as a method of drawing boundaries, negotiations between the two states on the maritime boundary delimitation are likely to be executed focusing on certain circumstances in the Yellow Sea in the working-level process. The most conflicting elements include basepoints, resources, and coastlines as a verification factor for proportionality.

2-2. Relevant Circumstances

2-2-1. Basepoints

China issued the "Declaration on the Territorial Sea" in 1958 claiming that the baseline for measuring the breadth of its territorial sea is the straight lines connecting basepoints on the mainland coast and on the outermost of the coaster islands. This was specified in Article 3 and Article 15 of the "Law on the Territorial Sea and the Contiguous Zone" adopted in 1992 in which 49 basepoints adjacent to its mainland coast, and 28 basepoints for the Paracel Islands were created as basepoints for measuring its territorial sea. Out of them, those that may affect the negotiation between Korea and China regarding the maritime boundary delimitation of the Yellow Sea are basepoints 1-13, and according to a report of the U.S. Department of State, most of them are found not to meet the principles set forth in the United Nations Convention on the Law of the Sea (UNCLOS).[13] It is known that Korea notified to China its diplomatic position that it could not accept some basepoints of straight baselines, at least points 9 (Macaiheng, 麻菜珩), 10 (Waikejiao, 外磕脚), 12 (Haijiao, 海礁), and 13 (Dongnanjiao, 東南礁).[14]

Among the basepoints of straight baselines declared by China, those that may have the biggest impact on the maritime boundary delimitation between Korea and China include points 9, 10, 12 and 13. If points 9 and 10 are recognized, Korea will have a loss of approximately 5,671km², and if points 12 and 13 are recognized, Korea should take a loss of approximately 3,635km².[15] Points 9 and 10 are situated on a well-developed shoal about 80km off the coast of Yancheng in Jiangsu Province. Since these points seem to be situated on low-tide elevations or submerged sandbars at a distance exceeding the breadth of the territorial sea, it is necessary to accurately verify facts. Based on the survey done for this study, however, points 9 and 10 set by China are considered to be situated either on submerged sandbars or low-tide elevations that are submerged for most of the days of the year, even if they are above water irregularly. Thus, this needs to be discussed along with the legal status of low-tide elevations.

The UNCLOS states that where a low-tide elevation is situated wholly or partly at a distance not exceeding the breadth of the territorial sea, the low-water line on that elevation may be used as the baseline for measuring the breadth of the territorial sea, considering the breadth of the territorial sea as an important criteria to judge the proximity to the coastal line. It is notable that Article 1 and Article 2 highlight "at a distance not exceeding the breadth of the territorial sea <u>from the mainland or an island</u> (underlined arbitrarily by the author)" regarding a low-tide elevation, and this indicates that even if a low-tide elevation (B) is lying within the distance of 12 nautical miles from another low-tide elevation (B), and if elevation B is situated at a distance exceeding 12 nautical miles from the mainland or an island, then, elevation B has no territorial sea of its own. In other words, the articles reaffirm that in waters where low-tide elevations are scattered around, "leapfrog"[16] or "stepping stone"[17] methods of establishing basepoints by using one low-tide elevation located within the distance not exceeding 12 nautical miles as a medium to connect it to others situated outside are not allowable. The ILC also added "as measured from the mainland or an island" to Article 11 of the final "Convention on the Territorial Sea and the Contiguous Zone" in 1958 to prevent drying rocks and drying shoals from being used infinitely in a leapfrogging way, which is a reasonable action.[18]

Therefore, according to the UNCLOS, where a low-tide elevation is situated wholly or partly at a distance not exceeding 12 nautical miles from the coast, the low-water line on that elevation can be used as the baseline for measuring the breadth of the territorial sea. However, in waters where the straight baseline is already established, even if a low-tide elevation is situated within the distance of 10 nautical miles from the baseline, and if it is situated outside the territorial sea 12 nautical miles off the coast, the low-water line on that elevation cannot be used for measuring the breadth of the territorial sea. This is clearly shown in the article of the UNCLOS where the status of an low-tide elevation is defined as "from the mainland or an island."

After all, the convention limits the geographical value of a low-tide elevation for a coastal state to claim its maritime jurisdiction to coastal waters, and its ability to generate the territorial sea is relying on its proximity to the mainland or an island. In this respect, low-tide elevations are often called "parasitic basepoints."[19] It should be also noted that the distance or proximity applied here is limited within 12 nautical miles not from the straight baseline, but from the mainland or an island.[20]

Then, except the limited function of low-tide elevations to be used as basepoints for the territorial sea, is there any possibility that low-tide elevations in waters of which coastal formations are roughly convex in form can be used as basepoints to draw straight baselines? To answer this question, Paragraph 4 of Article 7 of the UNCLOS can be referred to. The paragraph states, "straight baselines shall not be drawn to and from low-tide elevations, unless lighthouses or similar installations which are permanently above sea level have been built on them or except in instances where the drawing of baselines to and from such elevations has received general international recognition (underlined arbitrarily by the author)," and this paragraph exactly reflects Paragraph 3 of Article 4 of the "Convention on the Territorial Sea and the Contiguous Zone" in 1958, and the underlined part is newly added considering the ICJ's *Fisheries Case* (UK v. Nor.)[21] in 1951, in which Norway established its straight baselines for measuring its territorial sea. It shows that the UNCLOS does not accept the use of low-tide elevations for establishing straight baselines in principle, but allows two exceptions including "lighthouses or similar installations which are permanently above sea level have been built on low-tide elevation," and "or except in instances where the drawing of baselines to and from such elevations has received general international recognition." This was stipulated for the purpose of eliminating any cases that artificial structures are being used to create their own territorial sea, and this is an exception to the general conditions of "a naturally formed area of land" and the possibility of drawing from high-tide elevations.

Other basepoints that may affect Korea's maritime boundary delimitation are point 12 and 13. The two basepoints are known as uninhabited islands situated approximately 69.9 nautical miles off the coastline of Shanghai. Scholars such as Allen and Mitchell point out that Haijiao and Dongnanjiao depart from the general direction of the coast, but prof. Jeanette Greenfield criticizes that such an argument is simply based on distance and is not sufficient to judge the general direction of the coast or proximity conditions, supporting the stance of China.[22] She argues that such basepoints should be judged based on their relations with other islands in the coast and the coastal lines of land. Prof. Greenfield's argument seems to be grounded on the fact that no clear dividing line exists due to numerous islands off the mainland of China, like the judgement of the ICJ in 1951, doubting whether to "constitute a clear dividing line between land and sea."[23] This is the logic that allows the use of straight baselines in geographical environments like the coastal area of China where islands are scattered like the judgement in 1951. Under the logic of prof. Greenfield, however, it is highly likely that straight baselines can be established by abusing the leapfrogging method that is restricted in principle, but allowed as an exception by Article 11 of the Convention on the Territorial Sea and the Contiguous Zone in 1958, and Article 13 of the UNCLOS. Although the Convention in 1958, and the UNCLOS limit using the leapfrogging method for establishing straight baselines only to "low-tide elevations," requiring further discussion, it is viewed that conditions such as "along the coast in its immediate vicinity" and "must not depart to any appreciable extent from the general direction of the coast, ... must be sufficiently closely linked to the land domain to be subject to the regime of internal waters" ensure that such conditions should be interpreted strictly to meet the initial intention of the UNCLOS. As mentioned above, it is because geographical locations of Haijiao and Dongnanjiao situated 69.9 nautical miles off the Shanghai coast cannot be by any means interpreted as "sufficiently closely linked to the land domain to be subject to the regime of internal waters."

2-2-2. Proportionality between Length of Coastlines and Area of Waters

Proportionality in maritime boundary delimitation can be used to verify the equity of the results in the final stage of delimiting maritime boundaries. Maritime boundary delimitation is to divide certain waters neither equally nor proportionately. Verifying proportionality itself is not a method of delimiting maritime boundaries. It is desirable to view proportionality as a means to verify whether it is necessary to adjust the results since it is believed that the length of the relevant coastline of each country or the proportion of seas allocated to each country is seriously unbalanced.[24]

The principle of proportionality was first formed in the process of delimiting continental shelf maritime boundaries based on the principle under which seas are governed by the land domain,[25] but it has been used broadly in the process of maritime boundary delimitation, viewed as an important relevant circumstance, and served as a basic element to equitably delimit maritime boundaries.

In the *North Sea Continental Shelf Cases* in 1969, the ICJ stated, "there could not be a question of rendering the situation of a State with an extensive coastline similar to that of a State with a restricted coastline," and added, "states whose coastlines are comparable in length have been given broadly equal treatment by nature." It went on to state, therefore, "it is unacceptable that a state should enjoy continental shelf rights considerably different from those of its neighbors merely because the coastline is roughly convex in form," laying a theoretical foundation for proportionality depending on coastlines.[26] In the *Tunisia v. Libya Case* in 1985, the ICJ stated, "the coast of the territory of the State is the decisive factor for title to submarine areas adjacent to it"[27] and went on to judge that proportionality is the basic principle for the equitable boundary delimitation between relevant states. In the case, the ratio of the coastlines was 31 to 69 (Libya/Tunisia), and that of the straight coastlines was 34 to 66. The final ratio for the maritime areas was calculated to be 40:60. The ICJ decided that proportionality was met in this case.[28] In the *Delimitation of the Maritime Area between Canada and France* (St. Pierre and Miquelon) case in 1992, the ratio of the coastlines was 15.3 to 1 (Canada/France), and the areas was finally divided by the ratio of 16.4 to 1, and the ICJ decided that proportionality was met in this case.[29] In the *Qatar v. Bahrain Case* in 2001, Qatar claimed that the ratio of the coastlines of Qatar and the principal islands of Bahrain should be 1.59:1, but the Court judged that the claim without an actual measurement was not substantial enough for adjusting the most equidistant line.[30] In the *Cameroon v. Nigeria Case* in 2002, the two states wanted to adjust the provisionally drawn line proportionally to the length of their coastlines, but the Court found that it was not substantial enough for relocating the equidistant line.[31]

Unlike precedents ruled by the International Court of Justice, it is difficult to find agreements between states in which the proportionality principle was clearly applied except some cases. It may be because many boundary delimitation agreements were not publicly disclosed due to the sensitivity of the results, but it can be also attributable to the fact that agreements themselves are subjectively decided with other factors combined together.[32]

Then, is there any possibility to apply the proportionality principle to the maritime boundary delimitation in the Yellow Sea? China claims that the ratio of the coastlines between China and Korea is approximately 1:0.8, but it is doubtful that the ratio is substantial enough for adjusting the provisionally drawn line. As shown above, the proportionality principle is not applying a measured ratio as it is, but it is just an adjustable factor against significant imbalance. Thus, even if the ratio claimed by China is accepted as it is, it seems to be not substantial enough for adjusting the provisionally drawn line.

Of course, from the perspective of Korea, it is not necessary to disagree the application of the proportionality principle. It is because there are several strategic approaches that Korea can adopt in claiming the length of coastlines. For instance, they can be measured from straight baselines or from low-water lines of the two states, or by recognizing the coastlines of uninhabited islands in the relevant waters, or by measuring the coastline that connects the southern land and Jeju Island. Each of the methods requires strategic analysis of gains and losses.

3. CHINA'S POLICY FOR THE EXPANSION OF ITS JURISDICTION

Another matter that should be noted regarding the maritime boundary delimitation in the Yellow Sea is China's policy for the extension of its jurisdiction in its laws. The extension of jurisdiction has been pursued and linked with the macroscopic national policies as it is in line with the military and political aspects. Research institutes and relevant government departments have been individually executing projects on relevant issues.

3-1. CHINA'S JURISDICTION EXPANSION POLICY

China started to develop a plan for maritime surveys on surrounding waters after the 1970s, and it is known that China had already finished geophysical and submarine topographic surveys on gravity, magnetic force and earthquake from the Bohai Basin to the northern continental shelf in the South China Sea in the early 1980s. For the duration from 1975 to 1985, China had conducted comprehensive surveys on geological and geophysical features on the continental shelf from the Bohai Sea to the East China Sea, and it had also executed the 908 Plan (Project for comprehensive surveys and evaluation on surrounding waters) by investing 240 billion won for the duration from 2004 to 2009 in order to prepare for the application of the extension of its continental shelf.

Along with surveys on the resources and geological structures of surrounding waters, China also enacted the Nautical Chart Protection Act in December, 2009, (enforced on March 1, 2010). The act aims to protect the ecosystem of islands and surrounding waters, but it should be also noted that China wanted to prepare for potential disputes with neighboring states over jurisdiction by protecting basepoints of its territorial sea and uninhabited islands.

3-2. MARITIME BOUNDARY DELIMITATION BETWEEN CHINESE LOCAL GOVERNMENTS

Another notable circumstance regarding the maritime boundary delimitation in the Yellow Sea is China's policy approach on the jurisdiction scope and boundary delimitation principles of local governments.

Since the necessity to address boundary issues between provincial (county) governments was raised in 1984, China's State Oceanic Administration established leadership teams (領導小組) for national maritime boundaries in April, 2000, and started to review policies and execution plans associated with maritime boundaries. Under this initiative, about 6,500 islands with an area of over 500㎡ became to play an important role as economic resources for technologies of fishing and marine science, and, unlike the past years, the authority for the management of waters has been clearly divided, which was based on the necessity to pursue economic, social and national benefits.

For the maritime boundary delimitation between local governments, the Chinese government had aggressively executed its initiative and established a decision-making structure. By the end of 2008, China completed the boundary delimitation between 8 provincial governments neighboring coasts in total, and boundaries between 233 county governments, 97% of the total counties, were established.[33]

In the "notice on the tasks associated with the county-level jurisdiction boundaries of waters for the General Office of the State Council,"[34] the jurisdiction scope of local governments was set as 12 nautical miles. It should be noted that even with the principle set forth by the State Council, some local governments approach the issue of the outer limit of their jurisdiction scope differently, which has a significant implication in terms of the validity of China's establishment of its territorial sea.

Some experts in local maritime boundary in China point out that it would cause no problem in viewing the territorial sea as the outer limit in areas of which outer limit of the maritime boundary is relatively close to their coastline, but that it would be unreasonable to view the areas situated relatively away from the coastline as the outer limit.[35] For instance, China set basepoints for the territorial sea both on Dashandao Island (達山島), situated off the southeastern coast of Rizhao City (日照市) in the Shandong Peninsula, and Sushandao Island (蘇山島), off the coastline of Rongcheng City (榮成市).[36] However, the straight baseline that connects the two islands is situated at a distance exceeding 20 nautical miles from the coastline, and if the outer limit of the territorial sea in the water is established with the outer limit of the boundary between relevant local governments, then the line will be situated about 30 nautical miles away from the coastline. From the perspective of local governments, it would be problematic in managing the waters under their jurisdiction, and efficiently enforcing laws. To consider the concerns, the People's Government of Shandong Province issued the "notice for the implementation of the notice on the tasks associated with the county-level jurisdiction boundaries of waters for the General Office of the State Council (魯政發[2002]33號)," adding a slight condition to the notice mentioned above (國辦發 12號). That is, in the original sentence, "the end point of the boundary shall be limited to the outer limit of the territorial sea (界線的終點止於領海外部界限)," the government added a word "可" as "界線的終點可止於領海外部界限 (underlined arbitrarily by the author)," meaning, "the end point of the boundary can be limited to the outer limit of the territorial sea." This is a new attempt on the scope of the jurisdiction boundaries.

Based on relevant regulations, China prepared policy grounds to set the end point in the waters of Shandong Province not as the outer limit of the territorial sea, but "to the baseline of the territorial sea." Based on this, the Shandong Provincial government is planning to set the outer limit of the maritime boundary delimitation between Yantai (烟台市) and Weihai (威海市); Yantai (烟台市) and Qingdao (青島市); Qingdao (青島市) and Rizhao (日照市) as the baseline of the territorial sea, not as the outer limit of the territorial sea.[37]

As straight baselines set by China are subject to the conditions of the UNCLOS, that is "the general direction of the coast" and "sufficiently closely linked to the land domain," it is possible to doubt that setting the outer limit of the maritime boundaries between Chinese local governments as the baseline of the territorial sea, not as the outer limit of the territorial sea violates the condition, "sufficiently closely linked to the land domain to be subject to the regime of internal waters."

4. COUNTERMEASURES: CONCLUSION

The UNCLOS, in its preamble, noted that the states parties to the convention were "conscious that the problems of ocean space are closely interrelated and need to be considered as a whole." From this statement, it can be said that this convention aims to extend the jurisdictional seas of coastal states, and manage seas comprehensively. This means that seas are no longer viewed simply as places to utilize, but that the world has turned the page to a new era of viewing seas as places to be comprehensively and spatially managed across various sectors including development and use, environmental protection and conservation, and security. This contains a possibility of expanding the conceptual definition of seas of a state from that of today. The meaning of maritime boundary delimitation for each state lies right here. It is the time Korea with a limited amount of resources should develop countermeasures for each stage to prepare for maritime boundary delimitation with a determined will to defend its jurisdictional seas. To this end, several measures are developed as follows:

First, an analysis of gains and losses needs to be conducted focusing on accessible methods while assessing economic values of relevant circumstances that can be considered between Korea and China. As pointed out in the body of this study, given that there is no special consideration in the maritime boundary delimitation in the Yellow Sea between Korea and China, it is highly likely that this will be approached, in the end, with the method of drawing a median line, and with the syllogistic approach applied to precedents ruled by the International Court. However, China's stance seems to utilize its arbitrary interpretation on the ambiguous methods of boundary delimitation set forth in the Convention, rather than to secure legal grounds or transparency, which is viewed to have no implication in the working-level process. In particular, unless it is viewed that there is no specific circumstances to be considered other than disputes between the two states over basepoints in the Yellow Sea, an approach of considering and quantifying all relevant circumstances to be raised by each country would rather become a cause to make directions and solutions for the maritime boundary delimitation between the two states more complicated.

However, one thing that should be noted in delimiting maritime boundaries in the Yellow Sea is to consider the optimal or maximum jurisdiction in analyzing circumstances associated with relevant waters. If all circumstances claimed by both states are accepted in the Yellow Sea that has indeed no special circumstance to be considered, the maximum jurisdiction will cause an imbalance in waters. Thus, it seems to be applied only restrictively. On the other hand, an approach to execute maritime boundary delimitation focusing on values prioritized by each state is desirable given that the two states will be able to secure their intended optimal jurisdiction based on the evaluation results on each water. Of course, the optimal jurisdiction here should be approached with the method of drawing a median line, and means an economic value comprehensively assessed with mineral resources, fishery resources, and maritime safety or defense.

To determine the optimal jurisdiction from this perspective, two preliminary surveys and approaches are required. First, it is necessary to conduct marine scientific research (or surveys) on relevant natural and social science features of surrounding waters including topographical and geological features, marine ecosystem, mineral and fishery resources, uninhabited islands and surrounding rocks. The fact that there is no special circumstance to be considered in the Yellow Sea on the continental shelf shared by the two states indicates that there is no geographical or non-geographical consideration for adjusting the median line. However, it is still necessary to conduct an internal assessment on geological structures including mineral resources as a precondition necessary to determine the optimal jurisdiction. Second, it is also necessary to conduct an analysis of gains and losses regarding the basepoints for the territorial sea claimed by China, or basepoints that can be utilized in determining the median line between the two states. Basepoints mean in general those for the territorial sea established by a coastal state for measuring the EEZ or the outer limit of its continental shelf based on its domestic law, but basepoints in maritime boundary delimitation can be interpreted to include those separately established or designated for maritime boundary delimitation. For this reason, the ICJ pointed out in the *Anglo-Norwegian Fisheries Case* that although domestic laws of a state are not covered by international law, areas such as seas are covered by international law on one side,[38] and that they become effective by international law.[39] In the *Romania v. Ukraine Case* in 2009, the ICJ reaffirmed this by stating that the issue of determining the baseline for the purpose of measuring the breadth of the continental shelf and EEX, and the issue of identifying basepoints for drawing an equidistance/median line for the purpose of delimiting the continental shelf and the EEX between adjacent/opposite states are two different issues.[40] From this perspective, it can be said that there is a possibility that China's action for drawing a median line in the process of delimiting the maritime boundary in the Yellow Sea can result in drawing a median line by ignoring basepoints between coasts, normal baselines and straight baselines, or certain controversial basepoints for the territorial sea, or that a median line can be drawn between the basepoints established by each state separately. Thus, it is urgently required to conduct an analysis of gains and losses focusing on already-discovered geographical status and basepoints for the territorial sea; basepoints that can be established; or potential strategic basepoints of Korea by connecting economically profitable waters.

Second, it is necessary to analyze and develop theoretical and working-level countermeasures to China's policies and actions associated with the maritime boundary delimitation and the extension of its jurisdiction. For instance, the maritime boundary delimitation in the Gulf of Tonkin that was signed between China and Vietnam in 2000 and became effective in 2004 gives a meaningful implication regarding China's unclear principles and approaches to maritime boundary delimitation. In the case, China highlighted the principle of equity outwardly, but focused on the half-and-half strategy in the actual negotiation process, taking the method of drawing a median line, and it was found that in the results of the negotiation the method was applied as well. China's view on Coco Island near Vietnam and Bach Long Vi Island (白龍尾島) in the Gulf of Tonkin is also a good example for analyzing the stance of China on legal grounds for the boundary delimitation of islands.

Third, it is necessary to promote cooperative relations between the two states in order to increase its function as a shared sea along with the expansion of marine scientific research on the surrounding waters of Korea for maritime boundary delimitation. The marine scientific research includes actions of internal surveys and interpretation for Korea to develop the strategies for maritime boundary delimitation internally. For promoting cooperative relations, cooperative research regarding the management of the waters in the Yellow Sea can be conducted. That is, such marine scientific surveys in the Yellow Sea are needed, even under the conflicts over jurisdiction between the two states, based on the directions of individual purposes including the necessity of managing waters and maritime boundary delimitation.

Notes

1. Prof. Oxman viewed that decisions in negotiating boundary delimitation, suggesting certain boundaries, consenting to reach an agreement, and agreeing on certain boundaries are all political decisions, and understood that court decisions with a binding force are also part of political decisions. Bernard H. Oxman, "Political, Strategic, and Historical Considerations", in J.I. Charney and L.M. Alexander, *International Maritime Boundaries, Vol. I (part I)* (Martinus Nijhoff Publishers: Dordrecht, 1993), pp. 10-11.

2. 梁熙喆 (Hee-Cheol), Yang, "從國際海洋劃界原則和實踐論中國EEZ與大陸架劃界問題 (A Study on the Issues of China's EEZ and Maritime Boundary Delimitation of Continental Shelf Through International Principles and Cases of Maritime Boundary Delimitation)," 法學博士學位論文 (Thesis for doctor's degree of laws), 國立臺灣大學校(National Taiwan University), 2006, p. 341.

3. Hee-Cheol, Yang, "The Role of the Sedimentary Deposits (silt line) from Rivers Flowing into the Sea in the Yellow Sea Maritime Boundary," *Ocean and Polar Research,* Vol. 31, No. 1 (2009), p. 33.

4. *Ibid.*

5. Donga Daily Newspaper (2006. 11. 9), Government briefing of the Ministry of Foreign Affairs, Jan. 26, 2007.

6. Joongang Daily Newspaper, "China-Japan Conflicts over East China Sea, why matters?," Sept. 22, 2005.

7. It is difficult to accurately measure the actual overlapped area between the Chinese mining field and Korea's Block 2 due to the different coordinate methods of the two, but it is reportedly about 80,000m².

8. Donga Daily Newspaper (Nov. 9, 2006).

9. Government briefing of the Ministry of Foreign Affairs, Jan. 26, 2007.

10. *Supra* note 2, p. 349.

11. The Submarine Mineral Resources Development Act enacted in 1970 was affected by the report on the geological exploration in East Asia in 1969 funded by the UNECAFE. The so-called "Emery Report" stated that the high possibility of oil and gas deposits in the Yellow Sea and East China Sea, triggering the ambition of states in Northeast Asia to develop resources. Korea swiftly took actions for the development of resources by enacting the Submarine Mineral Resources Development Act.

12. 28(3) UN FAOR Supp. 21, pp. 72-73; UN Doc.A/9021 (1973).

13. US Department of State, Straight Baseline Claim: China, *Limits in the Seas*, No. 117 (1996) referred.

14. David Chen, "Baselines for Territorial Waters," Window (May. 24, 1996), p. 28. Nak-jeong, Choi 『Why the Korean-Japanese Fisheries Agreement must be abolished?』 (Seoul, Sechang Publish, 2002), p. 218 Requotation.

15. The area was calculated using the UTM52 coordinate program of the KORDI called Evergreens.

16. R.R.Chuchill and A.V.Lowe, *The Law of the Sea, 3rd ed.* (Juris Publishing, 1999), p. 48.

17. Carleton, Chris and Schofield, Clive, "Developments in the technical Determination of Maritime Space: Delimitation, Dispute Resolution, Geographical Information Systems and the Role of the Technical Expert," *Maritime Briefing*, Vol. 3, No. 4 (2002), p. 38.

18. Gary Kinght and Hungdah Chiu, *The International Law of the Sea: Cases, Documents, and Readings* (Elsevier Applied Science: London/NewYork, 1991), pp. 144-145.

19. Clive Schofield, "Some Problems Relating to the Definition of 'Insular Formations' in International Law: Islands and Low-Tide Elevations," *Maritime Briefing*, Vol. 1, No. 5 (1995), p. 7.

20. Carleton, Chris and Schofield, Clive, *op.cit.*, p. 38.

21. *Fisheries Case (UK v. Nor.), Judgement of December 18th, 1951, ICJ Reports* 116.

22. Jeanette Greenfield, *China's Practice in the Law of the Sea* (New York: Clarendon Press, 1992), p. 69.

23. ICJ (1951), paras. 127-129.

24. *Case Concerning Maritime Delimitation in the Black Sea (Romania v. Ukraine)*, Judgment of 3 February 2009, para. 110.

25. *Supra* note 2, p. 173.

26. *North Sea Continental Shelf Case (1969), 8 International Legal Materials* (1969), para. 91.

27. *Tunisia v. Libya Case* (1985), para. 73.

28. *Ibid.*, para. 100.

29. *St.Pierre v. Miquelon Case* (1992), paras. 61-62.

30. *Qatar v. Bahrain Case* (2001), para. 243.

31. *Cameroon v. Nigeria Case* (2002), para. 301.

32. *Supra* note 2, p. 176.

33. 中國海洋年鑑編纂委員會, 前揭書, p. 141.

34. 國辦發 [2002] 12號.

35. 老鐵 (LaoTie), 『關於縣際間海域勘界有關問題的探討 (A Study on the Issues Associated with Maritime Boundary between Xian Governments)』(海域管理 (Management of Waters), 2008), pp. 55-56.

36. Point 6 on Sushandao (蘇山島), and point 8 on Dashandao (達山島)

37. *Supra* note 35.

38. 魏敏 (WeiMin), 海洋法 (*The International Law of the Sea*), (北京: 法律出版社 (Law Press China), 1995), p. 29.

39. In the case, the ICJ stated, "The territorial sea and its baselines belong to the sovereignty of a coastal state, and can be executed by its domestic law, provided that they are determined by international law as they are associated with the interests of other states at the same time. The determination of waters has always an international aspect, and they cannot be determined only with the will of a coastal state expressed in its domestic law. The boundary delimitation itself is absolutely an unilateral action since it can be done by a coastal state, but the validity of the boundary for other relevant states should be decided by international law." "*Anglo-Norwegian Fisheries Case, in Reports of Judgements, Advisory Opinions and Orders,*" *ICJ Reports* (1951), p. 132.

40. *Case Concerning Maritime Delimitation in the Black Sea (Romania v. Ukraine),* Judgment of 3 February 2009, para. 137.

SPECIAL REPORTS

International Military Tribunal for the Trial of the Major War Criminals in the Far East and Its Trial Verification and International Legal Issues

LEE Jang-Hie
Professor Emeritus
Hankuk University of Foreign Studies Law School, Seoul, Korea

1. JAPAN'S INTERNATIONAL MILITARY TRIBUNAL AND HISTORICAL IMPLICATIONS OF ITS TRIAL VERIFICATION

The allied forces agreed on signing the San Francisco Peace Treaty and the U.S.-Japan Security Treaty after Japan, a war crimes state, surrendered unconditionally on September 2, 1945 and agreed to accept the rulings of the International Military Tribunal for the trial of the major war criminals in the Far East (hereafter, "Tokyo Trial").[1] Thus, Japan reintegrated into the international society.

The Kono Statement, named after former Chief Cabinet Secretary Yohei Kono in 1993, was the first apology to the Korean women who were forced to work at Japanese military brothels during World War II.

However, after the conservative regime of Abe came back to power in 2012, the Japanese government went back on past promises with international society and denied legal responsibility for the Pacific War and embraced the "Colonial Modernization" theory. In February 2014, Japan's Chief Cabinet Secretary Yoshihida Suga said in the Japanese parliament that the Japanese government is considering reexamining testimony previously given by 16 former sex slaves (Koreans) which was used to draw" up the "Kono Statement."[2] The reason is that the Kono Statement[3] was the outcome of political bargaining between Republic of Korea (hereinafter, 'Korea') and Japan. It is highly likely that Mr. Abe will use the results of the reexamination of the Tokyo trials as grounds for the denial of Japan's war responsibility and as a springboard for revising the pacific Constitution that renounces war. This amounts to nothing more than a complete negation of Japan's past.[4]

Moreover, on November 14, 2015, Japan's ruling Liberal Democratic Party (LDP) will set up a war and history recognition verification committee reporting directly to Prime Minister Shinzo Abe to reevaluate the verdicts handed down by the International Military Tribunal for the Far East to Japan's World War II criminals.

This history verification committee is to reinvestigate the rulings of the Tokyo Trial in order to justify their past history. The fact that the Abe regime is refusing to apologize for the past wrongdoing of the Japanese government, denying legal responsibility, and pursuing militarization is of great concern in regards to peace in East Asia.

The fundamental cause of the conflict on past liquidation negotiations between Korea and Japan, including the matters of the comfort women, is that these negotiations got off on the wrong foot. The Taft-Katsura Agreement of 1905 laid the ground for the unequal Treaty of Annexation between Korea and Japan, which led to the colonialization of Korea. And failing to strictly punish war criminals during the Tokyo Trials (1946-1948) resulted in the revival of the war criminals as the main group of Japan's history. These people were deeply involved in the San Francisco Peace Treaty in 1952 and the Basic Treaty of Korea and Japan in 1965. They played a vital role in leaving the legacy of incomplete resolution of war crimes between Korea and Japan.

Germany, which was another war crimes state, complied with the rulings of the International Military Tribunal for prosecution and punishment of the major war criminals of the European Axis[5] (hereafter, "Nuremberg Trials")[6] on the basis of international law, which consisted of fair punishments for war criminals, and implemented corresponding legislations. These measures seemed to be harsh for Germany at the time but through this process, Germany was not only able to receive cooperation and trust from neighboring countries in overcoming its division but also was able to participate in the process of European integration as a leading country.

In 2012, the right-wing Abe regime is using the militarization doctrine and the denial of past wrongdoing for internal political gains. A primary example of militarization is Japanese government's attempt to amend Article 9 of Japan's Peace Constitution. A primary example of the denial of past wrongdoing is refusing to comply with the recommendations of the UN Human Rights Council and international society regarding the matters of the comfort women. The UNHRC and international society already stated that Japan's comfort women was a state crime against humanity and specifically a "crime of sex slaves that was carried out by the state" and that the Japanese government should compensate the victims and punish the criminals through special legislation.

The Japanese government, however, filed proof of the non-existence of compulsion regarding the matters of comfort women to the UNHRC, which contradicts the recent 12.28 Agreement between Korea and Japan in 2015.

Japanese government's attempt to reinvestigate the Tokyo Trial demonstrates that the Japanese government is denying the rulings of the Tokyo Trial as well as their crimes on the Pacific War and colonization. It is quite clear that these measures will have a negative impact on the resolution of unresolved past issues of the Imperial Japan.

The Agreement of December 28, 2015 has demonstrated that the Japanese government is denying legal responsibility regarding the issues of sex slaves during war times.

Even during the Tokyo Trial, the Japanese attorney defended Japan's war crimes and the rightists did not comply with the rulings. Japan's authorities released 15 war criminals, who were found guilty during the

Tokyo Trial, by adopting a resolution in the Diet.

The objective of this paper is to review the activities of the Japanese government's history verification body and to examine the logic behind the Abe regime's reinvestigations and denial of the Tokyo Trial and to refute this logic on the basis of international law.

2. JAPAN'S HISTORY AND WAR CRIME VERIFICATIONS ACTIVITIES

The Abe regime's intentions are to deny the illegality of Japan's colonial rule. This is shown in various activities of the history verifications body after Abe took office.

- On June 18, 2015, Inada Domomi (稲田朋美), the chair of Liberal Democratic Party (LDP)'s political affairs investigation committee, stated the following in a press conference:[regarding the Tokyo Trials] "the historical perceptions behind the rulings is too vague. The rulings should be verified by Japanese experts."[7]

- On November 12, 2015, the Abe regime announced that the LDP will reinvestigate the Tokyo Trials on the day of the 67th anniversary of the establishment of the Tokyo Trials. The LDP stated in a press release on November 15, 2015, the 60th anniversary of the LDP, that a war and history recognition verification committee should verify the Tokyo Trials, which will be directly accountable to Prime Minister Abe, and will be established within the month. In the afternoon of this day, reporters asked Chief Cabinet Secretary Suga Yoshihide whether this press release was true. Secretary Suga Yoshihide confirmed that it was true.

- On November 29, 2015, the history verifications body 『Office for Learning History and Thinking the Future』(hereafter, "Office") was established as a government agency directly accountable to the Prime Minister Abe, the president of the LDP. Daigak Sadagaz (谷垣禎一) was appointed as director of the Office.

− On December 3, 2015, Inada Domomi, the chair of the political affairs investigation committee, stated the following in a press conference: "We would like to have our first meeting on December with our advisors, observers, and professors in order to review the purpose and the management of the Office in order to exchange ideas at least once a year. Next year, we would like this meeting to develop into a discussion with invited lecturers once every month or two.

− On December 22, 2015, the first meeting of the Office was held in Tokyo.[8]

• Inada Domomi, the chair of LDP's political affairs investigation committee, stated that he wants to discuss about the Tokyo Trials as the agenda of the Office.

• More than 60 MPs and professors participated in the first meeting.

− On February 9, 2016, Special Appointed Professor Yamauchi Masauki (山內昌之) of Meiji (明治) University, an advisor of the Office, gave a lecture.[9]

• Prof. Masauki argued that historians, as well as politicians and diplomats, should fight against fabrication of history.

• Prime Minister Abe evaluated that his address to the nation for the 70th anniversary of the end of the Pacific War and the Korea-Japan Agreement regarding the matters of comfort women at the end of 2015 was an act of verifying the lessons and facts of history carried out by the politicians. The Japanese government claims that Japan's colonial rule was legal and in turn, denied legal responsibility, and every issue is, according to Article 2 Section 1 of the 1965 Korea-Japan Agreement, "finally and completely resolved."

This paper will analyze and evaluate how Japan's history verifying body is denying the rulings of the Tokyo Trial in the perspective of international law.

3. PROBLEMS OF THE TOKYO TRIAL

This section compares the rulings of the Tokyo Trials and the Nuremberg Trials and suggests some implications for the resolution of the past liquidation between Korea-Japan after war in the perspective of international law.

For example, during the Tokyo Trials, U.S. focused on its policy objectives (U.S. interests in Asia) rather than objective principles of international law and the position of the victims. Thus, it is problematic that the U.S. took a passive stance regarding after-war liquidation such as not punishing for crimes against humanity, exempting the Japanese Emperor from punishment, not prosecuting the commander of Japan's 731 Unit (a biological warfare unit), releasing 19 A-level war criminals, etc. The problems of the Tokyo Trials can be summarized as follows:

First, the efforts to converge the victims' positions were clearly lacking in the Tokyo Trials of 1946 compared to the Nuremberg Trials. The U.S., in particular, neglected crimes against humanity in the prosecution process and in turn, did not punish the war criminals properly and released them. As a result, war criminals in Japan have re-entered the Japanese society and their descendants greatly influenced the politics, diplomacy, and the economy of Japan. They are also in the way of past liquidation between Korea and Japan. For example, 6 A-level war criminals are settled in the Yaskuni Shinsa and Prime Ministers of Japan have been worshipping them. On the contrary, during the Nuremberg Trials, war criminals were prosecuted for their crimes against humanity and the rulings were executed domestically. In addition, follow-up legislation was made for relapse prevention.

Second, the Tokyo Trials have reflected more on the policy interests of the U.S. rather than legal liquidation. On the contrary, the formation of the court and the legal process were carried out equitably by four nations and the legal liquidation was relatively unbiased during the Nuremberg Trials.

Third, we need to analyze and question U.S.'s biased stance regarding Japan's responsibility during the Tokyo Trials in order to formulate policy tools and logic to alter the U.S.'s passive stance on this matter when making Korea-Japan past liquidation policies. The Tokyo Trial focused too much on U.S.'s policy on Asia rather than legal justice and allowed Japan's war criminals to reintegrate into the Japanese society. These criminals later intervened in the 1952 San Francisco Treaty which did not handle the matters on the compensation for Korean and Chinese victims of illegal colonial rule sufficiently. For example, the U.S. military government excluded the Japanese Emperor from punishment, released war criminals of Japan's 731 Unit's biological warfare and testing, released 19 level-A war criminals, only punished the military for the war crimes, left unresolved matters in the San Francisco Treaty, and neglected the revival of militarism[10] in Japan after the San Francisco Treaty. These matters must be resolved by revealing the cause and fault with objective evidence.

Forth, domestic studies on the Tokyo Trials are less developed than their foreign counterpart. The studies on the rulings of the Tokyo Trials must not be left to U.S. and Japan, and Korean scholars should actively participate in order to maintain objectivity in international research. Moreover, national efforts and support for these activities are required.

4. EVALUATION OF THE TOKYO TRIALS IN THE PERSPECTIVE OF INTERNATIONAL LAW

Despite the fact that the Tokyo Trials were biased in favor of Japan compared to the Nuremberg Trials, the LDP Office's arguments for reinvestigating the Tokyo Trials are not persuasive. The Korean and Chinese victims cannot tolerate this. In 1947, referring to the rulings of the 1946 Tokyo Trials, claims on U.S. and the Soviet Union's violation of the laws of war regarding the U.S.'s dropping of the atomic bomb and the Soviet Union's invasions have been made by the right-wing activists in

Japan.

The problem of fairness of court rulings during the Tokyo Trials and Nuremberg Trials that have been filed by Japanese and German scholars, the problem of ideological binding for the crime against peace, the problem of crimes against humanity, the problem of legal retrospection of Charter of International Military Tribunal are not objective problems in the perspective of international law. Principles of international law confirmed in the Tokyo Trials and the Nuremberg Trials have been adopted in the United Nations General Assembly in 1946 with a consensus[11] and these principles have been expressed in the 1949 Convention on Genocide and the 1951 European Convention on Human Rights.

Japan's responsibility on after-war issues is derivative and a part of the responsibility of war. The two issues should not be inversed and after war responsibility is not only a historic matter but it is a practical matter. It is also a significant matter related to peace in the Asia-Pacific region.[12] It is a great contradiction for the Japanese government to verify the rulings of the Tokyo Trials, which was biased in favor of Japan rather than victims of Korea and China in 2015. However, justice will be realized by reinvestigating the Tokyo Trials in order to punish the war criminals in the court of historical justice.

Comparing and reviewing the Tokyo Trials with the Nuremberg Trials in order to determine which country put more efforts in resolving after war problems [overcoming the past history] is very important in order not to repeat the failure of history. Like this, The German goverment concluded that the Holocaust was an anti-human crime and arrested and brought to trials all the related criminals. It cleared up the history with a sincere apology and punishment of those involved with the genocide.[13]

Regarding the legal issues claimed by Japan in the 1946 Tokyo Trials, the UN General Assembly adopted a resolution with principles of international law confirmed by the Nuremberg Trials and Tokyo Trials with consensus. Article 11 of the San Francisco Peace Treaty,[14] which came into effect in 1952 has promised that Japan will accept the rulings of the

Tokyo Trials.

The trial was legitimate. Due to the lack of precedence, there were concerns about the legal procedures and judicial issues. In fact, Indian jurist Radhabinod Pal acknowledged that the atrocities of the Japanese troops were evident but found the accused not guilty, as the tribunal was "the opportunity for the victors to retaliate." But the trials proceeded fairly, clearing away most of the concerns, and the principles that led the trials became established in international law. The idea of a "crime against humanity" became the basic framework through which many gruesome crimes would come to be punished.[15]

In this context, Japan's attempt to verify the rulings of the Tokyo Trials through history and war crime verifications committee on November, 2015 under direct supervision of the president of LDP is a violation of the 1946 UN General Assembly Resolution and the 1951 Genocide Convention.

Notes

1. Zachary D. Kaufman, "Transitional Justice for Tojo's Japan: The United States Role in the Estabilishment of the International Military Tribunal for the Far East and other Transitional Justice Mechanism for Japan after World War II," 27 Emory International Law Review, Vol. 27, 2013, pp. 756-773.
2. "Seoul condemns Tokyo's denial of history," The Korea Times, February 21, 2014.
3. For Abe government's awareness of the 'comfort women' issue, See-Hwan Doh, "Shinzo Abe's Denial of the Japanese Military Comfort Women's Issue and Challenges in International Law," Korean Yearbook of International Law, Vol. 2, 2014, The Korean Branch of the ILA, pp. 205-207.
4. "Turning back time," The Korea Times, March 1, 2014.
5. Trial of The Major War Criminals before The International Military Tribunal, Nuremberg, 14 November 1945-1 October 1946, Published at Nuremberg, Germany 1947. Volume 1, Official Text in the English language, Offical Documents.
6. Jang-Hie Lee, "A Comparative Study on the Nuremberg War Crimes Trial & the Tokyo War Crimes Trial from International Law Point of View," Journal of Northeast Asia History, Vol. 25, 2009, pp. 195-245.
7. LDP homepage-https://www.jimin.jp/news/press/chairman_pre/130994.html.
8. News 1, 2015. 12. 22.
9. Sankei Shimun, February 9, 2016.
10. Wang Xiliang, "Japanese war responsibility," Opening Symposium/Keynote Address-Panel 1, October 9, 2008, The 2nd International NGO conference on History and Peace, Seoul, Proceedings, p. 16.
11. UNGA, 95(1), Fifth plenary meeting, December 11, 1946.
12. See Supra note 10.
13. In December 1970, the then Prime Minister of West Germany Willy Brandt knelt down on the wet ground at the memorials in the Holocaust camp of Auschwitz near Warsaw and prayed crying out, "Oh, God What shall we do, the unforgivable sins we committed. Please forgive us." Chronik der Deutschen, Chronilk Verlag, 1983, pp. 1048-1049.
14. Article 11 of the San Francisco Peace Treaty states that "Japan accepts the judgments of the International Military Tribunal for the Far East."
15. "Japan's never-ending war," Korean Joongang Daily, December 4, 2015.

ROK-U.S. Nuclear Energy Agreement: The Republic of Korea Matures as a Nuclear Power Nation

WON Jae-Chun
Professor
Handong Global University, Faculty of Law / International Law School, Pohang, Korea

Abstract

Past agreements were, from a Korean perspective, restrictive and regulatory in nature, but the new agreement is better designed to foster long term cooperation on issues of mutual concern. This accord opens a way to further research on pyroprocessing and that could reduce nuclear fuel requirements. Korea may be able to also secure reliable supplies of nuclear fuel independent of the regional market situation. Moreover, Korea is authorized to produce low enriched uranium and enhance its scientific research and nuclear trade programs. Importantly, a high level bilateral commission was established to provide a decision making mechanism to address any rising issues of concern based on mutual cooperation.

1. INTRODUCTION

Cooperation between the Republic of Korea (hereinafter, 'Korea') and the United States concerning nuclear energy began with the "Agreement for Cooperation Between the Government of the Republic of Korea Concerning Civil Use of Atomic Energy" on February 3, 1956, and continued with the signing of the "Agreement for Cooperation between the Government of the Republic of Korea and the Government of the United States of America concerning Civil Use of Atomic Energy" on November 24, 1972. On April 22, 2015, the two nations updated their relationship with the "Agreement for Cooperation between the Government of the Republic of Korea and the Government of the United States of America concerning Peaceful Uses of Nuclear Energy." (hereinafter, the New Agreement)

2. CONTENTS OF THE NEW AGREEMENT[1]

2-1. ARTICLES

The New Agreement consists of a Preamble, twenty-one Articles, an Agreed Minute, and an additional Agreed Minute on High Level Bilateral Commission. The following table lists the articles.

Article 1	Definitions	Article 11	Enrichment, reprocessing, and other alteration in form or content
Article 2	Scope of cooperation	Article 12	Physical protection
Article 3	Cooperation on nuclear research and development	Article 13	No explosive or military application
Article 4	Transfer of information	Article 14	Safeguards
Article 5	Industrial and commercial cooperation	Article 15	Good faith and interests
Article 6	Nuclear trade	Article 16	Multiple supplier controls
Article 7	Transfer of nuclear material, moderator material, equipment and components	Article 17	Cessation of cooperation and right of return
		Article 18	Consultations and environmental protection
Article 8	Nuclear fuel supply	Article 19	Administrative arrangement
Article 9	Cooperation on spent fuel management	Article 20	Settlement of disputes
Article 10	Storage and retransfers	Article 21	Entry into force, duration and amendment

2-2. AGREED MINUTES

Following the main articles are a general "Agreed Minute" addressing implementation issues and a separate and more focused "Agreed Minute on High Level Bilateral Commission." The Agreed Minute on implementation includes sections on (1) coverage of agreement, (2) safeguards, (3) retransfers, (4) additional exchanges of information, (5) alteration in form or content, (6) arrangements for spent fuel management and disposition, and (7) enrichment.

The Agreed Minute on High Level Bilateral Commission primarily deals with four working groups operating under the direction of the Commission Chairs: (1) Working Group on Spent Fuel Management, (2) Working Group on Promotion of Nuclear Exports and Export Control Cooperation, (3) Working Group on Assured Fuel Supply, and (4) Working Group on Nuclear Security.

3. ANALYSIS OF KEY PROVISIONS

3-1. SPENT FUEL MANAGEMENT (ARTICLES 9 AND 10)

The New Agreement provides a potential path forward for pyroprocessing research, a technique which reuses spent fuel and could reduce the quantity of spent fuel wastes. The agreement also provides Korea with advance U.S. consent to retransfer spent fuel to certain countries for storage and reprocessing.

Korea has faced challenges in managing its spent nuclear fuels. During the negotiations, Korea pressed the United States to define a pathway for possible long-term or programmatic consent for Korea to conduct pyroprocess spent nuclear material fuel research. The New Agreement provides for further review of the issue based on the findings of the Joint Fuel Cycle Study. If the High Level Bilateral Commission agrees that pyroprocessing is technically and economically feasible and acceptable from a nonproliferation standpoint, the U.S. can give advance consent to these operations in Korea. This would not require an amendment to the agreement. Instead, U.S. consent would be given through a so-called subsequent arrangement process.[2]

The U.S. and the Korea have already been engaged in a cooperative program to develop practical solutions to the spent fuel storage problem. With the establishment of the working group on spent fuel management, it is expected that the two sides will intensify information exchanges and help each other find solutions to the pressing needs of both interim spent fuel storage and long-term waste disposal. Moreover, in Paragraph 3.2 of the Agreed Minute, the U.S. has given advance consent to the retransfer of spent fuel for storage and reprocessing to France, the United Kingdom, and additional countries as may be agreed upon in writing by the parties in the future.

3-2. NUCLEAR FUEL SUPPLY RELIABILITY (ARTICLES 8 AND 11)

The New Agreement allows production of low enriched uranium. Also, in principle, the U.S. will guarantee a supply of nuclear fuel in unusually sensitive market situations, such as periods of high demand by China or India.

The potential for long-term U.S. consent to the Korea's production of low enriched uranium is significant. Paragraph 2 of Article 11 provides that uranium subject to the agreement may be enriched up to a uranium isotope 235 level of 20% but only if the parties agree in writing on an arrangement to do so. Such an agreement could occur following consultations undertaken through the High Level Bilateral Commission.[3]

The Korea has depended on foreign services for purchasing, converting and enriching the uranium that is required for its nuclear power plants. Maintaining a consistent stream of nuclear fuel has long been beyond Korea's control because the nation's supply chain is subject to disruption by market forces and regional security situations. Accordingly, it was seen as crucial for the Korean government to secure nuclear fuel over a long term period.

In Article 8, the agreement stipulates that the United States shall endeavor to take such actions as may be necessary and feasible to ensure a reliable supply of low enriched uranium to the ROK. In addition, both countries agree to facilitate various cooperative efforts regarding the reliable supply of nuclear fuel, including the exchange of information on nuclear fuel markets and the potential disruptions to such markets.

3-3. KOREAN NUCLEAR EXPORTS (ARTICLE 6)

Regarding Korean nuclear exports, the New Agreement moves from a specific case-by-case consent model to a lump sum approach that will likely enhance the competitiveness of the nation's nuclear energy trade.[4]

The two sides agreed to facilitate industrial and commercial cooperation and promote nuclear trade. In Article 8, the U.S. agreed to facilitate the retransfer of low enriched uranium from the ROK to third countries. In addition, in Paragraph 3 of Section 3 of the Agreed Minute, the United States has given advance consent to the retransfer of unirradiated low enriched uranium; unirradiated source material; and equipment and components to third country destinations it has identified, provided the receiving country agrees to hold the transferred items subject to terms and conditions of the agreement for cooperation with the United States.

The clarity that the New Agreement brings to the export/import authorization process is a positive development. Paragraph 2 of Article 6 directs the United States to act on applications for export and import licenses and approvals for the transfer of technical data and assistance "promptly and without undue expense." Further, the agreement states that such authorization powers "shall not be used to restrict trade."

3-4. PRODUCTION OF RADIOACTIVE ISOTOPES (ARTICLE 3)

The New Agreement allows for the potential production of radioactive isotopes in Korea. In Section 5 of the Agreed Minute, each party grants consent to the other for the separation of radioisotopes from irradiated low enriched uranium at U.S. and ROK facilities listed in Section 1 of Annex I. Such production would still require additional agreements before it is authorized, but this level of consensus regarding the possibility of ROK produced radioactive isotopes is significant nonetheless.

3-5. ESTABLISHMENT OF HIGH LEVEL BILATERAL COMMISSION (ARTICLE 18, PARAGRAPH 2)

The New Agreement directs the formation of a joint consultation group with clear jurisdiction and decision-making authority. The High Level Bilateral Commission is to be led by the Korean Vice Minister of Foreign Affairs and the Deputy Secretary of Energy for the U.S. and should meet at least once each year, hosted alternately by the parties. The bilateral commission will have at least four working groups addressing (1) spent fuel management, (2) promotion of nuclear exports, (3) assured fuel supply, and (4) nuclear security. Additional working groups can be formed through written mutual agreement to address other topics relevant to peaceful nuclear cooperation.

This high-level commission is unprecedented under U.S. peaceful nuclear agreements and demonstrates the willingness of both parties to give serious senior-level attention to a broad range of interests. It is expected that a decision regarding pyroprocessing or enrichment would be made by this High Level Bilateral Commission.

4. OTHER THEMES OF THE NEW AGREEMENT

4-1. AFFIRMS SHARED PRINCIPLES OF NON-PROLIFERATION AND NUCLEAR SECURITY (PREAMBLE AND ARTICLE 12)

As host countries for the Nuclear Security Summit,[5] the ROK and the U.S. agreed to strengthen the global nonproliferation regime and enhance regional and international cooperation. By establishing a working group on nuclear security under the High Level Bilateral Commission, the New Agreement cooperatively builds upon that foundation to minimize the civil use of highly enriched uranium, slow the spread of weapons and materials of mass destruction, and address the emerging threat of cyber terrorism that targets nuclear facilities. The New Agreement also harmonizes with the latest safeguards and physical protection standards from the IAEA.

4-2. STRENGTHENS COOPERATION REGARDING NUCLEAR SAFETY AND ENVIRONMENTAL PROTECTION (ARTICLE 18)

In the New Agreement, both countries reaffirmed the importance of nuclear safety and agreed to strengthen their cooperation on nuclear research and development. Furthermore, the New Agreement requires both sides to hold talks on the advancement of nuclear safety standards. The Korea Nuclear Safety and Security Commission (NSSC) and the United States Nuclear Regulatory Commission (NRC) will provide the results of these talks to the High Level Bilateral Commission. Environmental protection concerns arising from nuclear activities are also addressed by the New Agreement.

4-3. RESPECTS SOVEREIGNTY (PREAMBLE)

The New Agreement's preamble clearly affirms the inalienable right of NPT parties to use nuclear energy for peaceful purposes. The cooperative steps taken were done so while acknowledging the sovereignty of the two nations. Press releases from both countries describe the end result as an exceptional agreement designed to secure greater autonomy for Korean nuclear activities. In addition, the New Agreement obligates each nation to respect the other's program regarding general nuclear activities. Importantly, the New Agreement significantly moves beyond the so-called "Gold Standard" that had limited Korea's nuclear development under past agreements.[6]

4-4. BETTER SECURES THE AUTONOMY OF KOREAN NUCLEAR RESEARCH AND DEVELOPMENT

The New Agreement removes barriers to research and development activities that utilize spent nuclear at specified ROK facilities, and it charts a path towards U.S. consent for additional nuclear research and development. The streamlining of the approval process is also a significant development.

5. CONCLUSION

The status of Korea as nuclear energy nation has been significantly elevated. Although the United States did not grant full consent to the use of highly enriched uranium or the reprocessing of used fuel, the New Agreement clearly moved beyond the paternalistic attitudes of the past and towards a more collaborative approach. The agreement is likely to help alleviate Korea's used fuel storage problem and ensure reliable access to enriched uranium, all while promoting the competitiveness of Korea's nuclear industry in a global market.[7]

This is not a comprehensive regulatory agreement that addresses all the issues and all the problems; rather, the New Agreement creates a sustainable decision making mechanism that can deal with issues of concern as they arise. Its tone is one of creative problem solving based on close communication and cooperation. The New Agreement will allow the two nations to flexibly address issues while upholding longstanding principles of peaceful use and non-proliferation.

Notes

1. Officially, the "Agreement for Cooperation Between the Government of the Republic of Korea and the Government of the United States of America Concerning Civil Use of Atomic Energy."

2. Yonhap news, *Seoul will create a working group on the nuclear deal with Washington*, http://news.naver.com/main/read.nhn?mode=LPOD&mid=sec&oid=001&aid=0007550852&isYeonhapFlash=Y, accessed February 23, 2016.

3. Hye-Sun Yoon, *New ROK-U.S. Civil Nuclear Cooperation Agreement: A closer look at Section 123 of the US Atomic Energy Act overcome the impasse*, 15(1) Journal of Law and Politics Research (2015), pp. 210-18.

4. Hye-Sun Yoon, *A comparative study for the New ROK-U.S. Civil Nuclear Cooperation Agreement: Focused on the renewal of the US-Japan Nuclear Cooperation Agreement*, 23(1) Seoul Law Review (2015), pp. 319-28.

5. The United States has hosted the Summit 2010 and the Summit 2016. The first and the fourth summit were held in Washington respectively April 12-13, 2010 and from March 31 to April 1, 2016. The ROK hosted the second summit in Seoul March 26-27, 2012.

6. The Gold Standard effected a total ban on reprocessing spent fuel or enriching uranium. Jae-Chun Won, *ROK-U.S. Nuclear Energy Agreement*, Korean Yearbook of International Law, Vol. 1 (2013).

7. Fred McGlodrick, *The New Peaceful Nuclear Cooperation Agreement Between South Korea and United States: From Dependency to Parity*, Korea Economic Institute, Special Studies Series No. 6 (Washington DC, 2015), pp. 9-42.

70 Years after WWII: International Legal Challenges for Establishing Peace Community in Northeast Asia

DOH See-Hwan
Research Fellow
Northeast Asian History Foundation, Seoul, Korea

1. INTRODUCTION

Year 2015 marked the 70th anniversary of the end of World War II and the Republic of Korea's (hereinafter, 'Korea') liberation from Japan and 50th anniversary of the Korea-Japan Treaty of 1965. Despite the historic significance of the year, Korea, Japan and China in Northeast Asia are not still free from serious historic tensions stemming from the legacy of the 20th century, let alone having a historical reconciliation or building a peace community for peace and prosperity in the 21st century. One of the most critical impediment to historical reconciliation is Prime Minister Shinzo Abe's administration which denies Japan's invasion and colonial rule and distorts and glorifies history under the banner of "breaking away from the post-war regime" and "historical revisionism."

Prime Minister Shinzo Abe declared a policy intended to deny the apologies of Japanese cabinets during his first term, and after winning the second term, he issued a statement on August 14, 2015. The statement and a series of actions was nothing but a move towards revising the post-war Peace Constitution and returning to pre-war militarism by claiming collective self-defense. This is evidenced by him denying the statement made by former Prime Minister Tomichi Murayama in 1995 and not stating that Japan's aggression caused the war, which is in the same line with denying its colonial responsibility and the definition of aggression itself.

What is noticeable here, however, is that the voices of the Historical Science Society of Japan and historical societies around the world call for terminating historic distortion regarding the Japanese military "comfort women" and acknowledging historic facts, and these voices are getting much stronger than Shinzo Abe's attempts to disregard historical truth and justice and historical revisionism. When Shinzo Abe passed responsibility saying "the issue of 'comfort women' should be left to historians and their studies," the academics in Japan and the world responded that "the forced mobilization of 'comfort women' for Japanese military is a historical fact."

Furthermore, in July 2015, Japan campaigned to add Meiji industrial sites, which include places where slave laborers were sacrificed for colonial rule and the war of aggression, to the UNESCO World Heritage list. This provocative action faded world peace and the meaning of the world heritage, and repeatedly infringed upon human rights. Contrary to this, on October 9, 2015, Japan expressed an extreme regret to China which registered Nanjing Massacre documents with the World Heritage, arguing that UNESCO should not be used for political advantages.

The series of Abe's provocative actions that run counter to building historical reconciliation and peace community in Northeast Asia show that repetitive human rights impingement against victims of Japanese colonial rule is still ongoing and Japan's claim that the Korea-Japan Treaty of 1965 is complete is another far-fetched move to block and rule out remedies for the victims of colonial rule.

2. REVIEW ON SHINZO ABE'S PERCEPTION ON HISTORY

2-1. CRITICISM BY THE HISTORICAL SCIENCE SOCIETY OF JAPAN

Regarding Shinzo Abe's statement on the 70th anniversary of the end of World War II which denied Japanese colonial rule and aggression and further distorted and glossed over history with the aim of "breaking away from the post-war regime" and "historical revisionism," the Historical Science Society of Japan criticized that the statement does not come to terms with Japan's responsibility as a perpetrator of war crime. Its self-righteous consciousness of history, not confronting the history of violence, is the tyranny of aggressors calling for the end of apologies.

In October 2014, in response to Shinzo Abe's remarks of "leaving the 'comfort women' issue in the hands of scholars involved in history studies," the Historical Science Society issued a statement on the existence of "comfort women" who were forcibly taken by the Japanese military. In May 2015, the Society initiated the joint statement of 16 associations of history scholars and educators, which called for ending the Abe regime's distortion of the "comfort women" issue. Against this backdrop, the Society's criticism on the Abe statement centers around the lack of any sense of subjectivity or responsibility with regard to Japan's role in the colonial rule and as the perpetrator of war crimes, denying its responsibility for aggression, and avoiding liability for "comfort women."[1]

2-2. ISSUES RELATED TO HISTORICAL CONSCIOUSNESS IN THE SHINZO ABE STATEMENT

First, the Abe statement lacks any sense of responsibility as the perpetrator. The statement includes four key words such as "aggression," "colonial rule," "reflection," and "apologies" being conscious of public opinion both at home and abroad. However, these words and phrases only appear within indirect references to statements by past prime ministers and explanations of Japan's post-WWII position, and not as Abe's own words. Moreover, because the statement leaves the subjects of "aggression" and "colonial rule" ambiguous, and because it does not specify that the war was induced by Japanese aggression, it neither identifies who exactly should "reflect," nor even addresses the issue of responsibility. This is typical of the Japanese government which has diluted and distorted Japan's accountability held for colonial rule and aggression. With misleading subjects, the statement itself becomes meaningless.

Second, the Abe statement denies Japan's role in colonial rule. While his statement sees 19th century Japan as a state that successfully defended its independence by rapidly modernizing in response to the perceived threat of European colonialism, it ignores the fact that it did so by violating the sovereignty of Korea and colonizing Taiwan. Furthermore, the statement claims that the Russo-Japanese war "gave encouragement to many people under colonial rule" at the beginning of the 20th century. On the contrary, the Russo-Japanese war was first and foremost a battle between Russia and Japan for supremacy over Manchuria and other parts of northeastern China, as well as the Korean peninsula. The war was fueled by imperialist ambitions, which allowed Japan to continually violate the rights of peoples who happened to live in the countries caught in the fighting. For example, during the Russo-Japanese war, Japan ignored Korea's declaration of neutrality and, upon taking control of Seoul, imposed the asymmetrical Korea-Japan Treaty. By absolutely avoiding any reference to these historical facts, the Abe statement undermines the notion that Japan bears responsibility for colonial rule, and creates the impression that the blame ultimately lies with the West.

Third, the statement denies any responsibility for the war caused by Japanese aggression. It reveals a problematic understanding of the historical circumstances of World War II. The Prime Minister constructs a historical understanding that justifies Japan's actions by portraying Japan as a passive victim of the West's economic blocs after the Great Depression, which left the country severely damaged and politically isolated. Just as with the Russo-Japanese war, this narrative seeks to shift focus away from the fact of Japanese aggression on the Asian continent and further obscure the subject of responsibility.

The fourth is evasion of responsibility for "comfort women." It avoids any direct mention of the "comfort women" issue, and instead glosses over the matter by briefly mentioning the harm caused to women in general by the war. Expressed this way, the "comfort women" issue is treated as though it were simply a general problem in war; this must be seen as an attempt to further evade the question of Japan's specific responsibility for the issue. No mention is made of instances such as forced labor of Chinese and Koreans and the massive killing of prisoners of war as well as civilians.

2-3. HISTORICAL RESPONSIBILITY

As pointed out in the statement of Historical Science Society, Japan ignored Korea's declaration of neutrality and took control of the Korean peninsula for colonization. Japan emphasizes a legitimate conclusion of the Korea-Japan Treaty without turning its eyes to a forcible nature of the treaty which allowed Japan's annexation of Korea. Based on this premise, the perception of the Japanese government on its annexation of Korea converted from being legitimate before the Tomichi Murayama statement in 1995, which reflected on its colonial rule and aggression and offered apologies, to being valid but unjust after the Murayama statement. Still, the view of valid but unjust basically falls into the criteria of legitimacy.[2]

Despite the statement of Prime Minister Naoto Kan in 2010 marking the centennial of Japan's colonization of Korea, which expressed that Japan's colonial rule was imposed "against the will of Koreans," it had limitation as it fell short of labeling colonization as illegal.

The statement made by Abe seemingly intentionally turned blind eye to the essence of resolving colonial rule and the harm it did since the statement was made on the 70th anniversary of the end of WWII and should duly serve its historical responsibility of remedying harms and damages of compulsory manpower draft and "comfort women" recruited for the Japanese military. This move is nothing more than avoiding its international legal responsibility: Japan's "state liability" held based on "legal investigation into historical truth" which stands at the heart of resolving "historical conflicts between Korea and Japan."

3. INTERNATIONAL PRECEDENTS FOR LIQUIDATING COLONIAL RESPONSIBILITY AND THEIR IMPLICATIONS

3-1. THE DUTCH GOVERNMENT'S COMPENSATION FOR INDONESIAN VICTIMS: RULING ON THE RAWAGEDE MASSACRE (SEPTEMBER 14, 2011)

On December 9, 1947, 90 Dutch soldiers led by Major Alphons Wijnen shot to death Indonesian soldiers and criminal suspects in summary execution based on informal interrogation in the course of performing "Clean-up Operation" in Rawagede village against 200-500 residents. Their bodies were left unretrieved.

The court in the Hague ruled on September 14, 2011, that the Dutch government was guilty and responsible for the massacre in Rawagede village, Indonesia on December 9, 1947.

The court ruled that the Dutch government was obliged to pay compensations to the victims and their families, and the compensations would be determined by subsequent due process. The Dutch government initiated negotiations with the relatives of the Rawagede massacre victims on November 23, 2011 and agreed to pay 20,000 euros (27,000 dollars) per person to the nine relatives of the victims.[3]

3-2. BRITAIN'S COMPENSATION FOR COLONIZATION OF KENYA: RULING ON THE MAU MAU UPRISING (OCTOBER 5, 2012)

The Mau Mau case about British colonial rule in Kenya involves the Kikuyu, Kenya's major ethnic group, who raised armed uprising for independence during British colonial rule from 1952 until 1961. The

Kikuyu activists attacked British settlers and government officials. In response, the British declared a state of emergency and ordered a strong counter-insurgency campaign. In the course of physically suppressing the fighters, unlawful detention, torture and harsh treatment including castration were inflicted.

The UK argued all liabilities for the torture by colonial authorities were transferred to the Kenya authorities upon independence in 1963, and after its argument was thwarted, it appealed saying the claim is not valid because of the legal prescription of the suit.

On October 5, 2012, the High Court ruled that "in the case involving the UK Foreign and Commonwealth Office, the plaintiff could only make a claim against the direct preparator in assumed violence case and the Kenyan colonial authorities, their employer at that time, but not against the British government." The court decided the government was legally held responsible for five accounts. First, the British government's responsibility does not transfer to the colonial authorities upon independence of Kenya. Second, the government is legally responsible for encouraging, aiding, condoning or colluding torture. Third, the UK government is not free from legal responsibility for the roles the government performed as the supreme colonial power for separate, independent interests. Fourth, the July 1957 "measure" by the Minister was equivalent to the one taken as a member of the UK government. Fifth, the government is held accountable for being negligent in not preventing nor intervening to stop systematic torture on the basis of having no obligation of protection.[4]

In June 2013, the UK government issued the statement of apologies by the Secretary of State for Foreign Affairs and the High Commissioner and announced that it would build a monument to commemorate the torture victims in Nairobi and pay compensations for 5,288 victims. On September 12, 2015, a statute commemorating the Kenyan movement for independence was established in Uhuru Park in Nairobi with the financial support of the UK.

3-3. IMPLICATIONS OF THE RULINGS

A review on the rulings of Rawagede case between the Netherlands and Indonesia and Mau Mau case between Britain and Kenya reveals that the decisions to come to terms with colonial accountability were made by the Dutch and British courts. Particularly, the governments of the Netherlands and Britain counter-argued based on the "legal prescription of summary execution and bringing the suit," but the courts ruled out their claims.

Furthermore, the court rulings highlighted "the grave violation of human rights has no statute of limitations," which is in line with the Convention on the Non-Applicability of Statutory Limitations to War Crimes and Crimes against Humanity, 1968. Also, monetary compensations given to victims by the colonial governments were taken as a solution to do justice, and sincere apologies were emphasized as a measure to come to terms of past atrocities. The court ruling that the colonial government is not free from legal responsibility for the roles the government performed as the supreme colonial power for separate, independent interests is considered as a decision to realize legal justice for historical facts.

4. REVIEW ON THE RULINGS ON COLONIAL RESPONSIBILITY

4-1. LIMITATION AND ISSUES OF POST-WWII COMPENSATION RULINGS IN JAPAN

Since the Cold War ended in the 1990s, changes of international political circumstances as a result of democratization in Asian countries and the voices of victims of colonial rule and war raised in Asia have led to the solidarity transcending borders calling for post-war compensation and subsequent filing of lawsuits. Under the Treaty of San Francisco and bilateral treaties, the Japanese government paid reparations to other nations, but it never agreed to pay compensation to individual victims. This stance caused a number of war victims in Asia to file lawsuits against the Japanese government.

Japan, however, has dealt with post-WWII compensation cases without considering the state liability for colonial rule and war of aggression, and the total number of cases reached 90 as of July 15, 2012. Among them, 10 cases involve "comfort women" victimized by the Japanese military, three of which are Korean victims. Regarding Korean forced labor victims, lawsuits were filed against Mitsubishi Heavy Industries in 1995 and Nippon Steel in 1997, but they were overruled at the Supreme Court of Japan.

4-2. JURIDICAL BACKGROUND OF RULINGS ON JAPANESE COLONIAL RESPONSIBILITY

Behind the historic rulings of the Korean judiciary including the Constitutional Court's 2011 ruling on constitutional appeal regarding "comfort women" and the Supreme Court's 2012 ruling on compensation for forced labor were the spirit of the age determined to overcome its grave past under colonial rule and build the Northeast Asian peace community.

First, the World Conference against Racism, Racial Discrimination, Xenophobia and Related Intolerance held in Durban, the Republic of South Africa, from August 31 to September 8, 2001 stated that "colonialism fostered intolerance related to racialism, racial discrimination and xenophobia and provided a path toward racialism, which was the ground for crime against humanity such as racial segregation in South Africa and genocide." It further declared that eliminating slavery and colonial rule which had tormented people and ethnic groups in Africa and Asia over hundreds of years was a historical challenge to tackle, and to realize this, the conference issued the action plan. The declaration applies to all colonial empires including Japan. The rulings on compensation for torture, atrocities and summary executions between Britain and Kenya in June 2013 and between the Netherlands and Indonesia in September 2013 and subsequent apologies and compensations given to victims marked a milestone on the way to ending and liquidating colonialism.

Second, international society has experienced changes in values from a traditional state-first philosophy to respect for human rights as a universal value of humanity. Reflecting on the cause of WWII, it was indicated that the aggression and atrocities committed by Germany and Japan were attributable to the traditional state-first philosophy in disregard of human dignity. With the advancement of international human rights law, today the view itself that perceives the violations against individual rights as those against the individual's nation is considered a mere fabrication or legal fiction and it is believed that individuals should not be forced to be sacrificed to promote friendship between nations. This is a significant change in international law in the context of strengthened diplomatic protection and individual claims for compensation. Third, in 2010, the centenary of Japanese annexation of Korea, 1,139 Korean and Japanese intellectuals issued a joint statement declaring the Japan-Korea Treaty of 1910 itself "null and void" based on the premise of "upholding historical truth and justice under international law." The joint declaration stated that the treaty draft, process of entering into the treaty, and annexation process were all wrongful, faulty, and unjust. In addition, under Article 2 of Treaty on Basic Relations between the Republic of Korea and Japan of 1965 which stipulates all treaties and agreements concluded on or prior to August 22, 1910 are already null and void, the joint statement emphasized that Korea's interpretation of the unjust annexation treaty, which was made as part of Japan's policy of aggression, as being unlawful and invalid in the first place should be acknowledged as a shared view. It also urged Japan to accept the academic society's efforts in the field of international law regarding colonial responsibility and crimes against humanity and to live up to the calls of the times by fundamentally reflecting on its history of aggression, annexation and colonial rule.[5]

4-3. RULINGS OF THE KOREAN JUDICIARY ON JAPANESE COLONIAL RESPONSIBILITY

First, on August 30, 2011, the Constitutional Court ruled the government's the omission to act is in violation of the Constitution that the Korean government has not resolved disputes regarding interpretation according to Article 3 of "Agreement on the Settlement of Problem concerning Property and Claims and the Economic Cooperation between the Republic of Korea and Japan." The disputes were about whether the rights to claim compensation made by Koreans whose dignity and human rights were gravely infringed upon by organized and consistent unlawful acts against humanity inflicted by Japan, extinguished under Article 2 Paragraph 1 of the Agreement. The ruling indicated the possibility and necessity of overtaking the colonial responsibility and decided that the government has a concrete and stipulated obligation of realizing claims against Japan and eliminate obstacles to recovering human dignity and values.[6]

Second, on May 24, 2012, the Supreme Court reversed the original trial court's ruling that recognized the Japanese court decision, which viewed the forcible mobilization of Korean nationals as lawful — under the normative perception that its colonial rule over Korea was legitimate — and which therefore ran against the essential values of the Korean Constitution including the legal tradition of the provisional government established following the March 1 Independence Movement that found such to be illegal. The court ruled that Japan is liable to pay compensation for its illicit acts against humanity and those directly associated with its colonial rule over Korea.[7] The core of the Supreme Court ruling is the illegal nature of Japanese colonial rule through the coerced annexation of Korea in 1910, which established legal justice on historical truth and provided a milestone to international human rights law by switching from a state-centric perspective to a human rights-centric one.

5. CONCLUSION: INTERNATIONAL LEGAL CHALLENGES

Marking the 70th anniversary of the end of World War II when Korea became liberated, as well as the 50th anniversary of the Treaty between Korea and Japan, the start point of discussion on relieving the victims of the Japanese colonial rule from the perspective of international law should be overcoming the position held by the Japanese government regarding completing the Korea-Japan Treaty, which has been strongly asserted as if it were a trump card, and holding the Japanese government accountable for its colonial rule. This is confirmed by the fact that individual studies of scholars around the world on Japanese military's comfort women and the Japanese colonial rule all boil down to a single voice pursuing historical justice.[8]

Nevertheless, the Japanese government has had the normative recognition that, as the forced annexation of Korea and Japan in 1910 was made by the conclusion of the Korea-Japan Annexation Treaty which was legal under the international laws of the time, Japan's forcible occupation of Korea and subsequent colonial rule made on this basis were also legitimate. It has denied its responsibility to compensate for illegalities against humanity involving its state power and other unlawful acts associated directly with its colonial rule; it has also been consistent in claiming that the conclusion of the Korea-Japan Basic Relations Treaty brought these issues to a complete end.

The Japanese government, after all, had no intention to fulfill its colonial responsibility in the first place; it believed its colonial rule over Korea was justifiable, viewing it as a "dispensation" for Koreans which helped modernize them. Focusing on "property" and "claims" as stipulated in Article 4, Paragraph (a) of the San Francisco Peace Treaty, the negotiations between Korea and Japan on postwar claims did not specify Japan's responsibility for colonial rule. This, paradoxically, left "colonial responsibility" as an issue unresolved and to be therefore addressed under the Korea-Japan Basic Relations Treaty.

Therefore, as the Korean judicature proclaims with historic rulings, the way international law should be heading with the goal of giving relief to the victims who suffered significant human rights infringement under colonial rule is to establish three contemporary principles of human rights, justice and peace in resistance to crimes against humanity where the Japanese colonial rule was involved.[9]

Marking the centennial of forcible annexation between Korea and Japan, the Joint Statement of intellectuals from the two countries suggests that getting the regional history right will lay the foundation for seeking a genuine process of historical reconciliation. Going beyond "negative peace" as a basic element of international laws premising an apology and compensation for colonial rule and war of aggression, we should now go for "positive peace" in which human dignity and rights are respected as universal values. This will make sure that another 50 years following the 50th anniversary of the Korea-Japan Basic Relations Treaty in 2015 serves as the starting point for working hand in hand to bring a Northeast Asian peace community into reality.[10]

Notes

1. Committee of the Historical Science Society of Japan, "Commentary on the Prime Minister's Statement on the 70th Anniversary of the End of WWII," September 14, 2015.

2. See-hwan Doh, "Considerations of the Korea-Japan Annexation Treaty from the Viewpoint of Historical Truth and International Law," The Korean Journal of International Law, Vol. 55, No. 4, 2010, pp. 13-47.

3. "The Netherlands apologies for Rawagede massacre, pays compensation" Dutch News. nl., December 5, 2011. <http://www.dutchnews.nl/news/ archives/2011/12/ the_netherlands_apologies_for.php>; Pyoung-Keun Kang, "A study on Judgment on compensation for Dutch colonial rule over Indonesia with specific reference to the Rawagede case," Korea International Law Review, Vol. 40, 2014.

4. Kavita Modi, "The Mau Mau litigation; colonial era reparations in Britaina-victory against the odds," Revisiting the fifty years of the agreement between south Korea and Japan IV, Northeast Asian History Foundation, 2015, pp. 147-157.

5. 2010 Joint Statement by Korean and Japanese Intellectuals, "1910 Korea-Japan annexation treaty is null and void."

6. Challenge against the Act of Omission Involving Article 3 of "Agreement on the Settlement of Problem concerning Property and Claims and the Economic Cooperation between the Republic of Korea and Japan," 23-2(A) KCCR 366, 2006Hun-Ma788, August 30, 2011.

7. Supreme Court Decision, 2009Da22549, 2009Da68620, Decided May 24, 2012.

8. Alexis Dudden, "Standing with Historians of Japan," February 6. 2015; "Full text of historians' statement on Japan's wartime sex slavery," Yonhap News, May 6, 2015.

9. See-hwan Doh, "Human rights, justice and peace," Korea Times, June 23, 2015; See-hwan Doh, "Shinzo Abe's Denial of the Japanese Military 'Comfort Women' Issue and Challenges in International Law," Korean Yearbook of International Law, Vol. 2, The Korean Branch of the International Law, 2015, pp. 203-225.

10. See-hwan Doh, "Japan's Colonial Responsibility under International Law: The Korean Supreme Court Decision of May 24, 2012," Journal of East Asia and International Law, Vol. 7, No. 1, 2014, pp. 254-255.

The Korean Courts: Arbitration-friendly or Arbitration-averse?

LEE Gyooho
Professor
Chung-Ang University School of Law, Seoul, Korea

1. INTRODUCTION

Whether courts of a country is arbitration-prone will be determined by how they get involved in arbitration process[1] and how easily they recognize and enforce domestic or foreign arbitral awards. Especially, this Special Report focuses on the latter, describing a controversial case called as KT Skylife case.[2]

In terms of the latter, the Korean Supreme Court has generally been said to be arbitration-friendly.[3] The Korean Supreme Court has continued to hold that the "public policy" exception to enforcement under the New York Convention should be narrowly interpreted to protect only "the most basic moral beliefs and social order of the enforcing country" in light of the necessity for foreseeability and legal certainty in transnational business transactions.[4] For instance, the Korean Supreme Court held that an arbitral award based on interest in USA than in England did not violate the Korean public policy even if the agreement was governed by English law.[5] Also, the Korean Supreme Court stated that court should not reexamine "the whole case as to whether the foreign judgment is in substantive right or wrong under the pretext of reviewing whether the judgment was procured through fraudulent means."[6]

As far as foreign arbitral awards are concerned, this Special Report covers an overview of recognition and enforcement of foreign arbitral awards.

Also, in terms of domestic arbitration, the Korean Supreme Court has interpreted "public policy" narrowly, holding that it was not a violation of the public policy for an arbitral award to interpret the law and the contract differently from a prior judgment of the Korean Supreme Court.[7] In connection with recognition and enforcement of domestic arbitral awards, the grounds for cancellation of arbitral awards needs to be delved into and thus will be explored, focusing on KT Skylife case.

In sum, the Korean Supreme Court has been proven to take arbitration-prone approach. This approach has been taken by the lower Korean courts. A good illustration is the appellate court's holdings in the following KT Skylife case.[8]

2. CANCELLATION OF ARBITRAL AWARDS IN THE REPUBLIC OF KOREA

Arbitration awards issued in the Republic of Korea (hereinafter, 'Korea') Korea must be recognized or enforced unless they fall under one of grounds for cancellation of arbitration award in accordance with Article 36 (2) of the Korean Arbitration Act. Accordingly, in terms of recognition or enforcement of domestic arbitration awards, the grounds for cancellation of arbitration award under the Korean Arbitration Act need to be discussed.

Article 36 of the Korean Arbitration Act prescribes the action for setting aside arbitral awards. Recourse against an arbitral award may be raised only by an action for cancellation of the arbitral award to a court.[9] The Korean Arbitration Act enumerates the four reasons which a party making an application bases his/her action for setting aside an arbitral award and the two reasons which a court finds, *ex officio*, to cancel the arbitral award. An arbitration award may be set aside by the court only if a party making an application for cancellation of the arbitral award presents proof that: (i) the party to arbitration agreement was under some incapacity under the law applicable to him/her, or the said agreement is not valid under the law to which the parties have subjected it, or failing any indication thereon, under the Korean law; (ii) the party making the application was not given proper notice of the appointment of an arbitrator or of arbitral proceedings or was otherwise unable to present his/her case; (iii) the award has dealt with a dispute not contemplated by or not failing within the terms of the submission to arbitration, or contains decisions on matters beyond the scope of the submission to arbitration; or (iv) the composition of the arbitral tribunal or arbitral proceedings were not in accordance with agreement of the parties, unless such agreement was in conflict with any mandatory provision of the Korean Arbitration Act from which the parties can not derogate, or failing such agreement, were not in accordance with the Korean Arbitration Act.[10] In terms of the said (iii), if the decisions on matters submitted to arbitration can be separated from those not submitted, only that part of the award which contains decisions on matters not submitted to arbitration may be set aside.[11] Also, an arbitration award may be set aside by the court if the court finds, *ex officio*, that the subject-matter of the dispute is not capable of settlement by arbitration under the Korean law or that the award is in conflict with the good morals and other forms of social order of Korea.[12]

In cases where arbitrators merely erred in fact-finding or their legal determination violates the Korean law and regulation so that the contents of an arbitral award can be regarded to be unreasonable, it is not safe to say that the award is in conflict with the good morals and other forms of social order of Korea. Rather, the legal wording means that the outcome which the award results in violates the good morals and other forms of social order of Korea.[13] The mere fact that an arbitral award differs from the decisions rendered by the Korean Supreme Court in the same type of cases depending on different interpretation of law and regulation or contract does not fall under the category in which the enforcement of the award is in conflict with the good morals and other forms of social order of Korea.[14]

3. RECOGNITION AND ENFORCEMENT OF FOREIGN ARBITRAL AWARDS IN KOREA

Recognition or enforcement of an award shall be confirmed by the judgment by a court.[15] The party applying for recognition or enforcement of an arbitral award shall submit the duly authenticated original award or a duly certified copy thereof or the original arbitration agreement or a duly certified copy thereof.[16] If the award or arbitration agreement is made in a foreign language, a duly certified translation into the Korean language shall be accompanied.[17] A domestic arbitral award shall be recognized or enforced, unless any ground for setting aside the award can be found. Recognition or enforcement of a foreign award which is subject to the New York Convention shall be governed by that Convention.[18] The recognition of a foreign judgment under Articles 217 and 217 *bis* of the Korean Civil Procedure[19] and enforcement of a foreign judgment under Article 26 (1)[20] and 27[21] of the Korean Civil Enforcement Act shall apply *mutatis mutandis* to the recognition and enforcement of a foreign award which is not subject to the New York Convention.[22] A Korean court will review an arbitral award, which was rendered in countries that are not a signatory to the New York Convention and tried to be enforced in Korea, in order to make it sure that the award meets the requirements for recognition and enforcement under Korean law. The requirements are as follows: (1) the award is final and conclusive; (2) the jurisdiction of the foreign tribunal is granted under international jurisdictional principles; (3) the Korean party was legally and timely served with the pleadings; (4) the award does not conflict with Korean public policy; and (5) there is a mutual guarantee by the foreign country where the award was rendered, or the requirements for recognition of a final and conclusive foreign award in Korea and the State of origin are not strikingly out of balance and substantially identical to each other in their material aspects.[23]

4. THE KOREAN COURTS' ARBITRATION-FRIENDLY APPROACH IN TERMS OF KT SKYLIFE CASE[24]

The KT Skylife case arose out of a contract between NDS Limited, a British data encryption software provider, and KT Skylife, a state-invested Korean digital satellite broadcasting company.[25] NDS, a subsidiary of Cisco providing conditional access systems (CAS), had been KT Skylife's CAS supplier since 2001. However, the contract between NDS and KT Skylife was terminated in 2009 when KT Skylife switched to another supplier. On August 6, 2010, KT Skylife applied for arbitration, seeking an award that the contract had been valid, that KT Skylife has a right to permanently use NDS's CAS software, and that NDS must pay damages for breach of the contract to KT Skylife. In this case, NDS applied for a counter-arbitration, seeking a declaration that the contract had been terminated and an order that requires KT Skylife to abide by Article 14.2 of the contract. Here, Article 14.2 of the contract stated that upon termination of the contract, KT Skylife "shall immediately cease using" the NDS software and related materials and "shall return the original and all copies" of the software and related materials to NDS.[26]

Article 16.1 of the contract states that its applicable law is the law of Korea. Article 16.2 of the contract prescribes that arbitration procedure is carried out in accordance with UNCITRAL Arbitration Rules, that the situs of arbitration is Seoul in Korea, and that arbitration procedure is conducted in English. Hence, KT Skylife case is a domestic arbitration case because the place of arbitration is in Korea on basis of Article 2(1)[27] and 38 of the Korean Arbitration Act.

Pursuant to UNCITRAL Arbitration Rules, the arbitration tribunal comprised of three well-recognized arbitrators issued an arbitration award favorable to NDS, stating that the contract was terminated and ordering KT Skylife to abide by Article 14.2 of the contract.[28] In this regard, the arbitration tribunal ordered KT to pay 24.8 billion Korean Won, unpaid CAS fees following the termination of the contract as well as NDS's legal costs, to NDS.[29]

In January 2013, the Seoul Southern District Court refused to enforce the arbitral award on the ground that it did not state the Article 14.2 obligation in sufficient detail to permit an administrative official to determine, without referring to other documents, the exact materials that KT Skylife was obliged to return and to cease using.[30] Acknowledging that Article 35 of the Korean Arbitration Act states that arbitral awards "shall have the same effect on the parties as the final and conclusive judgment of the court," the court held that an arbitration award can not be enforced unless it has the same level of particularity that is required for a court judgment.[31] The court's judgment was criticized as adding a new ground for refusing enforcement of the award that was not mandated by the applicable law.[32]

In January 2014, the Seoul High Court, in part, reversed the first instance court's judgment.[33] The Seoul High Court held that lack of particularity was not a ground for refusing an arbitration award under Articles 36 and 38 of the Korean Arbitration Act whereas the Seoul High Court agreed with the first instance court that the arbitral award "lacks the level of particularity for compulsory enforcement."[34] In this case, the main text and grounds of the award only stated that KT Skylife "must perform the obligation under Article 14.2 of the contract" without specifying its contents, subject and extent. As a corollary, the appellate court granted enforcement of the arbitral award, holding that even though the award could not be enforced in practice, the enforcement judgment would prove the court's recognition of the validity of the award and thus may provide for resolution of the dispute by encouraging the parties to abide voluntarily with the award.[35] The dispute settled following the Seoul High Court's judgment in favor of NDS, which issued its enforcement judgment. Hence, the KT Skylife case certainly shows the Korean courts' arbitration-friendly approach, following arbitration-prone tradition of the Korean Supreme Court.

Notes

1. Kap-You (Kevin) Kim & John S. Bang, Arbitration Law of Korea: Practice and Procedure, BAE, KIM & LEE LLC, pp. 235-44 (2012).
2. Judgment rendered by Seoul High Court on January 17, 2014, Case No. 2013Na13506.
3. *Id.* at 255-324; Grant L. Kim, Korea's "Bali Bali" Growth in International Arbitration, 15 Pepp. Disp. Resol. L.J. 615 (2015).
4. Judgment rendered by the Korean Supreme Court on April 10, 1990, Case No. 89Daka20252.
5. *Id.*
6. Judgment rendered by the Korean Supreme Court on February 14, 1995, Case No. 93Da53054.
7. Judgment rendered by the Korean Supreme Court on June 24, 2010, Case No. 2007Da73918.
8. Judgment rendered by Seoul High Court on January 17, 2014, Case No. 2013Na13506.
9. Article 36(1) of the Korean Arbitration Act.
10. Article 36 (2) of the Korean Arbitration Act.
11. Article 36 (2) 1 (c) proviso of the Korean Arbitration Act.
12. Article 36 (2) 2 of the Korean Arbitration Act.
13. Judgment Rendered by the Korean Supreme Court on June 24, 2010, Case No. 2007da73918.
14. *Id.*
15. Article 37(1) of the Korean Arbitration Act.
16. Article 37(2) of the Korean Arbitration Act.
17. Article 37(2) proviso of the Korean Arbitration Act.
18. Article 39(1) of the Korean Arbitration Act.
19. The Korean Civil Procedure Act was amended on May 20, 2014 (Act No. 12587, amended on May 20, 2014, effective on May 20, 2014) and came into effect starting from the same day. It intends to reflect the existing case laws. Articles 217 and 217 *bis* of the Korean Civil Procedure Act are as follows:

    Article 217 (Recognition of a Foreign Judgment) (1) a final foreign judgment or a foreign adjudication which has same preclusive effect as a foreign judgment (hereinafter, 'a final foreign judgment') will be recognized if the requirements of all of the following paragraphs are met:

    1. That an international jurisdiction of such foreign court is recognized in the

principles of an international jurisdiction pursuant to the Acts and subordinate statutes of the Republic of Korea, or to the treaties;

2. That a defeated defendant received, pursuant to a lawful method, a service of a summons or a document equivalent thereto, and a notice of date or an order, with a time leeway sufficient to defend (excluding the case pursuant to a service by public notice or similar service), or that he responded to the lawsuit even without being served;

3. That such final judgment does not violate good morals and other social orders of the Republic of Korea in the light of its contents and procedure;

4. That there exists a mutual guarantee or that the requirements for recognition of a final foreign judgment in the Republic of Korea and the State of origin are not strikingly out of balance and substantially identical to each other in their material aspects.

(2) a Korean court must make an *ex officio* examination as to whether the requirements prescribed in Paragraph 1 are met.

Article 217 *bis* (Recognition of a Final Foreign Judgment Awarding Damages)

(1) a Korean court can not recognize all or a part of a final foreign judgment awarding damages when it will result in the outcome which strikingly contravenes the essential orders of the Acts of the Republic of Korea and of the treaties acceded to by the Republic of Korea.

(2) when a Korean court examines the requirement prescribed under paragraph 1, it must take into account whether and to what extent the damages awarded by the court of origin serve to cover costs and expenses relating to the proceedings.

20. Article 26 (1) of the Korean Civil Enforcement Act provides that "A compulsory enforcement based upon the a foreign judgment or a foreign adjudication which has same preclusive effect as a foreign judgment (hereinafter 'a final foreign judgment') may be conducted only if a court of the Republic of Korea has permitted its compulsory enforcement by means of an enforcement judgment."

21. Article 27 of the Korean Civil Enforcement Act set forth as follows:

(1) An enforcement judgment shall be made without making any examination as to whether the judgment is right or wrong.

(2) A lawsuit seeking an enforcement judgment shall be dismissed if it falls under any of the following subparagraphs:

1. When it has not been proved that the judgment of a foreign court has become final and conclusive; and

2. When the foreign judgment fails to fulfill the conditions under Article 217 of the Civil Procedure Act.

22. Article 39(2) of the Korean Arbitration Act.

23. *Cf.* Terrence F. MacLaren, Arbitration-Overview, 5 Eckstrom's Licensing: Joint Ventures § 17:31 (2012).

24. Judgment rendered by Seoul High Court on January 17, 2014, Case No. 2013Na13506.

25. Judgment rendered by Seoul Southern District Court on January 31, 2013, Case No. 2012 Gahap 15979; Benjamin Hughes, Enforcement and Execution of Arbitral Awards in Korea: A Cautionary Tale, ASIAN DISP. REV., April 2014, at 95.

26. Hughes, *Supra* note 25, at 95.

27. Article 2(1) of the Korean Arbitration Act prescribes that "This Act shall apply to cases where the place of arbitration under Article 21 is in the Republic of Korea: Provided, That Articles 9 and 10 shall apply even in cases where the place of arbitration is not yet determined or is not in the Republic of Korea, and Articles 37 and 39 shall apply even in cases where the place of arbitration is not in the Republic of Korea."

28. Hughes, *Supra* note 25, at 95.

29. https://www.kdbdw.com/bbs/maildownload/2014100514221178 (last visit on April 10, 2016).

30. Judgment rendered by Seoul Southern District Court on January 31, 2013, Case No. 2012 Gahap 15979.

31. *Id.*

32. Hughes, *Supra* note 25, at 96.

33. Judgment rendered by Seoul High Court on January 17, 2014, Case No. 2013Na13506.

34. *Id.*

35. *Id.*

References

Kap-You (Kevin) Kim & John S. Bang, Arbitration Law of Korea: Practice and Procedure, BAE, KIM & LEE LLC xix, pp. 255-324 (2012).

Grant L. Kim, Korea's "Bali Bali" Growth in International Arbitration, 15 Pepp. Disp. Resol. L.J. 615 (2015).

Benjamin Hughes, Enforcement and Execution of Arbitral Awards in Korea: A Cautionary Tale, ASIAN DISP. REV., April 2014, at 95.

Terrence F. MacLaren, Arbitration-Overview, 5 Eckstrom's Licensing: Joint Ventures § 17:31 (2012).

A Study of Dokdo Sovereignty: International Law, Korean-Japanese Relations, and Challenges for the Republic of Korea*

PARK Hyun-Jin
Former Director
Dokdo Research Institute, Northeast Asia History Foundation, Seoul, Korea

1. INTRODUCTION

Immediately after the inauguration of the Republic of Korea (hereinafter, 'Korea') government in 1948, Shin Seok-ho, then Director of the National History Compilation Office, published in vernacular language a seminal article entitled *Of Dokdo's Affiliation.*[1] This ground-breaking paper was far-sighted in historical perspective, thorough in the presentation of historical evidence and material, and exhaustive in analysis. His incisive insights have long inspired subsequent researchers.

Shin's research was followed after an interval of some 20 years by Lee Han-key's *Korea's Territories* and Park Kwan-suk's *The Legal Status of Dokdo*, both published in 1969. In particular, the former has set the tone and example and laid the cornerstone for subsequent studies on international law and jurisprudence governing territorial, insular and maritime boundary delimitation disputes. And after a 30-year hiatus, a fresh impetus and outlook have been injected by an independent researcher into the

---

* H.J. Park, *Dokdo Yeongto Jukwon Yeongu* (Paju, Kyeonggido: Kyeongin Publishing Co., 2016. 3) [hereinafter referred to as "Park"].

otherwise lackluster progress in research.[2]

A Study of Dokdo Sovereignty has been undertaken against this background to further cultivate, articulate and supplement the ideas, propositions and theses developed in these pioneering studies. Such an enterprise may be relevant and opportune, considering the time lapse and the evolution of legal principles and international jurisprudence on the acquisition of territorial title. It has been intended, through this integrated historico-legal approach, to contribute to and enrich the tradition and legacy of Dokdo research.

2. THE METHOD AND THE STYLE

2-1. THE METHOD

From the late 19th century onwards, Imperial Japan had actively pursued aggression as an instrument of its militaristic expansionist policies, while amalgamating into its territory various Pacific islands and rocks. Under the cover the Russo-Japanese War (1904-1905), in January 1905 Tokyo's Ministry of the Interior, foreseeing the strategic value of Dokdo in advance of the Battle of Tsushima of May 1905 against the Russian fleet, directed Shimane Prefecture to appropriate Dokdo into its territory.[3]

With the benefit of hindsight, the War meant not only the harbinger of the Japanese-forced annexation of Korea, but, more importantly in our context, a prelude to its 1905 clandestine 'incorporation' of Dokdo.[4] For this reason, the Dokdo sovereignty issue would only be put into a better, clearer perspective when one combines a historical approach in the context of bilateral relations (chs. 1 & 12-13) with a legal analysis (chs. 2-11).[5]

In international territorial disputes resolved by adjudication or arbitration, evidence and proof speak, just as money talks in politics and ordinary life alike. And proving or purporting to prove an overwhelming superiority of Korean title to Dokdo required not just legal but historical reasoning in a diachronic perspective. The relationship between positive international law (rules) and history (historical facts), *e.g.* intertemporal law, has been discussed in a number of places.[6]

2-2. THE STYLE

Taking advantage of a rich, indigenous pool of expressions of the Korean language, attempts have been made to get to the point straightforward as much as possible without beating around the bush. The book therefore takes a down-to-earth approach to the contentious issues. Euphemism or roundabout has been shunned away, while short sentences have been preferred and practised throughout, if not always. For a clear and accurate presentation of analyses and arguments is considered essential for the integrity of legal scholarship.

Although rhymes, metaphor, simile and ironies[7] have been employed throughout the work to illustrate the point or draw analogies,[8] even when it looks like playing on words, no pun has been intended. Parallelism has been profusely mobilized to create an aura of contrast between the two subjects compared. The text, shorn of an authoritarian, pedantic or formalistic diction, is predominantly colloquial.

The plain, verbal and figurative but not unduly condescending style is in accordance with the legacy of Anglo-American case law. It is a heritage embedded in the common law tradition not to set up an artificial Berlin Wall between legal and ordinary speech. Indeed, distinction between legal and ordinary English is not as obvious and clear-cut, as one would envisage (thus probably named the common law).[9] This would enhance the overall accessibility and readability of the general readership incapable of benefiting from education, training and expertise in law.

3. ANALYSES, EVIDENCE AND MAIN LEGAL ARGUMENTS

3-1. CONTIGUITY/ADJACENCY/PROXIMITY, DEPENDENCY AND UNITY OF THE ULLEUNG ARCHIPELAGO

Is it admissible under current international law to invoke the geographical contiguity, adjacency or proximity of an island to another, for which sovereignty has been established for the claimant state, as the ground or basis for advancing claims to the former as well?

In the 1928 Island of Palmas arbitration, sole Arbitrator Max Huber stated: "The title of contiguity, understood as a basis of territorial sovereignty, has no foundation in international law," for "it is wholly lacking in precision."[10] He further pronounced: "[i]t is impossible to show the existence of a rule of positive international law to the effect that islands situated outside territorial waters should belong to a State from the mere fact that its territory forms the *terra firma* (nearest continent or island of considerable size)."[11]

Under this jurisprudence, contiguity, proximity or adjacency *per se* of an island to another may not, as a matter of principle, create a territorial title. However, Huber's *obiter dicta* above were in fact qualified by at least two provisos. First, in order for Huber jurisprudence to apply, a strict delimitation should not be "naturally obvious" between different parts of the islands forming an archipelago.[12] Another reservation Huber cited for denying geographical adjacency the status of territorial title was that there were no sufficiently frequent and precise precedents.[13]

Given these reservations, a smaller island's adjacency to another, bigger one is a factor to be reckoned with in the determination of sovereignty, since a smaller island may be identified as a dependency of the larger, adjacent one.[14] In the absence of hard evidence to the contrary in such a situation, presumption of sovereignty may be established in favour of an archipelago. This is particularly so, where the island was uninhabited, like Dokdo, for an extended period of time.

In an analogous context, the Permanent Court of Arbitration in the 1998 Eritrea/Yemen case advanced the unity theory in relation to various groups of islands in the Red Sea. The Eritrea/Yemen jurisprudence is relevant to and consistent with the Korean and Japanese practice relating to Ulleungdo and Dokdo which have geographically formed an archipelago ever since the ancient Usan Kingdom (于山國). Dokdo has been dependent upon Ulleungdo to act as one geographical, economic and political unit. This is further exemplified by the longstanding consistent state practice of both Korea and Japan.

3-2. THE SYMBOLIC ANNEXATION OF AND VIRTUAL EFFECTIVENESS OVER SMALL UNINHABITED ISLANDS

The symbolic annexation of Dokdo, as recorded in the National Geography (地理志) appended or annexed to the Annals of King Sejong's Reign (世宗實錄), combined with virtual effectiveness, was designed to confirm the original title to Dokdo established during the Silla Dynasty (57 BC-935 AD).[15] In its section of Uljinhyeon (蔚珍縣), the official geography gave a premier eye witness account of the two islands in the East Sea to demonstrate the Joseon government's perception and intention at the time:

> "The two islands of Mureung and Usan are located due east of the (Uljin) Hyeon in the midst of the East Sea. They are not so far away with each other and can be observed on a clear windy day…."

This premiere geographical account accords with the empirically observed facts and reality. Dokdo (Usan: 于山) is clearly visible from Ulleungdo (Mureung: 武陵) with the naked eye on a clear day.

3-3. The Late 17ᵗʰ Century Korean-Japanese Exchange of Letters as the Treaty Concluded in Simplified Form

The dominion over Dokdo was first put to the test in the late 17th century when Joseon and Japan were embroiled in the lengthy, tedious negotiations [Insular and Maritime Frontier Skirmish or Ulleungdo Jaenggye (鬱陵島爭界), 1693-1699].[16] In the course of the Exchange of Letters, Japan's Shogunate agreed in February 1697 to Joseon's title to Ulleungdo and acquiesced in Joseon's sovereignty over Dokdo.[17] In reaching agreement, the *special custom* of the distance principle was invoked and agreed to from both sides.[18]

The probative effect of the Exchange of Letters, deemed to be a *treaty concluded in simplified form* in modern international law,[19] are obvious and incontrovertible.[20] Japan, relinquishing any claim to both islands, had agreed to put an end to the Dokdo controversy. This was confirmed and became more evident in the 1870 Japanese Ministry of Foreign Affairs' document and the 1877 Japanese Office of Prime Minister's document, both of which renounced any claim to Dokdo. The effect of these documents is decisive, irreversible and irrevocable.

3-4. The 1951 Treaty of Peace with Japan

The 1951 Treaty of Peace with Japan has been a potential bone of contention over the interpretation of Article 2(a),[21] which did not include Dokdo from the territories to be returned to Korea or to be retained by Japan. On both sides of the Korea Strait, this provision has been invoked to draw water to one's own mill. But a treaty must be interpreted "in good faith in accordance with the ordinary meaning to be given to the terms of the treaty in their context and in the light of its object and purpose", with the context comprised of, *inter alia*, its preamble and annexes.[22]

Under this rule of treaty interpretation, the object and purpose of the Peace Treaty have clearly been stated in its preamble, *i.e.* to *settle questions still outstanding as a result of the existence of a state of war between them* (the Allied Powers and Japan).[23] On the other hand, the Peace Treaty text of Art. 2(a), as quoted above, did neither deny nor confirm Korean title to Dokdo. In these circumstances, a reasonable interpretation should therefore be no other than the following.

Under the Treaty, to which Korea was a third party like the People's Republic of China and the Soviet Union, the Allied Powers and Japan agreed to withhold an express, formal stipulation to simply acquiesce in the continued Korean possession and control of Dokdo.[24] It is all too evident that the Allied Powers had, upon Japanese surrender, recognized and administered the *status quo* of Korean sovereignty over Dokdo by proclaiming SCAPIN 677. Gen. MacArthur issued it in his capacity as the Supreme Commander of the Allied Powers (SCAP) on Jan. 29, 1946 in compliance with the Cairo and Potsdam Declarations and the Instrument of Surrender.[25] The instruction was illustrated in an appended reference map.

This line of reasoning can be reinforced by Japanese conduct and practice, as demonstrated in the Reference Map of Japanese Domain produced by the Japan Coast Guard in August 1951 for presentation to the Japanese Diet for consent to ratification of the Peace Treaty.[26] In this map, Dokdo was clearly located outside the perimeter of Japanese 'domain'. This Japanese map is interpreted as intended to conform to its obligations undertaken under not only the Cairo and Potsdam Declarations and the Instrument of Surrender but SCAPIN 677.

Interestingly enough, the Reference Map of Japanese Domain resembled SCAPIN 677 reference map,[27] corroborating the inference that the former consulted the latter. Another interesting point is that SCAPIN 677 map shows a dividing line across the Korean peninsula and the East Sea, while the Japanese map did not draw such a line to simply designate the entire peninsula as "朝鮮 Korea." Since Japan renounced all right, title and claim to Korea under Art. 2(a) of the Peace Treaty, all that concerned Japan at the time must have been where Japanese boundary was to be drawn in the East Sea.

It constitutes a cardinal principle of international law and jurisprudence that "when two countries establish a frontier between them, one of the primary objects is to achieve stability and finality."[28] A final point with regard to the Treaty must not be missed. By restoring back to Korea sovereignty over the Korean peninsula and its appurtenant islands under Art. 2(a), the Peace Treaty has endowed the Korean people with the right to reunification in their own right.[29]

3-5. THE ADMISSIBILITY AND PROBATIVE VALUE OF MAPS

International jurisprudence on territorial, frontier or maritime boundary delimitation disputes did not grant maps intrinsic legal force establishing territorial rights; Maps merely provide geographical information and of themselves cannot constitute the evidence of a territorial title.[30] Maps can acquire such legal effect only when they are annexed to and identified expressly in the document as its integral part (*certified maps*). Although in this case maps are deemed to embody the "physical expressions of the will of the State or States concerned,"[31] such legal effect does not arise solely from the intrinsic merits of maps.

As a corollary, maps were not recognized as embodying the *real intentions of the party or parties concerned*.[32] Maps *per se* did not enjoy the same status as a legal instrument involving the recognition or abandonment of territorial rights.[33] Admissibility as the evidence of a territorial title or right had effectively been ruled out for maps that are not annexed to and incorporated into a document. This adamant position of international jurisprudence was gradually mitigated to pronounce that varying degrees of weight may be attributed to maps.

Thus, even if maps have not been annexed to and incorporated into a document, they may still be granted a certain weight as evidence, depending on technical accuracy or reliability, impartiality or neutrality of their sources, and cogency.[34] *Reference/illustrative maps*, whether official or semi-official, that have been attached to the document, may also be endorsed as secondary evidence.[35] Finally, unofficial maps were recognized as admissible in the ICJ's 1953 Minquiers and Ecrehos case and 1986 Frontier Dispute between Burkina Faso and Mali.[36]

International jurisprudence on map evidence as explained above may now be applied to the admissibility of Dokdo maps. From the Korean side, Paldo Chongdo (八道總圖: Map of the Entire Eight Provinces),[37] printed circa 1531 and attached to the government-compiled Shinjung Dokgguk Yeogisungram (Newly Supplemented National Geography of Our Lands of Scenic Beauty) may be picked up as a reference map. This ancient official Korean map was not annexed to and incorporated into the book and was flawed in its identification of Ulleungdo and Dokdo, potentially vitiating its probative value. Nevertheless, such misrepresentation would not put a damper on its probative force embodying the "physical expressions of the will of the Joseon government.[38]

Most of official Japanese maps produced since the 18th century recognized Dokdo as belonging to Korea. For example, Kijukdo Yakdo (磯竹島略圖),[39] or Ulleungdo Chart, appended to the 1877 document of the Japanese Office of the Prime Minister, is of particular probative force, since it acknowledged facts unfavorable to Japan itself.[40] So would be the 1951 Reference Map of Japanese Domain, quoted above (sec. 3-4). These two Japanese official maps, when combined with SCAPIN 677 Map, will constitute three representative maps corroborating Korean title to Dokdo.

4. MODERN KOREAN-JAPANESE RELATIONS AND THE CHALLENGES AHEAD

4-1. KOREA AND JAPAN: SOCIETY AND CULTURE

Japan, a nation of islands, had long been cut off and isolated from the outside world until the 1868 Meiji Restoration. A *bona fide* hermit kingdom, Japan had been governed by the emperor and the samurai (武士)

class, as aptly described and analyzed in *The Chrysanthemum and the Sword* by Ruth Benedict in 1946. Domestic politics had been embroiled until 1600 in never-ending internal battles among regional daimyos (大名; feudal lords) for supremacy and eventual domination.

Ordinary people must have been exposed to the *rule by the sword*, with their lives consigned or relegated to a sort of the state of nature.[41] The birth of the polytheist religion of Shinto (神道), worshipping a multitude of souls and deities sacrificed in ceaseless battles, may have been associated with a harsh, brutal everyday occurrence of casualties. Strategic behavior may well have been encouraged or even praised as intelligent and virtuous, while 'synchronized' behavior may have been required under the unwritten code of conduct.

By temperament, natural or acquired, the Japanese tend to be reticent, prudent, enduring and obedient, compared with their relatively straightforward, emotional, short-tempered and independent Korean counterparts.[42] A Japanese civil society governed by the rule of law had probably been a long shot[43] and not in sight, at least until 1868. The rule of law must have been not only a fancy idea but a utopian dream, and was certainly not known to nor inherent in the samurai tradition of strategic thinking for survival and maximum gains.[44]

Contrasted with the isolated environment of Japan, the Korean peninsula was geographically almost wide open. Incessant invasions from the north and Japan had been a matter of ordinary occurrence. Joseon, the last Korean dynasty ruled by the Confucian literati, was incompetent, inefficient, helpless and, above all ignorant of the nature and meaning of the cataclysmic Industrial Revolution, not to speak of its potential impact on the existing global power structure and Joseon's future.

The ruling upper echelons of society were *en masse* dogmatic, obstinate and indifferent to practising reform, adaptation and innovation required for an evolutionary progress. Armed with the anachronistic feudal Confucian ideology and privileged only with vast vested power and right, Joseon's civil service was not perceiving, let alone predicting, what was going to happen. They were simply interested and actually engrossed in factional strife throughout to make their people and territory a scapegoat for what actually happened.

4-2. THE BONDAGE AND WEIGHT OF THE PAST

Due to its strategic location, the Korean peninsula had been the natural channel of communication and intelligence for Japan until the mid-19th century. The flow of information, knowledge and technologies emanating from the Asian continent was facilitated through this corridor. Korea had acted as the primary bridge for trade, traffic and cultural exchanges in its own right, and as a conduit for continental ideas, religions and institutions.

The rocky bilateral relations had been forged in the course of history dotted with unilateral invasions and aggressions, culminating in the forced annexation of 1910. Queen Myeongseong, the consort of King Kojong, had been brutally stabbed to death at Kyeongbok Palace in 1895 by a group of Japanese "diplomats," soldiers and rōnins (浪人) stationed in Seoul. No formal apologies have ever been offered. The relations were restored on paper in 1965 after the elapse of 20 years.

But relations soon started to sour again, marred this time by the grossly distorted Japanese perception of, *inter alia*, its aggressions, coerced annexation and ensuing colonial domination,[45] forced labor, enforcement of the rule to adopt Japanese names (創氏改名),[46] forced drafting of comfort women and various war crimes.[47] Japanese colonial policies had obviously been targeted at obliterating the Korean nation and identity, resulting ultimately in wiping 'Korea' off the map.

Fuelling the already souring relationship was the sporadic but recurring outpouring of debased and degenerate remarks by Japanese diplomats and conservative politicians. The upsetting public utterances were primarily levelled at disparaging Korean identity and distorting historical facts to justify Japanese aggressions and other wrongdoing.[48]

Their tentacles finally reached the authors of U.S. History textbooks, only to be met with a strong backlash from a global academic solidarity.

A medley of recurrent vulgar and trashy remarks have been caused by a collective gross misperception and distortion of the common history. Such an approach and attitude are not considered a self-love of one's own country. Patriotism should not be abused as the last refuge of a scoundrel, while nationalism should be based on the mutual recognition of the right of nations to self-determination.

4-3. A MORAL SOCIETY AND AMORAL STATE VS. A MORAL STATE AND AMORAL SOCIETY

Despite their long-running relationship, Korea has been at loggerheads with Japan in historical perceptions. To the Korean mind, the benevolent slogan of the Commonwealth of Greater East Asia(大東亞共榮) belied Japan's incessant attempts to "escape from the islands" and concealed its territorial ambitions on the Korean peninsula as the stepping stone. A sustainable relationship cannot be built on such a manipulated campaign but on mutual trust and respect.

In 1947 Japan enacted the Peace Constitution featuring the renunciation of war (Art. 9).[49] The conservative Japanese government, however, vigorously disparaging it as one imposed by the occupation authorities, has been spearheading its reinterpretation and ultimate abrogation that would pave the way for going to war in its own right. The problem is that they used to repudiate historical facts relating to aggression, war crimes and wartime atrocities, causing concern about Japanese intentions and ambitions.

If we take the painful and tragic lessons of the calamitous Pacific and Second World War seriously, utmost caution should always be exerted in the exercise of the threat or use of force, even if necessitated by the circumstances and justified by the law. It should always be exercised in a transparent and responsible manner in accordance with the established rule of law and the law of war.

Whenever in doubt, the two countries should go back to the *original position* of 1965 having enabled them to strike an accord to say goodbye to their unfortunate past. Efforts to narrow the perception gap should continue in the spirit of justice, fairness and friendship. The other option for the two countries is to follow the model of *prisoner's dilemma*, that is to say, betray each other and go one's own way to obtain a maximum gain.

5. LAW AND HISTORY

5-1. TOWARDS LIBERTY, JUSTICE AND PEACE

History is about records, interpretation and evaluation. History, in short, belongs to the realm of memories and lessons. History is about "seeing the past through the eyes of the present and in the light of its problems."[50] All history is thus contemporary history, according to Italian historian Benedetto Croce (1866-1952). We may not speak of historical laws or prediction based upon generalized historical facts. This does not necessarily mean that we cannot invoke historical tendencies and inferences as a useful and valid guide to human conduct and evolution.[51]

It is submitted that human history has evolved, if not entirely linear, towards the expansion of freedom and justice. Although the evolutionary march of the human society along the lines of rationalism were on and off obstructed and interrupted by some extremists, nevertheless, backpedaling has not been leniently condoned. Human reason and conscience have not allowed war crimes, piracy, slave trade, apartheid, terrorism, crime against peace and humanity, or gross injustice to prevail.

The recurring debased remarks by Japanese politicians constitute no other than an outright insult to the Korean independence and its identity. Provocative claims to Dokdo are conceived as an outright challenge to the Korean territorial integrity,[52] enshrined in the United Nations Charter [Art. 2(4)]. Such a stance is against and in breach of the basic conditions of a democratic rule of law state.

No nation can defy or resist historical insights which have guided mankind as a lighthouse shining through the sea of darkness. No state could afford to jump into a higher stage of evolution without innovative thinking and cooperation in this era of revolution in information communication technologies. This would only be possible on mutual understanding and appreciation. Such a common perception and attitude would help both overcome hurdles to mutual trust and cooperation.

5-2. RETROACTIVE LEGISLATION

The principle, *Nulla poena sine lege* (Latin for "no penalty without a law": 罪刑法定主義), is a basic requirement of the rule of law. It follows from this that one cannot be punished for doing or failing to do something that was not prohibited by law at the time of having committed the act or omission(nonfeasance). Criticisms and objections have been levelled in this context at the Nuremberg and Tokyo Charters[53] for their respective retroactive application. Granted the principle, it is also true that there is no rule without exception.

Indeed, law is not simply a body of rules applying mechanically to wrongful, illegal acts or omissions. It is a body of binding norms intended to realize or restore substantive justice and fairness based on universal conscience and reason.[54] The two Charters were adopted to declare and confirm belatedly international peace and security and human dignity as the paramount values of international law that cannot be compromised under any circumstances. The Charters represented the collective conscience of mankind and embodied the dignity of their elevated soul.[55]

These evolutionary developments in legal doctrines and principles have borne testimony to the incessant advance of history and justice, fighting against and overcoming any form of injustice and discrimination. What should therefore be blamed is not the retrospective application of rules itself but human incompetence and short-sightedness of having failed to foresee such inhumane crimes and ensuing dire consequences.

5-3. THE RULE OF LAW

The rule of law is the professed goal and ideal of a democratic society, domestic or international. As if to emphasize its status as a model rule of law state, Japan had offered in 1954 to refer the Dokdo question to the International Court of Justice. And the conservative Japanese government is now tampering or tinkering with the revision of the 1947 Constitution to pave the way for waging war by itself. In order for Japan to invoke the rule of law, however, some prior conditions should be met in our view.

Japan, *qua* a civilized state, should first make clear its position on and offer sincere apologies for, *inter alia*, the Savage-like 1895 assassination of Queen Myeongseong, the 1923 massacre of Koreans residing in Tokyo amid the Kanto earthquake, and the whereabout of Gen. Ahn Jung-geun's remains. This would serve as the litmus test for Japan's genuine intention to wash hands with its wrongful past. "Better late than never" is a maxim in point.

6. THE WAY AHEAD

Proving Korean title to Dokdo still leaves more work to be done, including but not limited to the delineation of the relations between and the legal hierarchy among different territorial titles, the presentation of incontrovertible evidence of effective control, *i.e.* continuous display of state authority over an extended period of time, the ascertainment of the legality and validity of Japanese Shimane Prefecture's alleged incorporation of Dokdo in 1905,[56] and the legal status of Dokdo under the 1998 Korean-Japanese Fisheries Agreement.

Again, this book has focussed on the substantive law of international jurisprudence governing the acquisition of territorial sovereignty. It is therefore deficient in the study of the procedural aspect of the adjudication of territorial disputes, such as the presentation of evidence and arguments, written and oral proceedings, and intervention by third parties, etc.

A balanced approach would require due emphasis and weight to be accorded to the procedural part of international adjudication.

7. CONCLUSION

The Korean Independence Day which falls on August 15 is an English translation of 'Gwangbok-jeol' (光復節), literally meaning the 'anniversary of restored light'. By implication, the colonial period has been relegated as the days of darkness. If history is any guide, it would be this. Barring a religious kingdom, there has existed no eternal empire on earth. Only has there been the rise and fall of great powers. History also teaches us that there is no such thing as strategic ambiguity or diplomatic ambivalence, as far as territorial sovereignty is concerned.

Korea's easternmost island of Dokdo is a standing memorial bearing witness to the memories of a military watchtower and submarine communication cables built or laid by Japanese navy in late 1905 shortly after the Battle of Tsushima against the Russian fleet. It is a vivid token of Japanese infringement of Korean territorial integrity, just as Hiroshima is a painful reminder of the apocalyptic greed and violence. This is why Dokdo has been identified as the 'icon of national liberation and independence,'[57] symbolizing Korea's inherent, patrimonial territory.

To overcome the unfortunate past, to deter any recurrence and to move forward along the path of long-term cooperation and mutual benefits, a common perception of history is essential. Building sustainable bridges of mutual trust and respect is the next step to "normalizing" bilateral relations. Only sustained actions deeds could eliminate deep-seated misgivings and corroborate genuine intentions. All in all, both countries should remember, reflect on and take the painful lessons of the tragic past.

Notes

1. See H.J. Park, The Ulleungdo-Dokdo Field Research Expeditions of 1947 & 1952-1953 Evidencing Korea's Effective Control, Korean Journal of International Law, Vol. 60, No. 3, 2015, p. 61, 67-69 & 95 (English abstract).

2. Hong-ju Nah, A Study of Territorial Sovereignty over the Dokdo Islets in Light of International Law [Dokdo-eui Yeongyu-Kwon-e-gwanhan Kukjebeop-jeok Yeongu] (Seoul: Beopseo Publishing Co., 2000) and the two papers, published in 2009 and 2012, respectively, in the Journal of Dokdo [Dokdo Yeongu], which focussed on SCAPIN 677 (1946. 1. 29) and the Japanese Prime Minister's Executive Order No.24, 1951. 6. 6.

3. Shortly after the alleged incorporation, Japan constructed a military watchtower on Dokdo and laid submarine communication cables connecting Dokdo and Masue (松江) on Shimane Prefecture, mainland Japan.

4. Park, p. 39.

5. The Korea Herald, New book offers comprehensive study of Dokdo sovereignty, 2016. 4. 13, p. 30.

6. Park, pp. 250-252, 309-312, 518-521 & 693-717.

7. Imperial Japan exercised extraterritorial enforcement jurisdiction over Japanese criminals responsible for the brutal, savage-like assassination of Queen Myeongseong on Oct. 8 (Aug. 20 by the lunar calendar), 1895 at Kyeongbok Palace in Seoul. While exercising also judicial jurisdiction, Japan conducted a show trial for those Japanese mob assassins at Hiroshima to acquit them all for reasons of insufficient evidence. That is why Japan has been portrayed in the book as a 'would-be civilized state that administered their own arbitrary rule of law in the name of justice.' See Park, p. 44 & 52. No official apology has thus far been offered for that unprecedented, unparalleled heinous crime.

8. Chief Cabinet Secretary of Japan (内閣官房長官) Suga Yoshihide (菅義偉) once portrayed as a 'terrorist' Gen. Ahn Jung-geun of the Korean Righteous Army who had shot Ito Hirobumi to death at Harbin Railway Station in 1909 for having masterminded the forced conclusion of the 1905 Ulsa Dictate in breach of Oriental peace. Gen. Ahn's act had been intended to restore and realize the inherent right to self-determination, a fundamental right of a nation under customary international law. The question was thus raised: "Was Gen. George Washington having fought against the British colonial rule a terrorist as well?" See Park, pp. 44-55.

9. See H.J. Park, Anglo-American Law and Allusive Style and Skills: The Fair, Flair and Figure of Speech, Legal Fiction and Euphemism in the Common Law and English Legal Writings, Peophak Yeongu (Legal Research), Vol. 18, No. 3, 2008, p. 249, 279

(English abstract).

10. Island of Palmas arbitration, 1928, 2 United Nations Reports of International Arbitral Awards (1949), p. 831, 869; H.J. Park, The Proximity, Dependency and Unity of the Ulleung Archipelago as Evidence Creating Presumption of Effective Control, Korean Yearbook of International Law, Vol. 2, 2015, p. 69, 73.

11. Palmas arbitration, *ibid.*, p. 854.

12. Palmas arbitration, *ibid.*, p. 869; Park, p. 115, n.6.

13. Palmas arbitration, *ibid.*, p. 854.

14. The Minquiers and Ecrehos case, ICJ Reports, 1953, p. 47. For a distinction between proximity, dependency and unity, see H.J. Park, *supra* note 10, p. 69,

15. Park, pp. 223-226; F.A.F von der Hydete, Discovery, Symbolic Annexation and Virtual Effectiveness in International Law, American Journal of International Law, Vol. 29, 1935, p. 448 & G. Schwarzenberger, Title to Territory: Response to A Challenge, American Journal of International Law, Vol. 51, 1957, p. 308.

16. H.J. Park, Ahn Yong-bok towers over Dokdo, in The Korea Herald & Park Hyun-jin (eds.), Insight into Dokdo (Paju, Gyeonggi-do: Jimoondang, 2009), p. 196; H.J. Park, The Evidentiary Value of the 17th Century Korean-Japanese Exchange of Letters Agreeing Tacitly on the Former's Title to Dokdo and on the Maritime Frontier Based on the Special Custom of Distance Criteria, Korean Journal of International Law, Vol. 58, No. 3, 2013, p. 131, 165(English abstract).

17. Park, pp. 313-316; H.J. Park, *supra* note 10, pp. 72-73.

18. Park, pp. 328-330.

19. Park, ch.5 & ch.6, pp. 315-316; H.J. Park, The Legal and Evidentiary Status/Value of the Treaties Concluded in Simplified Form in International Territorial/Maritime Delimitation Adjudication: The ICJ's 'Judicial Activism'(1951-2005) over the Interpretation of Minutes, Agreed Minutes and the Exchange of Notes/Letters, Korean Journal of International Law, Vol. 58, No. 2, 2013, p. 95, 127.

20. Park, pp. 316-319.

21. "Japan, recognizing the independence of Korea, renounces all right, title and claim to Korea, including the islands of Quelpart, Port Hamilton and Dagelet."

22. A combined reading of Art. 31(1)-(2), The Vienna Convention on the Law of Treaties.

23. Treaty of Peace with Japan (with two declarations). Signed at San Francisco on September 8, 1951 and entered into force on April 28, 1952, 136 UNTS No. 1832, 1952, p. 46, preamble.

24. Park, pp. 371-373; H.J. Park, SCAPIN 677 as an International Legal Instrument Constituting both a Root and Evidence of Korean Title to Dokdo, Korean Yearbook of International Law, Vol. 1, 2014, p. 123, pp. 130-131.

25. Park, pp. 373-379; H.J. Park, SCAPIN 677 as an International Legal Instrument

Constituting both a Root and Evidence of Korean Title to Dokdo, *ibid.*, pp. 124-127.

26. Park, p. 386.

27. See the two maps in Park, p. 378.

28. Park, pp. 346-348, esp. n.162, quoting The Temple of Preah Vihear (Cambodia v. Thailand), Judgment, ICJ Reports, 1962, p.6, 34.

29. Park, pp. 402-404.

30. Frontier Dispute (Burkina Faso v. Mali), Judgment, ICJ Reports, 1986, p. 554, 582, para. 54; Palmas arbitration, *supra* note 10, pp. 853-854.

31. Frontier Dispute, *ibid.*

32. Eritrea/Yemen arbitration, PCA, 1998 & H.J. Park, Map evidence galore against Japan's Dokdo claims, in The Korea Herald & Park Hyun-jin, Insight into Dokdo, *supra* note 16, p. 216, 224.

33. Palmas arbitration, *op.cit.*, pp. 853-854; Park, p. 456.

34. Frontier Dispute, *op.cit.*, paras. 55-56; Temple of Preah Vihear, *supra* note 28; Park, pp. 461-463; H.J. Park, The Legal Status and Probative Value of Maps and Charts in International Adjudication on Territorial/Boundary Disputes, Korean Journal of International Law, Vol. 53, No. 1, 2008. 4, p. 61, 93 (English abstract) & H.J. Park, Title to Dokdo as Interpreted and Evaluated Chiefly from Changing International Jurisprudence on Map Evidence, Korean Journal of International Law, Vol. 52, No. 1, 2007, p. 89, 124(English abstract).

35. Polish-Czechoslovak Frontier case (Questions of Jaworzina), PCIJ, Series B, No. 8, 1923, p. 18; Park, p. 465.

36. Park, pp. 467-470.

37. See Park, book jacket & p. 475.

38. Park, Title to Dokdo as Interpreted and Evaluated Chiefly from Changing International Jurisprudence on Map Evidence, *supra* note 34, p. 126.

39. See Park, p. 470 & 472.

40. Palmas arbitration, *supra* note 10, p. 852; The ICJ's 1953 Minquiers and Ecrehos case & 1986 Nicaragua case.

41. T. Hobbes, Leviathan (1651; Penguin Books, 1988), Chapters XIII–XIV.

42. The Japanese do rarely lay bare their bosom, with refusals uttered almost always in a polite, restrained and 'diplomatic' diction.

43. See *supra* footnotes 7-8.

44. Park, pp. 44-45, quoting Montesquieu, De l'esprit des lois (The Spirit of the Laws).

45. The International Court of Justice(ICJ) landed a declaratory coup de grâce judgment on the controversy surrounding the legality of colonial domination in its Advisory Opinion in the 1971 Namibia (South West Africa) case. Park, p. 82.

46. See Wikipedia, "Sōshi-kaimei", at https://en.wikipedia.org/wiki/S%C5%8Dshi-

kaimei (visited 2016. 7. 27).

47. The Hankook Ilbo, "Abe at the Heart of Degrading Remarks," 2015. 8. 18, at http://hankookilbo.com/v/6959bb391cc041bca55a6e9e0608cbda (visited 2016. 7. 23).

48. In 2005 the Japanese ambassador to Korea made claims to Dokdo at the heart of Seoul to strike a nerve and to provoke outbursts of public furor in this country. H.J. Park, Insight into Dokdo, *supra* note 16, p. 15 (Introduction).

49. "The Japanese people forever renounce war as a sovereign right of the nation and the threat or use of force as means of settling international disputes." To this end the article provides that "land, sea, and air forces, as well as other war potential, will never be maintained."

50. E.H. Carr, What is History? (London: Macmillan, 1961; Penguin Books, 1964), p. 21.

51. Carr, *ibid.*, pp. 68-69. Even science has been concerned with a process of change and development based not on isolated facts but on a chain of events. Carr, *ibid.*, p. 57.

52. H.J. Park, Insight into Dokdo, *supra* note 16, p. 23.

53. The 1946 Charter of the International Military Tribunal for the Far East (CIMTFE) was adopted to try the leaders of the Empire of Japan for three types of crimes: "Class A" (crimes against peace), "Class B"(war crimes), and "Class C"(crimes against humanity). No Japanese national was prosecuted for Class C crime under the Charter. Wikipedia, Crimes against humanity, at https://en.wikipedia.org/wiki/Crimes_against_humanity (visited 2016. 7. 23); Park, pp. 604, 610 & 614.

54. Park, p. 604.

55. Park, pp. 614-615.

56. As already indicated above (sec. 2-1), Japan attempted in 1905 to encroach upon the established Korean title to Dokdo in a series of governmental and civilian acts meticulously contrived and secretly prosecuted under the cover of the Russo-Japanese War. The alleged 1905 measure was neither published in the Japanese Official Gazette, nor notified to Joseon. Disguised as lawful and innocent, the alleged incorporation was no other than an act of aggression on the established sovereignty. See H.J. Park, Japan's Military Occupation and Clandestine Incorporation of Dokdo: The Legality, Validity and Admissibility of A Provincial Government's Incorporation, paper presented at the Dokdo Society's annual seminar (Seoul's History Museum, 2015. 10. 8).

57. Remarks by Korean Minister of Foreign Affairs Byeon Young-tae in response to the Japanese proposal in 1954 to refer the Dokdo issue to the International Court of Justice.

RECENT DEVELOPMENTS

The Republic of Korea's Response against IUU Fishing by Korean Vessels

PARK Young-Kil
Senior Researcher
Korea Maritime Institute, Busan, Korea

1. INTRODUCTION

The Republic of Korea (hereinafter, 'Korea') is one of the leading distant water fishing states in the world of which vessels actively fish all over the world's oceans in the EEZ of other states and in the high seas. In 2014, it has 261 distant water vessels owned by 54 companies, producing 628,261 M/T, an amount of 1,185,507 million won.[1] Korean people did not pay much attention to Illegal, Unreported and Unregulated (IUU) fishing[2] activities of its distant water fishing vessels until the preliminary designations over Korea as an IUU fishing state by the US and the EU. They criticized occasionally Chinese illegal fishing activities which were widespread in the territorial sea and EEZ of Korea.[3] Thus many Korean people felt shameful when they heard the news about the designations of Korea as IUU fishing country. Unfortunately it seems the Korean government did not take the IUU fishing itself seriously at that time, in particular by its distant water fishing vessels, although international communities had been given their best shot to reduce the IUU fishing, even regarding it as an *enemy of all mankind. Fortunately, however, the government responded to 'yellow card' warnings given by the US and the EU by reforming relevant institutions quickly and effectively. According to a report by Greenpeace, IUU fishing by Korean vessels had been happening in the*

Pacific Ocean, Oceans near West Africa and the Antarctic Ocean; the report listed 34 cases of IUU fishing by Korean fishing vessels between 2006 and 2012.[4]

2. PRELIMINARY DESIGNATIONS OF IUU FISHING STATE BY THE US AND THE EU

In January 2013, the US identified Korea along with 9 other countries as having been engaged in IUU fishing based on violations of international conservation and management measures during 2011 and/or 2012.[5] The US pointed out in particular that Korea was not effectively controlling its nine fishing vessels authorized to fish in the CCAMLR Convention Area, and believed that "Korea's sanctions against the operator, vessel and master were inadequate, given the seriousness of the illegal activity." It also mentioned that the pending amendment raising the maximum fine for a violation from approximately USD 4,660 to USD 18,450 by itself is not enough of a disincentive to discontinue such profitable illegal activity.[6]

The relevant act for the US measure is the High Seas Driftnet Fishing Moratorium Protection Act (Moratorium Protection Act), which was amended by the Magnuson-Stevens Fishery Conservation and Management Reauthorization Act of 2006. According the Moratorium Protection Act, it has three-step procedures: The first step is Identification, identifying nations engaged in IUU fishing activities; the second step is Consultation, working collaboratively with identified nations on actions to address the activities for which they identified; the third step is Certification, issuing certification decisions based on the actions of the nations.[7] If a nation receives a negative certification at the last step, it may "result in denial of the US port access for fishing vessels of that nation, and potential import restrictions on fish or fish products."[8] Korea exported fisheries product to the US about USD 200 million a year in 2012 and 2013.

In November, the European Commission (EC) also named Korea as a preliminary IUU country, along with Ghana and Curacao in the Netherlands Antilles.[9] It accused Korean fishing companies of engaging in IUU fishing repetitively in West African waters. In the decision, the EC concretely pointed out that 19 Korean vessels committed serious IUU infringements during 2011 and 2012, which includes fishing without a valid licence, authorization or permit issued by the flag state or the relevant coastal state, using falsified coastal state administrative documents, falsified or concealed markings, identity or registration etc.[10] It also indicated that Korea failed to fulfil its flag state obligations under international law,[11] pointing out among others that there were no Fishing Monitoring Center (FMC), no compulsory VMS tracking in Korea.

The EC decision is based on European Council Regulation No.1005/2008, which is considered as the strongest measure against IUU fishing in the world. According to this regulation, the EC notifies a country of the possibilities of its being identified as non-cooperating country, as a preliminary nature. Then, the EC should give to the country concerned adequate time to answer the notification and reasonable time to remedy the situation. If a country fails to discharge the duties incumbent upon it under international law to take action to prevent, deter and eliminate IUU fishing, it may be identified as a non-cooperating third country which leads to trade measures. One of the most powerful measures among trade measures is to ban fisheries products caught by the country's vessels from being imported to the EU. In case of Korea, export of all fisheries product to EU, which amount to about USD 100 million a year, would be banned.

3. KOREA'S RESPONSE AGAINST IUU FISHING ACTIVITIES BY KOREAN VESSELS

It did not take long time for the Korean government to consider the situation seriously in which the US and the EU designated preliminarily Korea as an IUU fishing country. Korean government decided to respond positively against IUU fishing activities done by Korean vessels in order to avoid final designation. Thus, it has positively negotiated with the US and the EU and tries to accept their requests. During the consultation or cooperation with them between 2013 and 2014, Korea has established an effective system to eradicate IUU fishing activities by Korean vessels. The following are main measures of them.

3-1. Amendments of Distant Water Fisheries Development Act

Distant Water Fisheries Development Act is the core act among others to deter, eliminate and prevent IUU fishing by Korean vessels. The Korean government revised this Act twice over the past two years to comply with international standards, accommodating the requests from the US and the EU.[12] Under the first amendment, as a strong deterrent against IUU fishing activities, serious violations are regarded as a criminal offense with imprisonment up to five years or a fine of at least KRW 500 million (USD 45,000). It also strengthened significantly its monitoring, control and surveillance (MCS) capacity and reinforced sanctions on IUU fishing activities. All distant water fishing vessels of Korea are now required to carry vessel monitoring system (VMS), which enable satellites to track their movements. Before the amendment, the obligation to carry VMS was applied only to vessels fishing in waters in which the international fishery organizations control or to vessels catching fish stocks which are managed by international conventions or agreements. Korean officials monitor VMS at a 24-hour fisheries monitoring center (FMC) in Busan that opened in May 2014. The government also addressed all vessels to be fitted with an electronic logbook system, which allow vessels to share real-time information on catch and fishing operations.

3-2. REVISION OF NATIONAL PLAN OF ACTION

The Korean government submitted its revised National Plan of Action to Prevent, Deter and Eliminate IUU Fishing (NPOA-IUU) to FAO in October 2014. The EC Decision in November 2013 also mentioned that Korea did not update its NPOA-IUU since its first submission in 2005. International Plan of Action to Prevent, Deter and Eliminate IUU Fishing (IPOA-IUU), which was adopted in 2001 by FAO, recommends that every state updated its NOA-IUU every four years.[13] Thus, the submission of the revised NPOA-IUU was the expression of a strong will of the Korean government to respond against the IUU fishing. The NPOA-IUU of Korea includes state responsibilities, flag state responsibilities, coastal state measures, port state measures, internationally agreed market-related measures, measures to be implemented through RFMOs and special requirements of developing countries.

3-3. STRENGTHENING MONITORING, CONTROL AND SURVEILLANCE (MCS)

A comprehensive system that tracks the entire chain of catching, transshipment, landing, processing, wholesale and retail trades of fish and fisheries products should be established to maximize the effectiveness of MCS.[14] For the MCS, the Korean government strengthened port state inspections which were devised at the same level as required by Port State Measures Agreement.[15] For example, the Korean government uncovered 7 IUU fishing vessels among 701 vessels when it inspected all vessels from 31 January to 31 December 2014 that wanted to load fisheries products in Korean port and use the port. It prosecuted the uncovered Korean vessels according to relevant acts and banned port entry for those foreign vessels. It also completed to equip all distant water fishing vessels with VMS in March 2014, and started to run Fisheries Monitoring Centre in May 2013, which is situated in Busan.

3-4. MEASURES TO BUILD CREDIBILITY ON THE CATCH CERTIFICATE

The Korean government tried to build credibility on the catch certificate issued by it. It amended Regulation on Issuing the EC Catch Certificate and Process Certificate in May 2014,[16] which aims to regulate details required to export fisheries product to the European Community. The government inspected VMS information from FMC with logbook linking with the system to issue the catch certificate. As the result, it suspended the issuance of the catch certificate to vessels of which VMS is not working and illegal vessels.[17]

3-5. REINFORCING EDUCATION AND TRAINING PROGRAM AND INTERNATIONAL COOPERATION TO ERADICATE IUU FISHING

As a capacity building for officials, the Korean government sent officials who take charges of the catch certificate to FMC of the EU member states to learn the operation, and distributed manuals to issue the certificate. It also developed textbooks and videos on IUU fishing, and created a new course on IUU fishing at a compulsory education program on fishing boat crews.

In order to eradicate IUU fishing, the Korean government has closely cooperated with coastal states and NGOs. It established hot lines with Guinea and Guinea-Bissau in Western Africa and in June 2014 signed an MOU with Environmental Justice Foundation (EJF) to renew efforts to curb IUU fishing in West African Waters.[18] The Korean government, as one of some region-specific measures, bought 18 vessels, worth 9.9 billion Korean Won (equivalent to $9 million USD or 7.8 million Euro), that have been operating in West Africa and scrapped them as part of a vessel de-commissioning programme in 2015.

4. CONCLUSION

Thanks to a series of significant and effective measures taken by Korean government to deter, eliminate and prevent IUU fishing following the 'yellow cards' given by the US and the EU in 2013 separately, Korea was lifted from the preliminary list of IUU fishing countries in 2015.[19] Right after the removal from the IUU fishing list of the EU, Vice Minister of Oceans and Fisheries of Korea Kim Young-suk, now the Minister, told the following: "The EU's lifting of Korea from its list of IUU nations was possible through the concerted efforts by all concerned government agencies. We should not be complacent with the delisting. The government will make every effort to prevent the nation from being named as IUU nation again by thoroughly eradicating illegal fishing practices here."[20] Also Steve Trent, executive director of EJF rightly evaluated on the efforts of Korean government to respond against IUU fishing as follows: "South Korea's efforts to stop illegal fishing are unprecedented and demonstrate a clear intent to deliver national, regional and international leadership to combat IUU fishing which devastates marine environments, biodiversity, fish stocks, livelihoods and food security. We hope that the EU's yellow card sanction will be soon lifted, having done its job, and South Korea can take on a role as a regional leader in the fight against IUU fishing, inspiring others to act."[21]

Notes

1. The Ministry of Oceans and Fisheries, The Result of Distant Water Fishing (Single) in Distant Water Fishing *Statistical Survey in 2015*, p.78. The survey is based on facts of 2014. The number of the vessel was dramatically decreased in 2014: 316 in 2011, 323 in 2012, 318 in 2013 and 261 in 2014.
2. IUU fishing.
3. The Coast Guard and Fisheries Management Service of Korea arrested 568 illegal vessels of China in 2015. Ministry of Public Safety and Security, Weekly Paper for Policy Explanation (7 January 2016). Website: http://www.mpss.go.kr/home/news/press/press/?boardId=bbs_0000000000000047&cntId=680&mode=view&category=.
4. Greenpeace, Report on IUU Fishing by Korean Distant Water Fishing Vessels, April 2014. Visit to: www.greempeace.org/korea.
5. NOAA Fisheries, Improving International Fisheries Management: Report to Congress, January 2013, p. 3. The report was produced by the National Marine Fisheries Service (NMFS), a line office of the National Oceanic and Atmospheric Administration (NOAA) in the Department of Commerce. The other 9 states are as follows: Colombia, Ecuador, Ghana, Italy, Mexico, Panama, Spain, Tanzania, and Venezuela. Visit to: http://www.nmfs.noaa.gov/ia/iuu/msra_page/2013_biennial_report_to_congress__jan_11__2013__final.pdf.
6. *Ibid.*, p. 25.
7. Refer to NOAA website: http://www.nmfs.noaa.gov/ia/iuu/msra_page/msra.html.
8. *Ibid.*
9. European Commission, Commission Decision of 26. 11. 2013 on notifying the third countries that the Commission considers as possible of being identified as a non-cooperating third countries pursuant to Council Regulation (EC) No. 1005/2008 establishing a Community system to prevent, deter and eliminate illegal, unreported and unregulated fishing.
10. *Ibid.*, para. 22.
11. *Ibid.*, para. 31.
12. The first amendment was on 30 July 2013, came into force on 31 January 2014. The second one was on 6 January 2015, came into force on 7 July 2015.
13. The IPOA-IUU is the first international voluntary instrument formulated to address IUU fishing specifically.
14. The Ministry of Oceans and Fisheries of Korea, NPOA-IUU of Korea, 2014, Chapter 4. (7).

15. Korea is going to ratify the agreement in January 2016.
16. Ministry of Oceans and Fisheries Regulation No. 36. Amended on 21 May 2014.
17. Ministry of Oceans and Fisheries, "EU, Final Revocation of IUU Fishing State on Korea," Press Release on 23 April 2015.
18. *Ibid.*
19. Korean was removed from the list in February 2015 by the US and by the EU in April 2015.
20. The Korea Times, "EU removes Korea from illegal fishing list," 21 April 2015. Visit to: http://www.koreatimes.co.kr/www/news/biz/2015/11/123_177449.html.
21. Roo Price, "South Korea takes 'bold' stance against IUU fishing" in Fishing News International (The date was not appeared on the web.). http://fishingnewsinternational.com/south-korea-takes-bold-stance-against-iuu-fishing/.

International Trade Disputes in the Republic of Korea

LEE Jaemin
Professor
Seoul National University School of Law, Seoul, Korea

The Republic of Korea (hereinafter, 'Korea') practice of international law in the field of international economic sector continued to be active in the year 2015. At the World Trade Organization ("WTO"), Korea was involved in three direct disputes. Two of them were brought by Korea against the United States and one was brought by Japan against Korea. The two disputes brought by Korea involved antidumping and countervailing duty imposition by the United States against Korean residential washers, and antidumping duty imposition by the United States against Korean special steel products, respectively. A dispute brought by Japan against Korea involved Korea's import restriction of Japanese food products in the wake of Fukushima nuclear power plant disaster.

The first case, *United States-Anti-dumping and Countervailing Measures on Large Residential Washers from Korea* (DS464), completed its panel proceeding in 2015. In the panel report circulated on March 11, 2016, Korea prevailed in major issues of the antidumping aspect of the dispute, while it saw a largely mixed outcome on the countervailing duty front of the dispute. With respect to the second case, *United States - Anti-Dumping Measures on Certain Oil Country Tubular Goods from Korea* (DS488), the panel was composed on July 13, 2015, and the panel meetings are expected to take place in 2016. On May 21, 2015, Japan filed a request for consultation with Korea concerning Korea's import restrictions on food products from Japan. In *Korea-Import Bans, and Testing and Certification Requirements for Radionuclides* (DS495), Japan claimed that Korea's import restrictions constitute violation of certain provisions of the WTO's SPS Agreement. A panel was established on September 28, 2015, followed by its composition on February 8, 2016. This is the second WTO dispute between the two countries since the first one involving Japan's countervailing duty investigation against Korean DRAM manufacturers in 2006.

In addition, in 2015 Korea also actively participated in other countries' disputes as a third party including *Brazil-Certain Measures Concerning Taxation and Charges* (DS497). Korea was an active participant in other countries' direct disputes when they involved trade remedy measures or other types of border measures because of its systemic interest in those issues.

On the front of Free Trade Agreements ("FTAs"), Korea has ratified and brought into effect four major FTAs in 2015. They were FTAs with China, Canada, New Zealand and Vietnam. Obviously, the FTA with China triggered intense national debates due to the volume of trade with China who is Korea's largest trading partner since 2006. With conclusion of these FTAs in 2015, the total number of FTAs of Korea, as of the end of 2015, reached 16 with as many as 53 countries. Likewise, Korea continued to explore the possibility of joining the Trans-Pacific Partnership ("TPP") in 2015, whose negotiation was finalized in October 2015, followed by disclosure of the text in November 2015 and signing of the agreement in February 2016. Korea also actively participated in the negotiations of another mega-FTA, Regional Comprehensive Economic Partnership ("RCEP"), spearheaded by China. TPP and RCEP, as mega-FTAs, continued to draw keen attention in Korea due to the possibility of their rule making function in the trade sector.

On the other hand, as the number of Korea's trade agreements increases, foreign attention is also being focused on how Korean domestic courts incorporate and apply the provisions of trade agreements in cases brought before the Korean judiciary. In *Case Concerning Revocation of Limitation of Operating Hours for Certain Retailers* (Supreme Court of the Republic of Korea, 2015Du295, Nov. 10, 2015), a dispute involving local governments' measures to impose a bi-weekly close-down requirement for large-size retailer shops, the Korean Supreme Court basically held for the local governments, the defendants in the dispute. This case was brought by owners of large retailers who were subject to the bi-weekly mandatory close-down requirement of the local governments at issue. Under the requirement, these stipulated retailers were ordered to close down their business twice a month. The measure at issue was an implementation, on the level of respective local governments, of the enabling act (*Act on the Development of Distribution Service Business of 2013*), and its enforcement decree (*Enforcement Decree of the Act on the Development of Distribution Service Business*).

The plaintiff retailers argued that the ordinances of the local governments pronounced under the Act and the Enforcement Decree violate Korean Administrative Law principles (*i.e.*, abuse of discretion and disproportionate regulation) and the WTO's *General Agreement on Trade in Services* ("GATS") and the *Free Trade Agreement between Republic of Korea and the European Union* ("Korea-EU FTA") (*i.e.*, regulation not authorized in the schedules of specific commitments applicable to services trade). As the measure attempts to regulate retail distribution service provider operating in the Korean market, and as one of the plaintiffs is owned by an EU corporation, the dispute referred to the schedules of specific commitments of the GATS and the Korea-EU FTA.

The local governments at issue, the defendants, were various district offices of the Seoul Metropolitan City Government. The defendants issued respective ordinances following the enactment of the Act and the Enforcement Decree in 2013. The purpose of the Act and the Enforcement Decree was to maintain "good order in the distribution service industry," "health right of the employees working in the distributions service industry," and "the co-prosperity of the large corporation and Small and Medium Enterprises ("SMEs")," to name a few. In particular, the Act authorizes the heads of respective local governments to impose a close-down requirement not exceeding twice a month. The local governments thus adopted their respective ordinances mandating two close-downs per month for large retailers operating within their jurisdiction.

In the proceeding of the Seoul Appeals Court, the plaintiffs prevailed: the court decided that the ordinances of the local governments constitute violation of Korean Administrative Law principles because they constitute abuse of discretion on the part of the agency and a disproportionate burden on certain corporations in the industry. In addition, the court also found that the measure constituted violation of the GATS and the Korea-EU FTA because of a deviation from the schedules of specific commitments that Korea had submitted. In its decision of November 10, 2015, however, the Supreme Court of Korea, reversed the decision of the Seoul Appeals Court on both counts, remanded the case back to the lower court for reconsideration. In the decision, the Supreme Court held that the challenged ordinances were within the discretion of the local governments as empowered by the Act and the Enforcement Decree, and that they managed to maintain the conflicting interest between those regulated and that of the society at large. Thus, the Supreme Court found them to be compatible with the Administrative Law principles requiring "reasonable regulation" by a governmental agency.

With respect to the issue of possible violation of international trade agreements, the Supreme Court basically held that as international agreements these cited trade agreements create rights and obligations *only* for the contracting parties (*i.e.*, governments of the contracting parties). As such, according to the Court, the plaintiffs, as private corporations, do not possess the right to bring legal action before the Korean domestic court based on the trade agreements at issue. The Court thus basically dismissed the claim of the plaintiffs to the extent that it referred to trade agreements without reaching the merit, that is, whether or not the said measure constituted violation of schedules of specific commitments. So, in a sense, in this high-profile dispute attracting attention from the European Union and the United States, the Supreme Court managed to avoid addressing the difficult issue of evaluating the measures from the perspective of trade agreement obligation. Based on this decision, the Supreme Court remanded the case back to the lower court for further consideration.

All in all, the finding of the Supreme Court may arguably be a correct interpretation of the Korean Administrative Law principles. It is not entirely clear, however, whether the judgment can also be found to be consistent with the general understanding of treaty obligation imposed on Korea. Similar issues will continue to be raised in Korean domestic court as the web of trade agreements is becoming more complex both in terms of quantity and in quality. The judgment of November 2015 will raise more questions and issues when new disputes involving trade agreements are brought for the review by Korean courts.

In the area of investment disputes, Korea saw robust activities in 2015. Throughout 2015, Korea continued to participate in its first investment arbitration case at ICSID, a case brought by Lone Star on November 22, 2012 under the 2007 Korea-Belgium Bilateral Investment Treaty ("BIT"). The U.S. equity fund claims that Korean tax authorities and financial regulatory bodies adopted action and omission which constitute violation of certain provisions of the BIT. Major hearings took place in 2015, and it is expected that the final award will be released in late 2016 or in 2017. The final award will draw a great deal of attention from the general public as the first case of investment arbitration involving Korea.

In addition, two more investment arbitrations were initiated against Korea in 2015. On May 20, 2015, a Dutch company called Hanocal, owned by Abu Dhabi-based International Petroleum Investment Company, brought an investment arbitration against Korea under 2003 Korea-Netherlands BIT. In *Hanocal Holding B.V. and IPIC International B.V. v. Republic of Korea* (ICSID Case No. ARB/15/17), the claimants challenged the alleged tax levied on the 2010 sale of the claimants' controlling stake in Hyundai Oilbank, a petroleum and refinery company based in the city of Seosan, and argued that the taxation measure constitutes violation of the said BIT.

Another dispute raised in 2015 involves an Iranian investor. In a third investment arbitration involving Korea, *Mohammad Reza Dayyani and others v. Republic of Korea*, Iranian electronics company Entekhab Group filed a notice of arbitration against Korea on September 14, based on 1998 Korea-Iran BIT. The claimants challenge the Korea Asset Management Corporation's termination of an agreement for the sale of a majority stake in Daewoo Electronics to the claimants and the alleged non-return of the claimants' US$50 million deposit. The three pending investment arbitrations indicate that Korea is likely to see more investment disputes in the future involving various governmental regulation and policies.

The Arbitration Reform Bill of the Republic of Korea for the Hub for International Arbitration

KANG Pyoung-Keun
Professor
Korea University School of Law, Seoul, Korea

1. INTRODUCTION

The Republic of Korea (hereinafter, 'Korea') has been a Model-Law country since 1999 when she incorporated almost all the provisions of the UNCITRAL Model Law on International Commercial Arbitration ("the Model Law") of 1985 in amending the Korean Arbitration Act ("KAA") of 1966.[1] The Arbitration Reform Bill ("the Bill") of 2015 is another effort to incorporate the provisions of the Model Law which were newly inserted as the Model Law was amended in 2006. Furthermore, the Bill is proposed to make the Republic of Korea an attractable venue for international arbitration and to promote the use of arbitration in Korea as a means to settle disputes by agreement between the disputing parties without those disputes to be referred to the proceedings before the courts. The Bill is to extend the scope of the arbitrability of disputes, to loosen the requirements of arbitration agreement, to streamline the regime of provisional measures by an arbitral tribunal, and to allow an arbitral award to be recognized or enforced by decisions by the competent courts.

2. MAIN POINTS OF THE BILL

2.1. EXTENSION OF THE PURPOSE AND THE SCOPE (ARTICLES 1 AND 3)

The subject matter of the dispute is to be broadened to cover any claim under property law and any other non-pecuniary claims subject to settlement between the parties. Under the current KAA (Korean Arbitration Act), it is arguable whether the disputes arising out of competition laws, intellectual property rights under patent laws, or other borderline disputes involving entities under public laws are arbitrable.

2.2. RELAXATION OF FORMAL REQUIREMENTS FOR ARBITRATION AGREEMENTS (ARTICLE 8)

The article 8 of the Bill reflects the Model Law as amended in 2006 which relaxed formal requirements of arbitration agreements in writing. Under the Bill, the intention of the parties to arbitrate may be found in a contract concluded orally or by performance, or in an exchange of letters, telex, telegrams, or other means of telecommunication which provide a record of the agreement. It seems paradoxical that the agreement in writing may include an oral agreement since arbitration agreement may be made by reference to the terms in writing.

2.3. DESIGNATION OF ARBITRAL INSTITUTION AS APPOINTING AUTHORITY (ARTICLE 12)

Under the Bill, an arbitral institution may be designated by a competent court upon request of a party to arbitration proceedings so as to appoint a sole arbitrator on whom the disputing parties fail to agree, or to appoint either one of the party-appointed arbitrators or the presiding arbitrator in arbitration with 3 arbitrators. Furthermore, the designated arbitral institution may appoint an arbitrator in cases where another institution or any other person designated to appoint an arbitrator fails to perform the function of appointing an arbitrator. It is not clear, however, as to whether the designated arbitral institution may entrust to another institution or any other person the role of appointing an arbitrator.

2.4. CHALLENGE TO ARBITRATOR'S REFUSAL OF JURISDICTION (ARTICLE 17)

On the basis of a valid and effective arbitration agreement, an arbitral tribunal has the authority to determine the merits of the dispute which is called an arbitral jurisdiction. When an arbitration agreement is enshrined in an arbitration clause contained in a contract, it is established that the challenges as to the validity of the main contract have no necessary impact upon the validity of the arbitration clause. Facing such challenges, the arbitral tribunal may determine whether it does or does not have jurisdiction: arbitrators are competent to determine their own competence.

The Bill allows a party to commence a court proceeding to challenge the arbitral tribunal's decision that it does not have jurisdiction. The Bill overcomes the criticism that one of the parties is compelled to commence court proceedings to vindicate its right to arbitrate. It is only possible under the current KAA that the court may be requested to decide on the challenge against the arbitral tribunal's decision on jurisdiction that it has jurisdiction. When the reviewing court decides that there is a jurisdiction, the arbitral proceedings shall be resumed. When an arbitrator refuses to resume the arbitral proceedings or does not want to do so, his mandate shall be terminated and a substitute arbitrator shall be appointed.

2.5. INTRODUCTION OF NEW REGIME OF INTERIM MEASURES OF PROTECTION (ARTICLE 18)

On interim measures, the Bill provides clearly for the arbitrator's competence to grant interim measures, the enforcement of arbitrator-granted interim measures, and the relationship between the courts and arbitral tribunals. The Model Law of 1985 has been amended in 2006 to follow the trend of interim orders being made by arbitrators. A new Chapter IV A of the Model Law as amended in 2006 is dedicated to detailed provisions on interim measures and preliminary orders.

The Bill incorporates almost all of those provisions on interim measures in the Model Law as amended in 2006, but not on preliminary orders which are a sort of ex part interim orders. The Bill does not incorporate Section 2 of the Chapter IV A of the Model Law as amended in 2006. As a result, those provisions on preliminary orders are absent in the Bill with regard to the issues of modification, suspension, termination, provisions of security, disclosure, costs and damages. Furthermore, the Bill lacks the provisions on court-ordered interim measures in support of foreign arbitration which was newly inserted in the Model Law when it was amended in 2006.

The introduction of new regime of interim measures ordered by arbitral tribunals is meaningful because no such orders have not been recognized or enforced under the Korean Law to which only a formal award may be recognized or enforced. Unlike the Model Law, however, interim measures may only be made in the form of order or decision under the Bill. In addition to that, it is not clear whether the Bill envisages that an interim measure ordered by an arbitral tribunal sitting abroad may be recognized or enforced, since it lacks the words of "irrespective of the country in which it was issued, subject to the provisions of Article 17 I" from the Article 17 H of the Model Law as amended in 2006.

2.6. JUDICIAL ASSISTANCE IN TAKING AND PRODUCTION OF EVIDENCE (ARTICLE 28)

In general, arbitral tribunals have a broad power to conduct a process for document disclosure or production, or take evidence. The disclosure powers of the tribunals do not extend to non-parties or third-parties, since such powers originating from the arbitration agreement are confined to the parties to that agreement. In Korea, a tribunal may not order non-parties to give testimony at a hearing or to produce documents. Such order is left to a competent court which is authorized to compel non-parties to give testimony or to produce documents.

For the purpose of efficiency in taking evidence, the Bill allows the arbitrators to participate into disclosure process taking place under the auspices of the court at the request of the tribunal, and to get judicial assistance from the court in enforcing their disclosure orders. Under the Bill, the court may subpoena a party or non-party to an arbitral proceeding to provide testimony at a hearing before the tribunal or provide documents with it. A tribunal may withdraw an adverse inference against a party where a party without satisfactory explanation fails to produce a document or other relevant evidence following a request for production to which he did not object or an order by the tribunal to produce documents.[2]

2.7. ALLOCATION OF THE COSTS OF ARBITRATION AND THE AWARDING OF INTEREST (ARTICLE 34 (2) AND (3))

The Bill empowers an arbitrator to make costs award by providing him with a broad discretion as to how to deal with costs of arbitration. The arbitrator may have regard to all relevant circumstances when determining the allocation of the costs of arbitration incurred by the parties in the preparation of the arbitral proceedings. It is, however, uncertain whether the parties are free to agree that one party shall bear the whole costs of the arbitration whatever the outcome of the arbitration may be, what are the costs of arbitration, what costs are recoverable, whether the loser pays rule applies, whether interest may be awarded on costs. Given the lack of express provisions in the Bill, it is safe to say that the parties should agree clearly with regard to the allocation of the costs of arbitration, and that the relevant rules of an arbitral institution should be thoroughly consulted with when the quantification of the costs of arbitration is to be made.

The Bill enables an arbitrator to award interest in making an arbitral award. Under the Bill, an arbitrator may award interest under his discretionary power for the period between the date of the award and the date when the award is paid. Arbitrator's discretionary power to make award of interest is to be found in the rules of an arbitral institution such as Article 52(3) of Korean Commercial Arbitration Board (KCAB) Rules for Domestic Cases. It is, however, not clear from the Bill whether interest may be awarded for the period up to the award, whether an arbitrator awards either simple or compound interest at his discretion, and whether statutory limits on the rate of interest with regard to court proceedings are also applicable to an arbitration sitting in Korea.[3]

2.8. Recognition and Enforcement of Arbitral Awards (Article 37)

The Bill ensures that an arbitral award shall be recognized unless there is any ground for refusing recognition of the award. The court shall make an order of recognition or enforcement of the award upon the application of a party. Where there is a ground of refusal for recognition of the award to be considered, or where an application for declaration of enforcement of the award is made, the court shall set the date of oral hearing or examination where the parties are to participate. Therefore, a trial with a full hearing is not always necessary for having an award to be recognized or enforced under the Bill. When the court decides not to conduct a full hearing, however, there shall be an examination process.

A party may initiate an immediate appeal procedure against an order for recognition or enforcement of the award. Contrary to the court proceedings, the filing of an immediate appeal does not have the effect of staying the enforcement of the award. The appeal court may order the lower court's enforcement process to be suspended or continued with the provision of security until the immediate appeal has been decided upon.

Notes

1. The Bill was proposed by the Government on October 8, 2015. The Legislation and Judiciary Committee decided to submit the Bill to a plenary session of the National Assembly on December 8, 2015.
2. IBA Rules on the Taking of Evidence in International Arbitration (2010), Articles 9.5, 9.6.
3. It is not clear whether the article 34(3) of the Bill may change the attitudes of the Korean Supreme Court with regard to the application of the statutory limits on the rate of interest with regard to court proceedings. The Supreme Court ruled that an arbitral award decided on the basis of such statutory limits would not be contrary to public policy or other good morals. Supreme Court of Korea, Judgment, 2004Da67264, May 13, 2005.

Reforming the Law of International Civil Jurisdiction: Committee Proposal

JANG Junhyok
Professor
Sungkyunkwan University School of Law, Seoul, Korea

1. INTRODUCTION

The Private International Law Reform Committee was created in the International Legal Affairs Department of the Ministry of Justice in June 2014 and has since worked on drafting a set of comprehensive provisions on international jurisdiction in civil matters to be included in the Private International Law.[1] Its final meeting was held in December 2015, and the Committee Draft will be made public in due course. The pending reform is expected to bring meaningful changes to the current law.

For the past 50 years, Korean law of international jurisdiction has heavily relied on case law, in the absence of comprehensive legislation in this field. In the Supreme Court's view, the internal jurisdiction provisions in Korean Civil Procedure Act[2] are unfit to automatically perform the "double function" of regulating both internal and international jurisdiction, which is typical of the territorial jurisdictional provisions found in continental European civil procedure laws. The internal jurisdiction provisions in this Act contain such rules and criteria that cannot be extended to regulate international jurisdiction. Moreover, such elements are so mixed and intertwined with those elements that can play the double function; in some provisions, they coexisted in a single statutory sentence.[3]

This state of things, born out of Korean legislator's relative disinterest in international jurisdiction in early years, created an urgent need to create a separate set of rules for "international jurisdiction." Nevertheless, one can only find a limited number of scattered provisions which expressly regulates international jurisdiction in the Private International Law: Arts. 12 and 14 provides for Korean courts' jurisdiction over foreigners in the case of disappearance of persons and declaration of incapacity, respectively; Arts. 27 (paras. 4 to 6) and 28 (paras. 3 to 5), newly introduced in 2001, constitute a separate regime for international jurisdiction in consumer and labor contracts. Otherwise, Korean courts have had to manage with the method of selective analogy from internal jurisdiction rules. In 2001, the legislators attempted to streamline this law-finding process by introducing the general clause of Art. 2, which declares guiding principles and urges the courts to engage in the law-finding task in a more transparent manner. This temporary measure was preferred by the drafters toward the end of 2000, when they still found hope in the Judgments Project at the Hague Conference of Private International Law. Korean drafters would wait for the final version of the multilateral convention, which can be a model for national legislation as well.

Since the 2001 reform, the Korean legislators came to realize the dim prospect of creating a mixed convention at The Hague. There was no reason to postpone national legislation any further. Japanese legislator moved first to create a separate set of rules of international jurisdiction in 2011.[4] In this background, the Korean Ministry of Justice approved the proposal of comprehensive legislation from the Korea Private International Law Association.

The Justice Ministry's first move was to commission a study on the "Possible Options of Reforming Private International Law" to a group of researchers and practitioners organized by the Korea Private International Law Association. This report was submitted to the Ministry in December 2012 and was formally published by the Ministry in February 2014. As its title implies, this report provides a comparative survey of foreign laws and also contains the contributors' ideas on possible legislative choices. The next step of the Ministry was to launch the Private International Law Reform Committee in June 2014. It had 19 meetings from June 2014 to December 2015, and also sought advice from experts outside the Committee. In February 2015, the Department of International Legal Affairs hosted a symposium to make a comparative survey in international jurisdiction in family, maintenance and succession matters and non-contentious cases.[5] Each of the three outside experts who participated in the February symposium presented an expert report and presented his or her own proposal in the three consecutive Committee meetings in June and August 2015.[6] In September and October 2015, the Korea Private International Law Association invited Chinese and Japanese scholars to the bilateral Korea-China and the Korea-Japan seminars to seek their opinion on the pending reform. The Committee closed its official activity after the final meeting of the 29th of December, 2015. Finishing touches are to be given to the wording before the wording of Committee Draft is finalized and submitted to the Ministry. If the process goes smoothly, the Ministry is expected to go through the public notice and hearing procedure through the year 2016.

In view of the tentative nature of the current wording of the Committee Draft, the present writer would like to confine this report to sketching principal characteristics of the Committee's reform proposal. While the present writer was a member of the Committee himself, the description and evaluations in this paper is his own and does not represent any official position of the Committee.

2. GENERAL APPROACH

The approach adopted by the Committee could be summarized as its strong internationalism and an attempt to accommodate existing case law. Throughout the Committee discussion, comparative law played a crucial role. The existing case law provided a starting point, which was then estimated in a comparative perspective. In proprietary matters, it was not difficult to find the principal source of reference. Indeed, the Committee was determined to accept, *i.e.*, universalize, the Hague Choice-of-Court Convention of 2005.[7] The Committee also found a strong appeal in the Hague Preliminary Draft of 1999,[8] taking it as representative of a global standard. Interestingly, the Hague Interim Draft as of 2001 did not receive much attention in the Committee. It may have been influenced by the attraction of the 1999 Preliminary Draft in terms of expertise and draftsmanship. The present process of the Hague Judgment Project was neither given a serious weight, presumably because the ongoing work at The Hague is limited to creating a single convention.

Meanwhile, the drafters found it relatively difficult to identify a single dominant model, which can be an easy point of reference, in the area of personal, family, and succession matters. The relevant Hague Conventions were given relatively less weight, unlike in proprietary matters, presumably because they were either highly developed multilateral regimes,[9] or relatively older conventions, or because there are existing statutory provisions which supposedly require minor revision.[10] Committee members also paid attention to the European Union Regulations, Swiss and German legislations, and the drafting process in Japan, but it was difficult to find a consensus on choosing a principal point of reference out of vastly diverging legislative choices. In this setting, the Committee began its discussion from the internal jurisdiction provisions[11] and particularly its reform draft of 2015,[12] the existing case law in international jurisdiction, or practical considerations in dealing with international cases in court practice. In matters where actual cases are scarce, the Committee had to devise a compromise between foreign legislative models. In the face of such complexity, the Committee adopted a relatively selective approach in defining acceptable bases of jurisdiction.

In regard of substance, the general approach of the Committee reveals some notable characteristics.

Firstly, the legal provisions of "international" jurisdiction shall stand separately from those distributing judicial tasks within a state. The resulting divergence of the rules of international jurisdiction from internal jurisdiction shall not be seen as a defect. In the drafters' view, the courts are supposed to determine international jurisdiction before regional jurisdiction, and the criteria for the two separate issues may safely diverge.

Secondly, the Committee Draft sought to propose a comprehensive set of provisions and thereby minimize legislative gaps. The drafters noted that the Hague Preliminary Draft does not itself provide a complete list of jurisdictional bases, but instead allowed for a grey area.[13] This understanding led the Committee to maintain an inclusive approach, particularly to property-based jurisdiction, activity-based jurisdiction and other possible topics of legislation. Substantive areas also became comprehensive, ranging from contracts, torts and other proprietary matters to the specific areas of commercial paper and maritime cases, and further to personal, family, and succession cases. However, the Committee Draft did not go on to present a complete, closed set of rules. The drafters also noted the need for a breathing space that may allow for adaptation and further development. A room for differentiation was also preserved for special areas such as insurance and passenger transport contracts, and trusts, by remaining silent to these matters. Here the courts' gap-filling technique will play an important role; where the court finds "there is no provision in the law or treaties," Art. 2 shall be invoked to seek analogy from internal jurisdiction rules.[14] Moreover, the Draft also expressly stipulates the doctrine of *forum non conveniens*. This partly open-ended nature of the draft may have been influenced by the flexible approach of the Hague Preliminary Draft of 1999, recognizing a "grey area" and retaining some options for further discussion.

Thirdly, the Committee proposes, after a prolonged discussion, to experiment with two important institutions of Anglo-American origin: activity-based jurisdiction and *forum non conveniens*. By accommodating them in their own system of direct jurisdiction rules, the drafters sought to make a more complete system, which the drafters thought was well illustrated by the leading example of the Hague Preliminary Draft of 1999.[15] The Committee also found it desirable to retain a degree of flexibility within the system, considering the intensity of the prospective change from a highly flexible system to one of strictly defined rules. Notably, the decision to include *forum non conveniens* was reached by a majority decision in the Committee; it is also expected to be a point of heated controversy in subsequent discussions.

3. INDIVIDUAL RULES

(1) The Committee Draft substitutes "habitual residence" for domicile, as the basis of general jurisdiction over a natural person. The use of this concept is not wholly new to Korean law. In the whole revision of the Private International Law in 2001, this connecting factor was introduced as a better alternative to domicile, both in conflict of laws and jurisdictions.[16] The Committee also abstained from stipulating the conditions for acquiring and losing it, so that this issue will be left to interpretation.[17] In this connection, attention is also required to the Korean Supreme Court's Exemplary Rule for Family Relations Registration No. 33[18] which offers a guideline for determining habitual residence in keeping the family relationship registry. This guideline is not part of the law but effectively directs the practice of family relations registry officers.

(2) The pending draft adopts multiple standards to define the bases of general jurisdiction over legal persons and other entities, adopting four alternative definitions: place of incorporation, statutory seat, principal place of business and place of central administration.[19]

(3) The Draft introduces activity-based jurisdiction in a modest form. The defendant's "continuous and organized" activity within the forum or directed to it shall create special jurisdiction in the same way as the defendant's local establishment.

(4) The Draft contains a series of provisions on jurisdiction *ratione materiae* for each type of legal relationship. However, these material-specific provisions are not intended as a complete, closed set of rules. The drafters have instead chosen to leave some matters for further elaboration by the courts. For example, the drafters withheld the idea of creating separate rules for insurance and passenger transport contracts, trusts, *negotiorum gestio*, and unjust enrichment in the special rules. The Committee members also decided to leave *forum necessitatis* unwritten, in order to guard against its possible overuse by the courts. In making this decision, they also noted a Suprerre Court precedent that might be read to have given light to this doctrine.[20]

(5) The Committee Draft accommodates jurisdiction based on the presence of property within a certain limit. The proposal will make clear that there should be a substantial connection between the dispute and the forum,[21] and the value of the property should not be "significantly small."

(6) The Committee Proposal largely accommodates the Hague Choice-of-Court Convention criteria on the condition of validity for a choice-of-court agreement and its legal effect. The working proposal abolishes the objective "reasonable relationship" requirement for upholding exclusive jurisdiction under the existing case law.[22]

(7) The pending reform proposal authorizes a relatively broad jurisdiction over related actions. On the one hand, the court having jurisdiction over one of the defendants will have jurisdiction over related claims against his/her co-defendants, in the same way as the Hague Preliminary Draft of 1999 and the Brussels I Regulations of 2000[23] and 2012.[24] On the other hand, however, the working proposal goes on to make this head of jurisdiction available to a forum having only special jurisdiction, as long as the related claim is against the same defendant. Such head of jurisdiction over "objectively" related claims at the court of special jurisdiction is unknown in many foreign laws and may be a concern for the defendant. The key to limit its function property lies in the express requirement of "mutually close relationship" between the claims.

In interpreting this requirement, proper attention should be paid to the general standard of "substantial connection" as provided in Art. 2 para. 1. Additionally, the doctrine of *forum non conveniens* may guard against a possible abuse of this jurisdiction.

(8) The Committee decided, by a majority decision, to accommodate the procedural complexity of having a *forum non conveniens* motion. But it is not yet clear how this institution with Anglo-American origin will function in Korean courts. If this motion is to be given a serious meaning and function, independently of the general attention given to the leading principles of international jurisdiction (Art. 2, para. 1), it may open up a variety of issues, such as relative importance of private and public interests, and the scope of judicial discretion and appellate review.

(9) In regard of marriage dissolution, the pending proposal takes a relatively strict position, even compared to the current practice of first-instance family courts. While both spouses' nationality constitutes a sufficient basis, plaintiff spouse's nationality or habitual residence, standing alone, does not. Neither is defendant spouse's nationality provided as a valid basis. In contrast, the Draft introduces a jurisdictional basis which is yet unknown in Korean case law: Korean courts will have international jurisdiction where the custodial parent and the minor child of both spouses habitually reside in Korea.

(10) The reform draft also contains separate rules on the constitution and dissolution of parent-child relationship, adoption, dissolution of adoptive parent-child relationship, child custody and contact rights, and maintenance claims. The proposed rules are relatively strict in defining the available bases. Notably, even a legally custodial parent cannot invoke jurisdiction of the courts of his habitual residence. Such a parent is only left with the exceptional grounds of the presence of the child's property coupled with the need of protecting the child, and the general doctrine of jurisdiction by necessity.

(11) The drafters' choice of jurisdictional bases is also selective in the area of in succession and wills. The Draft only mentions the decedent's

habitual residence and relevant property as available bases.

4. CONCLUSION

The Committee Draft for reforming the law of international jurisdiction will, if it becomes law, change the law significantly. With the introduction of a comprehensive set of clearly defined rules, the reform proposal will significantly diminish the degree of reliance on the general clause of Article 2. Particularly, analogy from internal jurisdiction rules will only be left with a marginal role.

While the Committee Draft basically reinforces its continental European root with its broadly defined rules, the Committee sought to strike an optimal balance between certainty and flexibility in two ways. Firstly, the Committee Draft strived to find a balance between the need to restrict exorbitant jurisdiction and the need to provide an accessible forum. For this reason, the drafters chose to retain a few potentially far-reaching bases of jurisdiction, particularly jurisdiction based on the presence of property, and jurisdiction over related actions filed at the court of special jurisdiction; the drafters goes even further to introduce activity-based special jurisdiction. Secondly, the Committee Draft accommodates the Anglo-American institutions of activity-based jurisdiction and *forum non conveniens* within its own system of direct jurisdiction rules. In doing so, the Committee was guided by the Hague Preliminary Draft of 1999 as well as the practical demand for a comprehensive set of rules with a degree of flexibility.

In contrast to the Committee's inclusive approach in proprietary matters, the Committee Draft reveals a relatively restrictive approach in defining available jurisdiction in personal, family, and succession matters. Ironically, parties to family and succession cases will have to rely on the unwritten doctrine of *forum necessitatis* or the individual provisions reflecting this doctrine relatively often.

Notes

1. *Kukjesabeob*, Law No. 6465 of 7 Apr. 2001. For its English translation, see Jounral of Korean Law, Vol. 1, No. 2 (2001), pp. 204-223 (by Prof. Kwang Hyun SUK); Yearbook of Private International Law, Vol. V (2003), pp. 315 ff. (by Prof. Kwang Hyun SUK). For its German translation, 70 RabelsZ (2006), pp. 342 ff. (by K.B. Pißler); StAZ 2006, pp. 270-273 (same); IPRax 2007, pp. 479-484 (by TSCHE Kwang-Jun). For an overview of the 2001 revision of Korean Private International Law, see Kwang Hyun SUK, *The New Conflict of Laws Act of the Republic of Korea*, 5 Yearbook of Private International Law (2003), pp. 99 ff.; K.B. Pißler, *Das neue IPR der Republik Korea*, 70 RabelsZ (2006), pp. 279 ff.

2. Arts. 2 to 31. These provisions of the current Civil Procedure Act (Law No. 6626 of 26 Jan. 2002) preserves and partly amends what was originally Arts. 1 to 28 of the Civil Procedure Code (No. 547 of 4 Apr. 1960), which essentially sought to preserve the corresponding Civil Procedure Code of Japan as transplanted during the colonial rule.

3. For example, Art. 8 of the Civil Procedure Act provides "place of performance" and simple "residence" as independent bases for any "lawsuit on proprietary right."

4. Act No. 36 of 2 May 2011 (Japan). For an English translation, see 54 Japanese Yearbook of International Law (2011), pp. 723 ff.; 12 Japanese Yearbook of Private International Law (2010), pp. 228-41; 13 Kokusai shiho nenpo (2011), pp. 47-60. Its Korean translation was published in 18 Korea Private International Law Journal (2012), pp. 541-548 (trans. by SHIM Hwal-Seob).

5. Prof. KIM Moonsook of Konan University (Kobe, Japan) and Prof. KWON Jae Moon of Sookmyung Women's University (Seoul, Korea) reported on jurisdiction over non-contentious matters and parent-child relationship, respectively. Jurisdiction in marriage relationship, maintenance and succession was surveyed by the present writer, which was thoroughly commented on by Prof. KIM Won-Tae of Chungbuk University (Cheongju, Korea).

6. Prof. KWON Jae Moon made a report on natural persons and parent-child relationship. Prof. KIM Won-Tae reported on matrimonial causes and succession. Prof. KIM Moonsook dealt with non-contentious matters.

7. Convention of 30 June 2005 on Choice of Court Agreements.

8. Preliminary Draft Convention on Jurisdiction and Foreign Judgments in Civil and Commercial Matters, adopted by the Special Commission on 30 October 1999 (Hague Conference of Private International Law, Enforcement of Judgments, Prel. Doc. No. 11).

9. Convention of 19 October 1996 on Jurisdiction, Applicable Law, Recognition, Enforcement and Co-operation in Respect of Parental Responsibility and Measures for the Protection of Children; Convention of 13 January 2000 on the International Protection of Adults. The Republic of Korea has not yet acceded to these Convention nor has been a member of their predecessors, la Convention du 5 octobre 1961 concernant la competence des autorités et la loi applicable en matière de protection des mineurs and la Convention du 17 juillet 1905 concernant l'interdiction et les measures de protection analogues.

10. Private International Law, Arts. 12 (declaration of disappearance), and 14 (declaration of incapacity), respectively.

11. *Gasasosongbeob* [Family Procedure Act] (Law No. 4300 of 31 Dec. 1990), Arts. 13, 22, and 26.

12. *Gasasosongbeob Gaejeong'an* [Family Procedure Act Reform Draft], Arts. 39, 44, 48, 85, 94, 99, 101, 106, 108, 111, 114, and 123. *Gasasosongbeob Gaejeong Wiweonhoe* [Family Procedure Act Reform Committee], *2015 Gasasosongbeob Gaejeong Jaryojib [2015 Materials for Reforming Family Procedure Act]* (Seoul: Beobweonhaengjeongcheo [Ministry of Judicial Administration], 2015).

13. Art. 17.

14. This language in parentheses, introduced in the Committee Proposal, will further clarify the role of this general clause. This added language should make clear that Art. 2 cannot be a residual source of a "catch-all" jurisdiction, as long as the matter in question is already dealt with in a concrete provision.

15. The Hague Preliminary Draft of 1999, known for its dominantly continental European flavor, accommodates activity-based jurisdiction in Art. 9, though in brackets, and the doctrine of *forum non conveniens* in Art. 22.

16. Arts. 3 (para. 2), 4, 37-39, 41-42, 45-46, and 49-50.

17. One writer proposes to require one year's duration to qualify as "habitual" residence. Kwang Hyun SUK, *Kukjesabeob Haeseol [Commentaries on Private International Law]* (Seoul: Pakyoungsa, 2013), p. 122 n. 12.

18. Issued on 10 Dec. 2007; became effective on 1 Jan. 2008. This Exemplary Rule effectively preserves its predecessor, the Supreme Court Exemplary Rule for Family Registry No. 596 of 5 Sep. 2001.

19. The part of the Draft incorporates Art. 3(2) of the Hague Preliminary Draft of 1999 without any revision. During the discussion in the Committee, a concern was raised about the propriety of mentioning "central administration" separately, but it was decided to retain it.

20. One way to read the Supreme Court decision of 29 May 2008, 2006Da71908, 91915 is that it upheld Korean jurisdiction on the basis of jurisdiction by necessity.

The present writer had earlier indicated this possibility. Junhyok JANG, *Special Jurisdiction in Korean Law of International Jurisdiction: Current Case Law in Proprietary Cases*, 18 Korea Private International Law Journal (2012), p. 12. Some commentators cites as an example of *forum necessitatis* the exceptional jurisdiction at the plaintiff's domicile in family matters, which has been recognized by the Supreme Court, for example, in the Supreme Court decision of 12 April 1988, 85me71. See, *e.g.*, Kwang Hyun SUK, *op.cit.*, p. 102 n. 93.

21. This requirement is in accord with the German Federal Supreme Court decision of 2 July 1991. BGHZ 115, 90, NJW 1991, 3092, IPRax 1992, 160. One writer supports this requirement *de lege lata*, by reference to the general requirement of "substantial connection" (Art. 2, para. 1 of the Private International Law). Kwang Hyun SUK, *op.cit.*, p. 81.

22. Supreme Court decision of 9 Sep. 1997, 96Da20093; Supreme Court decision of 28 April 2011, 2009Da19093.

23. Council Regulation (EC) No 44/2001 of 22 December 2000 on jurisdiction and the recognition and enforcement of judgments in civil and commercial matters, OJ 2001 L 12/1.

24. Regulation (EU) No. 1215/2012 of the European Parliament and of the Council of 12 Dec. 2012 on jurisdiction and the recognition and enforcement of judgments in civil and commercial matters (recast), OJ 2012 L 351/1.

CONTEMPORARY PRACTICE
AND JUDICIAL DECISIONS

Judicial Decisions in Public International Law (2015)*

LEE Keun-Gwan
Professor
Seoul National University School of Law, Seoul, Korea

Daegu District Court Decision No. 2010GAHAB13392 Rendered on 23 November 2012

Main Issue

Whether the recruitment (by an organ of the United States Forces in Korea) of a dependent of a United States civilian component member for the position of 'engineer resource management analyst' in disregard of the 'commitment' (made in a Memorandum of Understanding between Korea and the United States of America) to hire such a person "only when there are no Korean Nationals who are available and qualified as candidates" is amenable to sovereign immunity

Facts

In January 2001, Korea and the United States of America concluded a Memorandum of Understanding on Preferential Hiring of Korean Employees and Employment of Family Members. According to Article 1

---

* The cases presented in this section are selected and translated from "Korean Judicial Decisions Related to Public International Law" edited by Professor Chung In-Seop (School of Law, Seoul National University) as found in *Seoul International Law Journal*, volume 22 nos. 1 & 2. The editor of this section sincerely acknowledges Prof. Chung's great efforts at systematically documenting Korean practice in public international law.

of the Memorandum, United States Forces Korea ("USFK") will employ exclusively Korean Nationals for those civilian component positions that have been designated by USFK for occupancy by Korean Nationals as of the date of entry into force of this Memorandum of Understanding. Although those positions may be open to dependents of the US armed forces and dependents of civilian component members, the dependents will be considered for the vacancies only when there are no Korean Nationals who are available and qualified as candidates.

In 2009, the Daegu directorate of public works, which is part of USFK, hired Son, the wife of a United States civilian component member for the above-mentioned position. The plaintiff instituted a lawsuit with the Korean court located in Daegu, Korea, arguing that the decision of USFK was illegal for violation of the relevant provisions of the Memorandum.

Judgment

Decision on the Preliminary Objections is as follows:

(a) Contention of the Plaintiff

The plaintiff seeks the confirmation of nullity of the decision [of the defendant] to hire Son who is the wife of a United States civilian component member for the following reasons. According to the Memorandum of Understanding between the Republic of Korea and the United States of America on Preferential Hiring of Korean Employees and Employment of Family Members [signed on 18 January 2001] and the Regulations on Personnel Matters at issue in this case, the defendant is under an obligation to employ exclusively Korean Nationals for those civilian component positions that have been designated by USFK for occupancy by Korean Nationals. The defendant can hire dependents of the US armed forces and dependents of civilian component members, only when there are no Korean Nationals who are available and qualified as candidates. The plaintiff contends that the defendant's decision to hire the above-mentioned Son as Engineer Resource Management Analyst, in disregard of the fact that the plaintiff [who applied for the same position] is a Korean national, constitutes a violation of the Regulations, giving rise to nullity.

In response to the claim of the plaintiff, the defendant objects that the present case is subject to sovereign immunity and, furthermore, not meriting the interest of confirmation [of nullity], does not satisfy the legal requirements [for the institution of a lawsuit].

(b) Decision of the Court

1) The courts of Korea cannot exercise their jurisdiction in cases where foreign states, having engaged in private law acts, are brought before the courts as defendants, provided that there are special circumstances such as the existence of concern that, those private law acts undertaken within Korea either falling within or being closely connected with the sovereign activities of the foreign states, the exercise of jurisdiction could constitute an unjustifiable interference (Supreme Court, rendered by the full chamber on 17 December 1998 [case number 97Da39216]; Supreme Court, rendered on 13 December 2011 [case number 2009Da16766]etc.)

   [...]

2) In light of the facts ascertained above and the evidence referred to above, the following facts are established. ① The engineer resource management analyst whose main task is to assist the head of the Daegu directorate of public works in analyzing the budget and accounting matters, is a senior position, entitled to have a wide access to and review the materials on the budget and accounting of the directorate, ② the work of the Daegu directorate of public works, intended for the administration of the armed units of the defendant, amounts to sovereign activities for the performanc of which the task of the engineer resource management analyst plays an essential role, ③ the job descriptions of the engineer resource

management analyst such as review of budget information as contained in documents like the request for military purchase, analysis of the productivity and accuracy of performance by the employees, composing the list of data on costs of each project, monitoring of the yearly administrative budget by implementing stages, apportioning tasks among the employees and adjustment of their workload, provision of information on promotion, relocation, outstanding performance and requests made by individual employees, are closely connected with the sovereign activities of the defendant, ④ accordingly, the notice of inviting applications for the job in this case strictly limited the applicants to 'Korean nationals under current employment with the USFK who were hired through the Korean branch of the directorate of civil personnel resources.' This signifies that despite its appearance of hiring through open competition the process in effect amounted to switching to a new position or promotion within the USFK of certain current employees who had been hired through a specific agency. In consideration of these circumstances, the defendant's decision to hire Son among the applicants rather than the plaintiff is closely connected with the sovereign activities of the defendant, justifying the concern that should the courts of Korea exercise jurisdiction it would constitute an unjustifiable interference into the sovereign activities of the defendant. Accordingly, it is reasonable to hold that the hiring decision at issue in this case is amenable to sovereign immunity and that the courts of Korea being unable to exercise jurisdiction this case shall be dismissed."

Judgments at the Appellate Stages

On appeal to the appellate court, the Daegu High Court confirmed the judgment of the lower court. The appellate court addressed the question of whether the above-mentioned Memorandum of Understanding represented the waiver of sovereign immunity by the USFK as follows:

"The plaintiff, invoking the 2004 UN Convention on Jurisdictional Immunities, contends that the defendant waived his sovereign immunity by subscribing to the above-mentioned Memorandum of Understanding and the Regulations on Personnel Management. In light of the purpose, the drafting process and the concrete contents of the relevant documents, these documents invoked by the plaintiff should be interpreted that the defendant intended merely to open certain positions connected with the USFK exclusively for Korean nationals. They cannot be interpreted as waiving the interests arising from the sovereign immunity concerning the employment and selection of the workers. For these reasons, the court cannot accept the contentions of the plaintiff [concerning the alleged waiver of sovereign immunity]."

This judgment was again appealed. The Supreme Court of Korea, in a judgment rendered on 10 April 2014, confirmed the judgments of the Daegu High Court.

Gwangju High Court Decision No. (JEONJU)2011NA1311 Rendered on 15 November 2012

Main Issue

Whether the dismissal of an associate manager, a Korean national, of a buffet restaurant located within a USFK base in Gunsan, Korea, is amenable to sovereign immunity

Facts

The plaintiff, a Korean national, had worked as associate manager at Loring Club, a buffet restaurant located inside a USFK base in Gunsan, Korea. She had been hired on a temporary contractual basis. On dismissal, the plaintiff instituted a lawsuit with the Jeonju District Court, alleging the illegality of the dismissal. Through the National Court Administration [an agency in charge of matters relating to judicial administration], the first-instance court had the Korean consulate in the United States serve the court documents including the duplicate of the process on the United States Attorney General. The defendant did not appear for the proceedings conducted at the first-instance court. The court proceeded to declare that the plaintiff won the case by dint of the rule of constructive admission of the case due to non-appearance. At the next instance, the issue of whether the Korean courts can have jurisdiction in a case where the United States of America appears as defendant was addressed.

Judgment

"The defendant objects that the dismissal in this case constitutes the essential part of the military and sovereign activities of the defendant and that in accordance with the principle of sovereign immunity this suit cannot fall under the jurisdiction of the Republic of Korea, not satisfying the legal requirements.

It is a principle [of international law] that according to customary international law, sovereign acts of states should be immune from the jurisdiction of the courts of other states. However, this does not mean that even private law acts of states should be immune from the jurisdiction of other states. Accordingly, the Korean courts can exercise jurisdiction in cases where a foreign state appears as defendant in respect of its private law acts, unless there are special circumstances such as the existence of concern that, those private law acts undertaken within the Korea territory either falling within or being closely connected with the sovereign activities of the foreign states, the exercise of jurisdiction could constitute an unjustifiable interference (Supreme Court, rendered by the full chamber on 17 December 1998 [case number 97Da39216]).

Let us now evaluate the defendant's objection in the light of the legal principle just described. Based on the facts not in contention between the parties, the testimony offered by [Ms. Sung] in this case and the oral pleadings as a whole, the following facts can be regarded as established: Loring Club is a buffet restaurant located within the Gunsan base of the USFK; not only the members of the USFK, but also any person having access to the Gunsan base can use the said Club; there being no actual restrictions on access to the Loring Club, Korean nationals can have access to it; the defendant, having been in charge of managing and running the club as an associate manager working for the general director and the deputy director of the club, was dismissed. Taking into account the relevant factors in a comprehensive manner such as the function and actual activities of the Loring Club, the position and job description of the plaintiff and the extent of connection between the sovereign activities of the United States of America and the work of the plaintiff, the dismissal in this case should be regarded as a private law act engaged into as a subject of private economic activity on an equal footing to ordinary citizens, rather than an administrative law act undertaken by the United States of America as a subject of public authority. Furthermore, the connection with the sovereign or military activities of the United States of America cannot be considered as that close.

Consequently, the exercise of jurisdiction by the Korean courts in this case will not carry the risk of constituting an unjustifiable interference into the sovereign activities of the United States. Therefore, the Korean courts are entitled to exercise their jurisdiction in this dispute regarding dismissal where the United States of America appears as defendant. The objections raised by the defendant should be rejected."

SUPREME COURT DECISION NO. 2015DU295 RENDERED ON 19 NOVEMBER 2015

Main Issue

Whether an ordinance promulgated by a ward ('*Gu*' in Korean) of Seoul ordering the 'superstores' located within the ward to suspend their operation from 12 a.m. [*i.e.* midnight] until 10 a.m. and also ordering these stores to be closed for business on the second and fourth Sundays of the month violates the provisions of the General Agreement on Trade in Services and the Korea-EU Free Trade Agreement concerning the prohibition of market access restrictions

Facts

On 25 August 2014, the head of Dongdaemun ward of Seoul promulgated an ordinance to the above-mentioned effect. The legal basis for this ordinance was provided by Article 12 *bis* of the Distribution Industry Development Act that purports to, among others, protect the small- and medium-sized stores from the fierce competition posed by the superstores and the right to health for the workers of the superstores that opened for 24 hours every day. The superstores affected by the ordinance included the two Dutch companies, that is, Home Plus Ltd. and Home Plus Stores Ltd. [whose parent company is Tesco] to which the two international agreements applied.

Seoul High Court, in its decision rendered on 12 December 2014 (Case No. 2013Nu29294), declared the ordinance illegal for either overstepping the boundary of discretion or abusing discretion because, among others, it violated the provisions concerning the prohibition of market access restrictions as provided for in the two international agreements. This judgment was appealed and the Supreme Court decided the case in a grand chamber.

Judgment

"According to the reasoning of the appealed judgment, the measures taken by the defendant were illegal because they either overstepped the boundary of discretion or abused discretion since ① the defendant either did not exercise discretion or was negligent in using it by either completely failing to balancing the public interests against the private interests or omitting those factors that should have been included into this balancing exercise, ② there was a violation of the principle of proportionality because the losses arising by way of impairment of, among others, the defendant's freedom of business ascribable to the measures being impeached in this case overwhelmed the public benefits accruing from the measures, and ③ the measures violated the provisions concerning the prohibition of market access restrictions of the General Agreement on Trade in Services and the Korea-EU Free Trade Agreement (these two agreements will be referred to as "the Agreements").

The Agreements are international agreements that provide for the rights and duties between states. In the light of their contents and nature, the legal disputes arising in connection with these agreements are, in principle, to be addressed by inter-state bodies of dispute settlement. Unless there are special circumstances, these agreements do not have direct effects on private individuals. Therefore, it is not allowed for private individuals to institute lawsuits directly before the domestic courts *vis-à-vis* the governments of states parties to the Agreements on the basis of the alleged violation of the relevant provisions of the Agreements. Neither is allowed for private individuals to put forth the violation of the relevant provisions of the Agreements as an independent cause for nullification of the measures (Supreme Court judgment rendered on 30 January 2009, case number 2008Du17936).

Let us proceed further to the analysis of the relevant provisions of the Agreements relied on by the plaintiff. The 'prohibition of limitations on the total number of operations or on the total quantity of output' as provided for in the Agreements purport to prohibit the very acts of restricting market access, in the relations between states, by imposing limitations on the total number or the total quantity. It is difficult to see why the measures under contention in this case, purporting to regulate a part of business activities of large-scale stores that were already granted market access without any discrimination between Korean and foreign businesses, fall within the purview of prohibited measures foreseen in the relevant provisions of the Agreements.

Judicial Decisions in Private International Law (2015)

RHO Tae-Ak
Presiding Judge
Seoul High Court of Korea, Seoul, Korea

1. PRIVATE INTERNATIONAL LAW

1-1. INTERNATIONAL JURISDICTION

1-1-1. SUPREME COURT DECISION 2012DA4763
DECIDED JANUARY 15, 2015 [PROHIBITION ON OBSTRUCTION OF BUSINESS]

Main Issue

Non-exclusive License of Employee Invention and International jurisdiction

Summary of Decision

As a preliminary question of a claim of prohibition on obstruction of business, in a raised case if A company can obtain a non-exclusive license of a patent right or a utility model right being registered overseas based on an employee invention about a patent right or a utility model right registered in Korea, which is completed according to the contract of employment service made by B and A company, because the employee invention was completed in Korea by B, and whether A company can obtain a non-exclusive license or not, which has nothing to do with its coming into existence or validity/invalidity of a patent right or a utility model right, thus which is not belong to court jurisdiction of the nation (being) registered or being registration claimed, therefore, in the above-mentioned party and/or case, the Korean court shall have an international jurisdiction due to its substantial connection with the Republic of Korea (hereinafter, 'Korea').

1-2. GOVERNING LAW

1-2-1. SUPREME COURT DECISION 2012DA4763
DECIDED JANUARY 15, 2015 [PROHIBITION ON OBSTRUCTION OF BUSINESS]

Main Issue

Governing law being applicable to an Employee Invention

Summary of Decision

1. The issues of an attribution and succession, an acquisition by employer and/or a right of compensation claim by employee on the patent right receivable in an employee invention correspond to the relationship of right and duty based on the employment relationship between employer and employee. Therefore any right and duty occurred from an employee invention, which has nothing to do with the formation, validity/invalidity or cancellation of patent right necessary for registration *in rerum natura* even any legal relations containing foreign factors, shall not be applicable to Article 24 of Private International Law('PIL') which stipulates the principle of territoriality for jurisdiction or the protection of intellectual right based on it.
2. The patent right receivable of an employee invention in every countries occurs from the identical invention which can be evaluated as a social fact practically based on an employment relationship, it is necessary for unified interpretation by relevant laws of the country having jurisdiction

of employment relationship against legal relationship originated from an employee invention for protection of interests of the parties and/or legal stability. After taking every factors into consideration, it is reasonable to regard it as the law to be determined according to Section 1, Section 2 etc. of Article 28 of PIL based on governing law of the employment contract in relation to the governing law being applicable to the legal liaison relationship regarding an employment invention. And this legal principle of law shall be applied to the utility model in like manner.

1-2-2. SUPREME COURT DECISION 2012DA108764
DECIDED JANUARY 29, 2015 [COLLECTION]

Main Issue

1. If set-off in common law of the United Kingdom can be applied to governing law with respect to the requirement and effect of set-off

2. Governing law regarding the set-off possibility of passive claim

Summary of Decision

1. As there are legal set-off of Common Law and equitable set-off of Equity in set-off legal system of the United Kingdom, the legal set-off of Common Law among them does not require restraint the related matters between both claims etc., however, which alleviates its prerequisite comparing with equitable set-off of Equity and may be executed as counter-argument of litigation, thus it is interpreted as having a character of adjective law; provided, however, that because legal set-off of Common Law also has a prerequisite of substantial law from the point of view that both claims become extinct at the equal amount by executing, it may be applicable as governing law with regard to requirement and effect of set-off. Therefore, the lower court's determination shall be justifiable by judging that both active claim and passive claim alleged by defendant as a counter set-off occur from time charter based on its

governing law as law of the United Kingdom, the set-off is principally subject to governing law of the claim in itself, thus legal set-off of Common Law of the United Kingdom is applied as a governing law with respect to requirement of set-off.

2. Even though the legal relationship regarding factor and effect of set-off between claims having foreign character has been interpreted and applied according to the governing law of set-off, in the event creditor carries out the credit execution under the provisional attachment or garnishment and/or order of collection according to Korean Civil Execution Act ('CEA'), as it is related to the issue of the effect of provisional attachment or garnishment as a execution procedure if the 3rd debtor (garnishee) having a counter–obligation under the provisional attachment or garnishment may counterclaim against creditor of provisional attachment or garnishment as a set-off against debtor, unless special circumstances, which shall be decided based on CEA etc. in principle, not based on governing law of set-off.

1-2-3. Supreme Court Decision 2012DA79866
Decided February 26, 2015 [Refund Guarantee]

Main Issue

The legal character and governing law of duty to restitution burdened by recipient of money due to loss of effect of judgment of provisional execution

Summary of Decision

1. Whereas the duty to restitution burdened by recipient of money is a restitution of unjust enrichment in its nature due to loss of effect of judgment of provisional execution by judgment of appellate court after payment was made based on judgment of lower court by provisional execution sentence, as loss of effect of judgment of provisional execution is not retroactive, such a duty to restitution is a debt limit acknowledged

by Civil Procedure Act ('CPA') based on concept of equity which tries to restore restitution to the extent that provisional execution is not existed from the beginning, thus which shall not come within the purview 'in case of unjust enrichment occurred from the execution based on legal relationship by the parties' stipulated in the provision of Article 31 of Private International Law.

2. Therefore, the lower court's decision to exclude plaintiff's allegation that the law of the United Kingdom is applicable to the ratio of loss incurred by delay of application for return of provisional payment because provisional payment is not occurred in its nature from the execution based on legal relationship by the parties but based on the judgment by provisional execution sentence of the court, and to apply Section 1, Article 3 of Act on Special Cases concerning a civil enforcement shall be reasonable.

1-2-4. SEOUL HIGH COURT DECISION 2014NA4127
DECIDED JUNE 2, 2015 [MONEY](NOT APPEALED)

Main Issue

The governing law of subrogation right of a creditor

Summary of Decision

1. The plaintiff, a Chinese corporation, alleges that it executes the subrogation of receivables claim of price of goods which a debtor has against the defendant, a Korean corporation, for the purpose of perpetuation of price of goods against the debtor, a Chinese corporation.

2. As the subrogation right of creditor is a right of substantive law being able to subrogate the debtor's right for the purpose of perpetuation of creditor's claim, it shall be decided with a priority according to the governing law of a relevant claim whether to have a creditor acknowledged such right of substantive law or not, and the subrogation right as a governing law of a right, being an object of a subrogation, shall

be acknowledged.

3. The governing law of preserved credit alleged by the plaintiff against a debtor is altogether the Chinese law, and the governing law of claim on goods price by debtor against the defendant, being an object of a subrogation, is the Korean law.

As, therefore, the Chinese law and the Korean law are applied by reiteration in executing the subrogation right of creditor in this plaintiff's case, if the Chinese law and the Korean law allow to execute the subrogation right of creditor, and to satisfy all the requirements, then the subrogation right shall be executed against the defendant.

1-2-5. SEOUL HIGH COURT DECISION 2014NA37752,
DECIDED SEPTEMBER 22, 2015 [TRANSFER OF CHATTEL] (APPEALS DISMISSED)

Main Issue

The governing law on Trust aiming at Lawsuit

Summary of Decision

1. As the plaintiff, people of Laos, claims delivery of jewel being possessed by people of Cambodia against the defendant, a Korean, there is foreign character in this case, thus the governing law shall be determined according to the Private International Law (PIL).

2. Above all, with respect to whether the Korean court has the international jurisdiction, having a look at that the defendant is residing in Korea with an official address, the place of jewel in this case is Korea at present, the plaintiff filed this suit at the Korean court because of necessity needed in execution with judgment from the Korean court, and the defendant does not quarrel over its jurisdiction, it shall be acknowledged that the Korean court has the international jurisdiction because the plaintiff's claim has a substantial connection with Korea (Refer to Article 2, Private International Law). As long as this litigation has justly continued at the Korean court, the procedure is regulated by the Korean adjective law, being *lex fori,*

whether the trust aiming at lawsuit alleged by the plaintiff is allowed or not is belong to the issue of standing to sue, thus the governing law about the above-mentioned controversial issue shall be under the Korean Civil Procedure Act.

1-2-6. Seoul South District Court Decision 2015NA50175, Decided September 11, 2015 [Cancellation of Fraudulent Behavior] (Appeal Dismissed)

Main Issue

Cancellation of fraudulent action and governing law

Summary of Decision

1. As the plaintiff alleges that the contract of sales made by a Korean and the defendant, a foreigner having Chinese nationality, in this case shall be canceled because of fraudulent action, the governing law in this case is considered with priority.
2. It is assumed that with respect to the contract, the chosen law explicitly or impliedly by the party shall be as governing law, however, if the party does not choose the governing law, it shall be applicable to the law of the most closely related country regarding the contract, and in case of the contract aiming at the right of real estate, it shall be applicable to the law of the most closely related country where such real estate is located according to Clause 1 of Article 25 and Clause 1, Clause 4 of Article 26 of Private International Law. As the issue of this litigation is whether the contract of sales in this case is subject to fraudulent action or not, and the real estate, object of trading, in this case is located in Korea, thus the Korean law shall be the governing law of this litigation.

2. INTERNATIONAL BUSINESS TRANSACTIONS

2-1. Supreme Court Decision 2014DA40237
Decided January 29, 2015 [Damages, etc.]

Main Issue

As, in case of opening Letter of Credit(L/C) trading, the person-in-charge of filling out and issuing airway bill on the transportation of export freight filled out and issued each airway bill in contrast to its content of the original differently, if the domestic bank which trusts the filling-out of airway bill, being the original for consignor, and refuses the payment against export draft of the L/C establishing bank whereas the domestic bank purchased the documents of export draft and airway bill etc. thus the right of transfer for security on export freight can not be executed, then whether there is a responsibility of compensation or not consequently.

Summary of Decision

In light of Clause 1, Clause 2 of Article 6, Article 11, Clause 1, Clause 4 of Article 12, Clause 1 of Article 13 of the Agreement of Unification Code in International Air Transportation amended in 1955 in Hague, in the trading, the system of which exporter issues the export draft with attachment of airway bill and requests to purchase it to domestic bank, and the domestic bank which purchased it requests the collection to the L/C establishing bank, thus export price is settled, if the consignee of airway bill is the L/C establishing bank, then the L/C establishing bank has the right of delivery on the freight at the destination, as a result the right of delivery is functionalized as a guarantee for price for export. And if the domestic bank purchasing export draft assigns the freight accompanied by purchasing export draft as a security for payment of debt which the exporter burdens against the domestic bank with respect to the trading with exporter, as agreed, as the domestic bank acquires the right of transfer for security, if in case of the above-mentioned trading, the L/C establishing bank, being consignee of airway bill, refuses the payment of export draft and the recipient of airway bill or freight, then the disposal right on freight is restored to the exporter, being consignor, and the domestic bank executes the right of transfer for security against the freight, and get repaid the purchase price of export draft paid to the exporter through the execution of the right of transfer for security. Therefore the person-in-charge of filling out and issuing airway bill on the transportation of export freight in the object of opening L/C trading shall have a duty to avoid the discordance with the content of original airway bill, if in violation of such duty, filled out and issued each airway bill in contrast to its content of the original differently, and the domestic bank which trusts the filling-out of airway bill, being the original for consignor could not execute the right of transfer for security on export freight in case of refusing the payment on the export draft of the L/C establishing bank whereas the domestic bank purchased the documents of export draft and airway bill etc. from the exporter, then there shall be responsible for compensation for the damage incurred to the domestic bank for the reason.

2-2. SUPREME COURT DECISION 2014DA88215
DECIDED MAY 28, 2015 [RECOURSE AMOUNT]

Main Issue

The criteria in case of ambiguity about the request of including transportation or transportation brokerage only by the transportation brokerage business operator requested from transportation client

Summary of Decision

As the contract of goods transportation is established by agreed that one party moves the goods from one place to the other, thus the other party makes a certain payment of reward in this regard, who the transportation operator is in burden of the right and duty based on the contract of transportation is decided according to who takes over the transportation in relation to the transportation client. Therefore in case of the request made by the transportation client to the transportation brokerage business operator, if there is an ambiguity about the request of including transportation or transportation brokerage only, then it is decided whether the status of transportation operator is acquired together or not after seeking for the intention of the party, however, in case of vagueness of the intention, it shall be determined whether the transportation brokerage business operator took over the transportation from the transportation client or not according to logic and experience after taking it into consideration comprehensively that circumstance of entering into the contract then, name of issuer of Bill of Lading (B/L), payment method of shipping cost, practically performed work by the company requested on the transportation etc.

2-3. SUPREME COURT DECISION 2013DA3170
DECIDED DECEMBER 10, 2015 [DAMAGE, ETC.]

Main Issue

1. Whether the plaintiff, being consignor, is applied to 'holder acquired the prescribed B/L in good faith' or not according to Clause 2, Article 854 of Commercial Act('CA')
2. Whether the defendant, being a carrier, takes responsibility of tort or not because of issuing B/L by mistake after delivering the freight to the lawful consignee under the transportation contract

Summary of Decision

1. The Clause 1, Article 854 of CA prescribes that "In the event a B/L has been issued it is presumed that a contract of affreightment in a general ship has been concluded between a carrier and a consignor and cargo has been received or loaded as stated in the B/L," and the Clause 2 prescribes that "A carrier shall be deemed to have received or loaded cargo as stated in a B/L and shall take responsibilities of a carrier as stated in the B/L

to the holder who has acquired the B/L mentioned in Clause 1 in good faith." As the Clause 2, Article 854 of CA is a regulation for the protection of circulation of B/L and security of trading by protecting the 3rd party who acquired B/L in good faith other than the legal relationship between the carrier and consignee prescribed at Clause 1, it shall be reasonable to deem that the 'holder acquired the B/L in good faith' in this case is the 3rd party who acquired the circulated B/L with in good faith except the carrier and consignee, being the parties of the transportation contract.

2. As the B/L in this case was issued after the freight was landed at the destination and delivery was made to the lawful consignee under the transportation contract, therefore, this B/L shall be invalid. As the plaintiff, being the party under the transportation contract, has nothing to do with 'the holder acquired the B/L in good faith prescribed at the Clause 2, Article 854 of CA, even though the plaintiff held this B/L, the defendant shall not have a duty to deliver this freight based on the invalid B/L for the plaintiff in this case.

3. INTERNATIONAL COMMERCIAL ARBITRATION

3-1. SUPREME COURT DECISION 2013DA74868
DECIDED OCTOBER 29, 2015 [JUDGMENT OF EXECUTION]

Main Issue

The fixation of a party of arbitration agreement

Summary of Decision

1. Having a look at that the shareholder's agreement was made between plaintiff, defendant and/or Loanstar Fund 3, and that the terminology like 'parties' and 'shareholders' have been used separately, in case of using the terminology 'parties' in this shareholder's agreement, it includes

all of three companies signed at the shareholder's agreement, unless special circumstances, and as it is also the same in the arbitration clause prescribed the arbitration agreement in this case, it shall be reasonable that the plaintiff is included as the party of this arbitration agreement.

2. As the indemnity report separately made other than the shareholder's agreement contains the agreement that the prepayment receivable as a pretext of dividend and principal of interest of debt securities is returned by the defendant in some circumstances, that is, which contains the return contract as a precondition for the prepayment by the plaintiff in this case, this materializes the shareholder's agreement prescribing the dividend, debt securities and/or return of loans against shareholders, and it is the follow-up contract for the execution of shareholder's agreement, thus this dispute regarding the return of prepayment between the plaintiff and the defendant surrounding the indemnity report in this case shall not be the separate dispute irrelevant to shareholder's agreement but the dispute arising out of the shareholder's agreement or the dispute in connection with the application of shareholder's agreement. On the other hand, it shall be discrepant against the reasonable intent by the parties to interpret that the dispute regarding 'the return' is settled by the other procedure of dispute settlement while the dispute regarding 'distribution' of prepayment is settled by the arbitration, rather it shall be coincide with the intent of the parties to deem that all disputes with respect to distribution and/or return of the prepayment in this case is settled by the one dispute settlement, that is, by the arbitration according to the arbitration clause in this case.

3-2. SEOUL HIGH COURT DECISION 2014NA33194
DECIDED MARCH 18, 2015 [COST OF CONSTRUCTION] (NOT APPEALED)

Main Issue

The interpretation of the arbitration agreement

Summary of Decision

1. As the regulation on arbitration agreement of the Section 2, Article 3 of Arbitration Act follows the model act of UNCITRAL 1985 and the above-mentioned model act is evaluated as coincident with the New York Convention 1958, the issue of meaning of arbitration agreement and scope of its effect under the Arbitration Act shall be needed to make balance with the international interpretation.

2. In the precedent of the United Kingdom, there is a tendency to interpret the arbitration agreement broadly based on "the presumption of one-stop adjudication." As the stance of court is to interpret the specific expression used by the both parties towards revival of their intention, in making decision on the limit of effect of the clause of arbitration, the court applies to presume that the both parties have agreed to the one forum for dispute resolution. That is, in case of agreement on the clause of arbitration, it is presumed that they intend to settle the disputes by arbitration, and that they do not intend to settle by a number of other ways of dispute settlement including arbitration and litigation. If they are the reasonable parties, they never intend that there are two kinds of procedures eventually.

3. In case of ambiguity about the clause of arbitration in the United States of America, "a presumption in favor of arbitration" has been acknowledged. Whereas the intention of the party through arbitration shall be clear, all disputes shall not be settled through arbitration automatically because of the ambiguity on the limit of effect of the clause of arbitration. Instead, in this case, a presumption in favor of arbitration exists and it shall be possible to reverse as a clear evidence which the parties did not intend to use the arbitration. The Supreme Court of the United States of America made a decision that the Court shall interpret the intention of the party broadly unless the party reduced the limit explicitly with respect to the limit of arbitration agreement in Moses Cone Case[Moses H. Cone Memorial Hospital v. Mercury Construction Corp., 460 U.S. 1(1983)]. 'Moses Cone Presumption', being accepted

repeatedly in a lot of judgments, shall be the well-established regulation regarding the interpretation with respect to the limit of arbitration agreement.

4. Have a look at the relevant clause of Arbitration Act, the intent of judgment of Supreme Court, the international interpretation regarding arbitration agreement etc., the terminology 'which may arise out of this Agreement' prescribed at the clause of arbitration in this case shall have a more broad sense than the terminology 'which may arise under this Agreement,' and the terminology 'in relation to or in connection with this Agreement' shall be interpreted to include the dispute occurring from other agreement in relation to the agreement embracing the clause arbitration.

4. RECOGNITION AND ENFORCEMENT OF FOREIGN JUDGMENT AND ARBITRATION AWARD

4-1. SUPREME COURT DECISION 2013DA87055 DECIDED FEBRUARY 26, 2015 [JUDGMENT OF EXECUTION]

Main Issue

Whether the litigation claiming the judgment of execution has the competency to stand trial or not

Summary of Decision

As the plaintiff does not have the admissibility of a party because of not having the substance as not a corporate body but an incorporate body, the lower court's judgment of which the plaintiff's litigation claiming the judgment of execution in this case is illegitimate, shall be reasonable.

4-2. Supreme Court Decision 2015DA1284
Decided October 15, 2015 [Judgment of Execution]

Main Issue

1. If the final judgment of a foreign court etc. orders the compensation preserved the physical damage incurred to the party, whether the approval is restricted or not based on the Clause 1, Article 217-2 of the Civil Procedure Act ('CPA')

2. Under the pretext which has a trial on whether the result of approval on the final judgment by a foreign court etc. is violation of good morals or other public order, the overall review on what the final judgment etc. is right or wrong practically is allowed or not

3. The way of making decision on whether the result of approval on the final judgment by a foreign court etc. is violation of good morals or other public order in Korea or not

Summary of Decision

1. The Clause 1, Article 217-2 of the CPA prescribes "The court shall not approve all or part of the relevant final judgment etc. if the final judgment etc. regarding compensation brings out the result in contrast to the Korean law or the basic order of international treaty entered into with Korea remarkably," as this is a regulation prepared for setting a limit to the appropriate range with respect to the foreign final judgment ordering the payment of compensation in excess of the limit of compensation like a punitive damage reimbursement or the approval of judgment on which the same effect is acknowledged, if the final judgment of a foreign court etc. orders the compensation preserved the physical damage incurred to the party, the approval shall not be limited based on the Clause 1, Article 217-2 of CPA.

2. According to the Section 2, Clause 2, Article 27 of the Civil Execution Act ('CEA'), the Section 3, Clause 1, Article 217 of the CPA, as it is the requirement of the approval and/or execution of the foreign judgment,

the point of which is not violation of good morals or public order in Korea by the acknowledgement on the effectiveness of the final judgment by foreign court or judgment on which the same effect is acknowledged, under the pretext which has a trial on whether the result of approval on the final judgment etc. is violation of good morals or other public order, the overall review on what the final judgment etc. is right or wrong practically shall be not only in contrast to the Clause 1, Article 27 of the CEA prescribing "the judgment of execution shall be executed without making any examination as to what the judgment is right or wrong" but also the purport having a separate execution judgment system regarding the final judgment of foreign court etc., thus which shall not be allowed.

3. As the Section 3, Clause 1, Article 217 of the CPA prescribes one of the requirements of approval that the acknowledgement on the effectiveness of the final judgment by foreign court or judgment on which the same effect is acknowledged is not violation of good morals or public order in Korea, whether the result approving the final judgment etc. is in contrast to good morals or other public order in Korea or not shall be determined accordingly in light of the issue handled by the final judgment and its extent of relation to Korea, the effect of which the approval of the final judgment affects on the basic moral faith and public order to be protected by the order of local law in Korea at the time of making decision on approval herewith.

4-3. SEOUL HIGH COURT DECISION 2013NA2012912
DECIDED MARCH 24, 2015 [JUDGMENT OF EXECUTION] (NOT APPEALED)

Main Issue

The legality of delivery as a requirement of execution of foreign judgment

Summary of Decision

1. 'The written complaint or equivalent document and/or date of

notification or order' prescribed in the Section 2, Clause 2, Article 27 of the Civil Execution Act ('CEA') and the Section 2, Article 217 of the Civil Procedure Act ('CPA') means the complaint and/or summons necessary for initiation of proceedings, and to request that the defendant who lost a suit should have been served with such summons etc. in due course aims at protecting the defendant who lost a suit without acquiring an opportunity of defense in litigation, thus if not conforming the way, procedure of service prescribed for the purpose of giving the opportunity of defense to the defendant in the country where judgment is made, it shall not be deemed that the service in a lawful manner has been made herewith.

2. As the United States of America is a member nation of Convention on the Service Abroad of Judicial and Extrajudicial Documents in Civil or Commercial Matters, hereinafter 'Hague Convention'), thus the Hague Convention has a priority to the State law concerned with respect to the procedure of service, and Korea, by also joining the Hague Convention, makes it clear that the way of direct service of the document of litigation by mailing to the person who resides in Korea is not acknowledged through the counter-declaration against the Section 1, Article 10 of the above Convention, if the court of the United States of America, being a member nation of the Hague Convention, makes an international service to the defendant having an address in Korea, the Hague Convention shall be obeyed in the above-mentioned, it shall not be deemed as a service based on a lawful manner as prescribed in the Section 2, Article 217 of the CPA to serve in breach of the Hague Convention.

3. As the plaintiff brought a law suit to the court of the United States of America against the defendants seeking the payment in May 24, 2011, the fact that the Complaint and/or Summons have been served by an attorney of the plaintiff, Christopher A. McCormack, from the United States of America to the defendants in Korea by FedEx, international delivery service operator, in May 27, 2011, and the fact that above documents have been served to the defendants in Korea in May 30,

2011 is acknowledged. As the above-mentioned way of service made at the litigation of the United States of America was to make a delivery by an attorney to the recipient directly or by way of a special delivery service operator etc. not through a central public authority, which is the private service and the service by mail simultaneously, Korea raised an objection explicitly against the service by mail by joining the Hague Convention as mentioned above, it shall not be deemed as a lawful service as prescribed in the Section 2, Article 217 of the Civil Procedure Code (CPC) to serve to the defendants as above in this litigation of the United States of America because of breaching the content of the Hague Convention.

5. INTERNATIONAL BANKRUPTCY

5-1. SUPREME COURT DECISION 2012DA104526
DECIDED MAY 28, 2015 [OBJECTION OF FINAL CLAIM INSPECTION JUDGMENT ON REHABILITATION CREDITORS ETC.]

Main Issue

1. The decision on governing law in case of initiating rehabilitation procedures against the party who made a contract which contains foreign character

2. In case of not being an excessive compensation without deducting the intermediary interest in assessment on future loss in the law of the United Kingdom, whether the amount of damage is discounted with deduction of the intermediary interest or not (negative)

Summary of Decision

1. In case of initiating rehabilitation procedures against the party who made a contract which contains foreign character, whether the administrator could choose the execution or cancellation, termination or not when it comes to the mutual executory bilateral contract,

and whether the credit of compensation arising out of cancellation, termination of contract is revival credit or not is determined by Debtor Rehabilitation and Bankruptcy Act; provided, however, that the issue of limit of compensation due to the cancellation, termination of contract is a factor of substantive law with respect to the effect of contract in itself, and has nothing to do with the typical legal effect of insolvency, the governing law of the contract determined according to the Private International Law shall be applied.

2. As the assessment of future loss for a lump sum payment based on certain timing in the law of the Unite Kingdom is for the purpose of protecting the over-compensation or less-compensation by an adjustment for determining the fair compensation, in case of not being an excessive compensation without deducting the intermediary interest at the such assessment on compensation, it shall not necessarily have to discount the amount of damage with deducting the intermediary interest.

International Law-Related Resolutions of the 19th National Assembly with a Focus on Protection of Cultural Heritage and Restitution of Cultural Assets, Anti-Terrorism and Free Trade Agreement

CHUNG Min-Jung
CHOI Jeong-In
Legislative Research Officer
National Assembly Research Service, Seoul, Korea

The resolution adopted by the National Assembly of Republic of Korea (hereinafter, 'Korea') is an expression of legislative will. The National Assembly can be influential in the direction of foreign policy initiatives through resolutions.[1] Total 56 resolutions were adopted at the plenary assembly, after the deliberation of various standing or select committees, in the first half of the 19th Session (May 30, 2012 - May 29, 2014) and the second half (May 50, 2014 - February 2, 2016). The resolutions of the National Assembly of Korea that are related to international law are primarily under the auspices of the Foreign Affairs and Reunification Committee (standing committee).

The National Assembly of Korea uses the rhetoric of international law as practical art of persuasive discourse because international law is considered shared logic and common understanding. For example, Article 53 of the Charter of the United Nations (hereinafter referred to as the "Charter")[2] was referred to in the *Resolution condemning the Abe administration's decision to use collective self-defense*, to which the number of States Parties is 193 as of April 12, 2016.[3] In the *Resolution calling for the return of looted Korean Chosun Dynasty's Great-General's Helmet and Armor in the Tokyo National Museum,* [4] was the United Nations Educational, Scientific and Cultural Organization (UNESCO) Convention on the Means of Prohibiting and Preventing the Illicit Import, Export and Transfer of Ownership of Cultural Property (hereinafter referred to as the "UNESCO Convention")[5] mentioned. The UNESCO Convention has 131 States Parties as of April 12, 2016.[6]

This paper sets forth selected resolutions related to the protection of cultural heritage and the restitution of cultural assets, anti-terrorism and free trade agreement. The resolutions related to territorial sovereignty, international criminal law and state responsibility, and the use of force was previously addressed. The resolutions related to human rights, and other international law-related resolutions will be subsequently introduced. The resolutions introduced here are primarily geared towards urging the country complained against by the National Assembly to enact legislation and specific measures regarding the issue, encouraging the Korean government to use active diplomacy to this end, and promoting alliance with the international community for resolution.

1. PROTECTION OF CULTURAL HERITAGE AND RESTITUTION OF CULTURAL ASSETS

The main source of international law concerning protection of cultural heritage is the Convention concerning the Protection of World Cultural and Natural Heritage (hereinafter referred to as the "World Heritage Convention").[7] The number of its States Parties is 191 as of August 15, 2014.[8] The UNESCO Convention is the primary source of international law concerning the recovery of stolen cultural property.

The looting of national cultural treasures such as Korean Chosun Dynasty's Great-General's Helmet and Armor during times of forceful occupation is a distinct threat to the integrity and unity of national cultural heritages. That's why the restitution of cultural assets is properly categorized in the same way that the protection of cultural heritage is categorized in this paper.

1-1. RESOLUTION URGING DESIGNATION OF SEODAEMUN PRISON AS A UNESCO WORLD HERITAGE

On April 29, 2012, the National Assembly adopted a resolution requesting the Korean government to make best efforts to add the Seodaemun prison to the List of the UNESCO World Heritage.

The National Assembly urged the Korean government to inscribe the Seodaemun prison into its tentative list,[9] to prepare a nomination with the invitation of expert consultants and extraction and accumulation of academic materials in case that the UNESCO conducts the fieldwork and assessment, and to support appropriate local government for the nomination and grant funding not exceeding the amount allowed in the budget.

It called for strong support and cooperative alliance from the international community for the World Heritage List inscription of Seodaemun prison in order to protect the cultural heritage of universal value such as human rights and peace.

Seodaemun prison is a historic site embodying a piece of history of the East Asian colonialism in the early 20th century and the development of Korean democracy immediately after the emancipation from colonialism. The World Heritage List inscription of Seodaemun prison is an urgent matter for two reasons; firstly, the Republic of Korea has an obligation under the World Heritage Convention to embody the constitutional spirit and to promote universal value; and secondly, the Republic of Korea has a policy need to respond to and to actively restrain Japanese right-wing movements.

1-2. Resolution Condemning the Japanese Government's Attempt to Nominate Detention Facilities Where People of the Chosun Dynasty were Forcibly Held in Custody for the UNESCO World Cultural Heritage List

On May 12, 2015, the National Assembly adopted a resolution condemning the Japanese government's attempt to nominate 28 heritage sites related to the industrial revolution of the Meiji period, containing 11 detention facilities where people of the Chosun Dynasty (a predecessor state of the Republic of Korea) were forcibly held in confinement, for the UNESCO World Cultural Heritage List, and defining it as diplomatic provocation that would have a severely negative impact on peace and security of the Northeast Asia.

Noting that Japan submitted a tentative list which includes 7 facilities where it is recognized that 57,900 Korean people were held in custody, which exposed Korean people who ended their lives in pain to ridicule, by palliating a painful history with a mere word of industrial revolution, the National Assembly warned the Japanese government that it should reserve sincere repentance and a responsible attitude to the first priority.

The National Assembly urged the Korean government, respectful of the resolution of the National Assembly, to take a firm stance against the Japanese government's attempt to process the UNESCO World Cultural Heritage List inscription, to condemn the Japanese governmentand also to rectify the situation using all diplomatic means necessary in order to deter a recurrence of Japan's denying invasion.

1-3. Resolution Calling for the Return of Looted Korean Chosun Dynasty's Great-General's Helmet and Armor in the Tokyo National Museum

On December 10, 2013, the National Assembly adopted a resolution requesting the Korean government to ask the Japanese government to make an investigation in a good faith for determining if the Korean Chosun Dynasty's Great-General's Helmet and Armor was illicitly transferred during the period of the Japanese occupation, and also urging the Korean government, given that the item was turned out to be illicitly trafficked to Japan, to offer a request for repatriation based on the UNESCO Convention.

The Korean Chosun Dynasty's Great-General's Helmet and Armor that currently reside in the Tokyo National Museum, are presumed to have been looted by the Japanese businessman named Okura Takenoske during the period of the Japanese occupation. They are important artifacts closely related to the national identity and therefore their ownership ought not to be transferred out of the country.

A series of resolutions adopted by the United Nations (hereinafter referred to as the "UN") and the UNESCO (*e.g.*, the resolution 3187 passed by the UN General Assembly on December 18, 1973) and the UNESCO Convention have continually established a statement of the return of cultural objects to nations of origin (or to the nations whose territory includes the sites from which they were last removed). According to the statement, the Korean Chosun Dynasty's Great-General's Helmet and Armor should be surrendered to the Republic of Korea, or a source country.

2. ANTI-TERRORISM

2-1. RESOLUTION CONDEMNING A SERIES OF TERRORIST ATTACKS COMMITTED IN PARIS, FRANCE, ETC.

On November 30, 2015, the National Assembly adopted a resolution condemning a series of terrorist attacks committed by various terrorist groups such as the Islamic State of Iraq and the Levant (hereinafter referred to as "ISIL") around the world.

On November 13, 2015, 130 civilians were dead in a series of gun shooting and suicide bombing terrorist attacks. On October 10, 2015, ISIL staged a massive terrorist attack in Ankara, Turky, killing 102 civilians. On October 31, 2015, a bombing terror attack against an aircraft flying in the Egyptian territorial air space took away the lives of 224 people all aboard.

The UN Security Council passed the Resolution 2249 in November 20, 2015, which called upon UN member states to take all necessary measure to eradicate the next possible terror attack, and each state such as the United States, Russia, China, and the Germany made a statement to condemn acts of terrorism.

The National Assembly vehemently condemned inhumane acts of terrorism, expressed condolence to terrorism victims and the victims' families, supported the efforts to restore the losses as a result of terrorist attack by various governments including the French government and the measures taken by the international society such as the resolution adopted by the UN Security Council, and urged the international community to shape common reaction strategy and cooperative counter-terrorism system to eradicate a terrorist attack.

Also the National Assembly called for the Korean government to actively participate in the international community's efforts to counter terrorism, to provide safety measures necessary to secure the Korean people abroad and a Korean consulate or embassy, and to make best efforts in being prepared for the preventive measures to address the domestic security challenges related to terrorist attacks.

3. FREE TRADE AGREEMENT

3-1. Resolution Urging Subsequent Negotiations of the Korea-China FTA

On November 30, 2015, the National Assembly adopted a resolution noting that the Free Trade Agreement between the Government of the Republic of Korea and the Government of the People's Republic of China (hereinafter referred to as the "Korea-China FTA") would have a huge spillover effect on national interests and therefore that the Korea-China FTA would subsequently require the incorporation of supplement or adjustment in order to maximize national interests, and urging the Korea government to commence subsequent negotiation with China in good faith.

According to the resolution, the National Assembly would continuously monitor the implement of the Korea-China FTA and deliver new proposals to the Korean government when the implementation of the Korea-China FTA is not compatible with the national interests, and therefore it urged the Korean government to subsequently negotiate with China in good faith and to try to incorporate the recommendations made by it in the Korea-China FTA.

Specifically, the National Assembly urged the Korean government to promptly initiate the subsequent negotiation for high-level liberalization for trade in services and investment.[10] Also it called for the Korean government to revisit and resolve, in good faith with the Chinese government, the issue concerning illegal fisheries, environmental matters such as the negative impact of minute particles of dust, sanitary and phytosanitary measures, and the gradual elimination of non-tariff trade barriers, etc., which were countered with objections from the National Assembly during its consideration and approval procedures for the Korea-China FTA.

Notes

1. It is not necessary for the National Assembly to adopt a resolution in the domestic realm where legislative intent can be fully addressed through amendments and the law-making process.

2. Under Article 53 of the Charter, the Security Council may authorize enforcement actions taken under regional arrangements.

3. UN Treaty Collection, *Status,* https://treaties.un.org/pages/ViewDetails. aspx?src=TREATY&mtdsg_no=I-1&chapter=1&lang=en, accessed 12 April, 2016.

4. The Chosun Dynasty had governed the Korean Peninsula as one country for over 500 years from 1392 to 1910.

5. November 14, 1920, 823 *U.N.T.S.* 231.

6. UNESCO, *States Parties,* http://www.unesco.org/eri/la/convention. asp?KO=13039&language=E, accessed 12 April 2016.

7. November 23, 1972, 1037 *U.N.T.S.* 151.

8. UNESCO, *States Parties Ratification Status,* http://whc.unesco.org/en/statesparties/, accessed 14 April 2016.

9. Nominations to the World Heritage List are not considered unless the nominated property has previously been included on the State Party's tentative list of the properties it intends to consider for nomination in subsequent years.

10. *See* Annex 22-A (Guidelines for Subsequent Negotiation) of the Korea-China FTA. The subsequent negotiations are supposed to be conducted based on a negative list approach, while the present Korea-China FTA lays out the positive list. Both Parties are supposed to commence the subsequent negotiations as soon as possible, but not later than two years following the date of entry into force of the Korea-China FTA.

International Ship Registration Act
[Act No. 13264, March 27, 2015, Partial Amendment]

The Editorial Board
Korean Branch of the ILA

1. REASON FOR AMENDMENT
[Partial amendment]

1-1. REASON FOR AMENDMENT

The purpose of this amendment is to expand the scope of international ships to be registered in order to secure the stabilized marine transportation means and strengthen the competitiveness of shipping industry, and delete the obligations of ship owners, etc. to put up in a ship a written document specifying the contents of collective agreement regarding a labor contract, etc. for foreign seamen and establish the foundation on the punishment and recovery of compensation for loss unfairly received by the owner, etc. of international ships essential to the nation, and increase the penalty amount to secure the practical effectiveness of punishment if the owner, etc. of international ships essential to the nation fails to comply with a summon order issued by the Minister of Oceans and Fisheries at the time of national emergency.

1-2. MAJOR CONTENTS

A. A ship operated by an ocean-going transport enterpriser among foreign ships chartered by an ocean-going transport enterpriser or by a person who registered the ship chartering service in accordance with the Marine Transportation Act Article 33 on the condition of acquiring a ship's nationality of the Republic of Korea (hereinafter, 'Korea') is prescribed as a ship to be registered, which is to extend the scope of ships to be registered (Article 3).

B. The provision obligating the ship owners etc. to put up in a ship a written document specifying the contents of collective agreement regarding a labor contract, etc. for foreign seamen and imposing a fine for default is deleted (Article 7 and Article 13 Paragraph 2 currently in effect shall be deleted).

C. The foundation on the recovery of compensation for loss unfairly received by the owner, etc. of international ships essential to the nation and the punishment thereby is established (Article 8-2 and Article 12 Paragraph 2 shall be enacted newly).

2. DESCRIPTIONS

Act No. 13264
Partial amendment act of the International Ship Registration Act

Part of the International Ship Registration Act shall be amended as follows.

Article 3 Paragraph 1 subparagraph 4 shall be prescribed as follows.

    4. A ship operated by an ocean-going transport enterpriser as a ship to be registered among foreign ships chartered by an ocean-going transport enterpriser or by a person who registered the ship chartering service in accordance with the Marine Transportation Act Article 33 on the condition of acquiring a ship's nationality of Korea

In the first part of Article 4 Paragraph 1, "a ship owner or an ocean-going transport enterpriser" shall be changed to "a ship owner, an ocean-going transport enterpriser or a ship-chartering service provider."

Article 7 shall be deleted.

Article 8 *bis* shall be enacted newly.

Article 8 *bis* (Recovery of compensation for loss) ① If a person who received the compensation for loss falls within any of the following cases, the Minister of Oceans and Fisheries shall recover the compensation for loss in whole or in part in accordance with the latter part of Article 8 Paragraph 4.

1. If the person received the compensation for loss in a false or other unfair way
2. If the compensation for loss is paid wrongly

② If the person obliged to return the compensation for loss in accordance with Paragraph 1 fails to return within time limit, the Minister of Oceans and Fisheries may collect the amount in a way of disposition for failure to pay national taxes.

③ The procedure and time limit for the recovery of compensation for loss in accordance with Paragraph 1 and other necessary matters shall be prescribed by a Presidential Decree.

"20 million won" in Article 12 Paragraph 1 shall be changed to "50 million won," and Paragraph 2 in the same Article shall be changed to Paragraph 3, and Paragraph 2 shall be enacted newly as follows.

② A person who received the compensation for loss in accordance with the latter part of Article 8 Paragraph 4 in a false or other unfair way shall be sentenced to imprisonment for 3 years or less, or a penalty amount not exceeding 30 million won.

Article 13 Paragraph 2 shall be deleted, and "in Paragraph 1 and Paragraph 2" in the same Article Paragraph 3 shall be changed to "in Paragraph 1."

Additional Provision

Article 1 (Enforcement Date) This Act shall be put in force six months after the date of its promulgation.

Article 2 (Applicability concerning Recovery of Compensation for Loss) The amended provisions of Article 8 *bis* shall apply starting from the first person who receives the compensation for loss after this Act is put in force.

United Nations Peacekeeping Operations Participation Act
[Act No. 13123 February 3, 2015, Partial Amendment]

The Editorial Board
Korean Branch of the ILA

1. REASON FOR AMENDMENT
[Partial Amendment]

1-1. REASON FOR AMENDMENT

As the status of the Republic of Korea in the international community has raised up recently, the frequency for the Korean armed forces to participate in UN peacekeeping operations increased. In most cases, these peacekeeping operations are performed in dispute regions or hinterlands hard to get to due to inconvenient traffic conditions, so it is prerequisite to establish the measures for systematic material cooperation and safety security. However, there is an aspect of deficiency in the material cooperation and safety security as shown in the case that although the Korean armed forces dispatched recently to dispute regions suffers from the deficiency in supplies, the supplies are not provided smoothly. Therefore, it is required to make a legal supplementation for this.

Accordingly, this amendment act intends to establish the basis provisions for material cooperation in order to ensure the smooth performance of peacekeeping operation and safety of contingent, and strengthen the control by the National Assembly in the process of dispatch of the Korean armed forces, and make assurance doubly sure for the establishment of safety measures.

1-2. Major Contents

A. "Material cooperation" means the activities for transferring and acquiring of materials required for peacekeeping operations of the contingent and participant personnel and the tasks necessarily incidental thereto and the protection of safety of the contingent, etc. (Article 2 No. 5 newly enacted).

B. The measures necessary for the safety security of contingent, the protection of personal safety for soldiers belonging to the contingent and participant personnel, the prevention of accidents and the prevention of disasters are included in a motion of request for consent submitted by the government to the National Assembly (Article 6 Paragraph 2 No. 7 newly enacted).

C. For the extension of dispatch period, it is required to submit a motion of request for consent to the National Assembly within 2 months before the existing period of dispatch comes to an end (Article 8 No. 3 newly enacted).

D. If the dispatch comes to an end, the government is required to submit a report on operation results to the National Assembly within 3 months after the dispatch comes to an end, and if there is a request for participation from the UN, or if the contents of dispatch mission is to be changed, the government is required to report this to the National Assembly (Article11 Paragraph 2 & 3 newly enacted).

E. The government may offer the material cooperation for peacekeeping operation, if necessary (Article 17 newly enacted).

2. DESCRIPTIONS

Act No. 13123
Partial amendment act of the United Nations Peacekeeping Operations Participation Act

Part of the United Nations Peacekeeping Operations Participation Act shall be amended as follows.

Subparagraph 5 shall be enacted newly in Article 2 as follows.

5. The term "material cooperation" means supporting or being supported by foreign governments/armed forces with materials necessary for peacekeeping operations and tasks necessarily incidental thereto, ensuring safety of the contingent, protecting safety of soldiers belonging to the contingent and personnel participating in peacekeeping operations, prevention of accidents and prevention of disasters, or transferring or acquiring such materials to or from foreign governments/armed forces.

Article 6 Paragraph 2 subparagraph 7 shall be changed to subparagraph 8, and subparagraph 7 shall be enacted newly in the same Paragraph.

7. Measures necessary for the safety security of contingent, the protection of personal safety for soldiers belonging to the contingent and participant personnel, the prevention of accidents and the prevention of disasters

Paragraph 3 shall be enacted newly in Article 8 as follows.

③ The government shall submit a motion of request for consent to the National Assembly in accordance with Paragraph 1 within 2 months before the existing period of dispatch for contingent comes to an end. Unless there is a request for the extension of dispatch from the UN after the government decision on the end of dispatch in accordance with Article 9.

"Report on operation" in the title of Article 11 shall be changed to "report, etc." and the contents except for the title of the same Article shall be included in Paragraph 1, and Paragraphs 2 & 3 are enacted newly in the same Article as follows.

② The government shall prepare and submit a report on operation results to the National Assembly within 3 months after the dispatch comes to an end.

③ The government shall report any of the following cases to the National Assembly.

1. If there is a request for participation in the peacekeeping operation from the UN

2. If the government intends to change the contents of mission for contingent

Article 17 shall be enacted newly.

Article 17 (Material Cooperation) ① The government may perform the material cooperation within the extent acknowledged necessary for the peacekeeping operation.

② The specific scale, procedure and other matters necessary for material cooperation shall be prescribed by a Presidential Decree.

Additional Provision

Article 1 (Enforcement Date) This Act shall be put in force six months after the date of its promulgation.

Article 2 (Applicability concerning the Consent of the National Assembly for the Dispatch of Korean Armed Forces) The amended provisions of Article 6 Paragraph 2 shall apply starting from the first submission of a motion of request for consent on dispatch (including a motion of request for consent on dispatch extension) after this Act is put in force.

TREATIES/AGREEMENTS CONCLUDED BY THE REPUBLIC OF KOREA

Treaties/Agreements
Concluded by the Republic of Korea*

1. MULTILATERAL

1-1. Enviroment

Amendments to Annexes A of the Stockholm Convention on Persistent Organic Pollutants
(Adopted May 10, 2013), (Entered into force November 27, 2015)**

Amendments to Annexes A of the Stockholm Convention on Persistent Organic Pollutants
(Adopted April 29, 2011), (Entered into force October 27, 2015)

1-2. Trade/Commerce/Industry

Amendment to the Product Specific Rules Set Out in Appendix 2 of Annex 3 of the Agreement on Trade in Goods under the Framework Agreement on Comprehensive Economic Cooperation among the Governments of the Republic of Korea and the Member Countries of the Association of Southeast Asian Nations
(Adopted November 18, 2014), (Entered into force May 1, 2015)

1-3. Labour

Maritime Labour Convention
(Adopted February 23, 2006), (Entered into force January 9, 2015)

---

* Treaties are found at the homepage of Ministry of Foreign Affairs, Republic of Korea, http://www.mofa.go.kr/trade/treatylaw/treatyinformation/bilateral/index.jsp?mofat=001&menu=m_30_50_40.

** Entered into force for the Republic of Korea

1-4. Nuclear Energy

Agreement Extending the Framework Agreement for International Collaboration on Research and Development of Generation IV Nuclear Energy Systems
(Adopted February 26, 2015), (Entered into force February 26, 2015)

1-5. Law Of The Sea/Fishery

Convention on the Conservation and Management of High Seas Fisheries Resources in the North Pacific Ocean
(Adopted February 24, 2012), (Entered into force July 19, 2015)

1-6. International Crime(Terrorism)

Protocol to Prevent, Suppress and Punish Trafficking in Persons, Especially Women and Children, supplementing the United Nations Convention against Transnational Organized Crime
(Adopted November 15, 2000), (Entered into force December 5, 2015)

Protocol against the Illicit Manufacturing of and Trafficking in Firearms, Their Parts and Components and Ammunition, supplementing the United Nations Convention against Transnational Organized Crime
(Adopted May 31, 2001), (Entered into force December 5, 2015)

Protocol against the Smuggling of Migrants by Land, Sea and Air, supplementing the United Nations Convention against Transnational Organized Crime
(Adopted November 15, 2000), (Entered into force December 5, 2015)

United Nations Convention against Transnational Organized Crime
(Adopted November 15, 2000), (Entered into force December 5, 2015)

1-7. Financial Agency

Articles of Agreement of the Asian Infrastructure Investment Bank
(Adopted May 22, 2015), (Entered into force December 25, 2015)

2. BILATERAL

2-1. FREE TRADE AGREEMENT

Free Trede Agreement between the Republic of Korea and Canada
(Signed September 22, 2014), (Entered into force January 1, 2015)

Free Trade Agreement between the Republic of Korea, of the One Part, and
the European Union and Its Member States, of the Other Part
(Signed October 6, 2010), (Entered into force December 31, 2015)

Implementing Arrangement for Economic Cooperation Pursuant to Chapter 13
(Economic Cooperation) of the Free Trade Agreement between the Government of
the Republic of Korea and The Government of the Socialist Republic of Vietnam
(Signed May 5, 2015), (Entered into force December 20, 2015)

Free Trade Agreement between the Government of the Republic of Korea and
the Government of the People's Republic of China
(Signed June 1, 2015), (Entered into force December 20, 2015)

Arrangement between the Government of the Republic of Korea and the Government
of New Zealand on Agriculture, Forestry and Fisheries
(Signed March 23, 2015), (Entered into force December 20, 2015)

Free Trade Agreement between the Government of the Republic of Korea and
the Government of the Socialist Republic of Viet Nam
(Signed May 5, 2015), (Entered into force December 20, 2015)

Free Trade Agreement between the Republic of Korea and the New Zealand
(Signed March 23, 2015), (Entered into force December 20, 2015)

2-2. MUTUAL RECOGNITION AND EXCHANGE OF DRIVING LICENSES

Agreement between the Government of the Republic of Korea and the Government
of the Republic of Lithuania on the Mutual Recognition and Exchange of Driving
Licences
(Signed October 14, 2014), (Entered into force January 22, 2015)

Agreement between the Government of the Republic of Korea and the Government
of Hungary on the Mutual Recognition and Exchange of Driving Licences
(Signed November 28, 2014), (Entered into force May 16, 2015)

Agreement between the Government of the Republic of Korea and the Government
of the Republic of Guatemala on the Mutual Recognition and Exchange of Driver's
Licenses
(Signed May 14, 2015), (Entered into force September 16, 2015)

Agreement between the Government of the Republic of Korea and the Government
of the Republic of Uzbekistan on the Mutual Recognition and Exchange of Driver's
Licenses
(Signed May 28, 2015), (Entered into force December 24, 2015)

2-3. COOPERATION FUND

Framework Arrangement between the Government of the Republic of Korea and
the Government of the United Republic of Tanzania Concerning Loans From the
Economic Development Cooperation Fund for the Years 2014 through 2016
(Signed March 25, 2015), (Entered into force March 25, 2015)

Arrangement between the Government of the Republic of Korea and the Government
of the Republic of Nicaragua Concerning a Loan from the Economic Development
Cooperation Fund for Juigalpa Wastewater Treatment Project
(Signed March 28, 2015), (Entered into force March 28, 2015)

Arrangement between the Government of the Republic of Korea and the Government
of the Republic of Madagascar Concerning a Loan from the Economic Development
Cooperation Fund for the Project for the Establishment of a National Disaster
Management Center in Madagascar
(Signed July 8, 2014), (Entered into force July 8, 2015)

Framework Arrangement between the Government of the Republic of Korea and
the Government of the Islamic Republic of Pakistan Concerning Loans from the
Economic Development Cooperation Fund for the Years 2015 through 2017
(Signed October 2, 2015), (Entered into force October 2, 2015)

Arrangement between the Government of the Republic of Korea and the Government of the Hashemite Kingdom of Jordan Concerning a Supplementary Loan from the Economic Development Cooperation Fund for the Jordan Research & Training Reactor Construction Project
(Signed October 28, 2015), (Entered into force October 28, 2015)

Arrangement between the Government of the Republic of Korea and the Government of the Republic of Mozambique Concerning a Loan from the Economic Development Cooperation Fund for the Firefighting Equipment Supply Project
(Signed November 5, 2015), (Entered into force November 5, 2015)

Framework Arrangement between the Government of the Republic of Korea and the Government of the People's Republic of Bangladesh Concerning Loans from the Economic Development Cooperation Fund for the Years 2015 through 2017
(Signed November 19, 2015), (Entered into force November 19, 2015)

Framework Arrangement between the Government of the Republic of Korea and the Government of the Republic of Ghana Concerning Loans from the Economic Development Cooperation Fund for the Years 2014 through 2016
(Signed December 10, 2015), (Entered into force December 10, 2015)

Framework Arrangement between the Government of the Republic of Korea and the Government of the Lao People's Democratic Republic Concerning Loans from the Economic Development Cooperation Fund for the Years 2016 through 2019
(Signed December 14, 2015), (Entered into force December 14, 2015)

Arrangement between the Government of the Republic of Korea and the Government of the Hashemite Kingdom of Jordan Concerning a Supplementary Loan from the Economic Development Cooperation Fund for the Naur Wastewater Treatment Project
(Signed December 14, 2015), (Entered into force December 14, 2015)

Exchange of Notes between the Government of the Republic of Korea and the Government of Mongolia
(Signed December 16, 2015), (Entered into force December 16, 2015)

2-4. Grant Aid Cooperation Project

Exchange of Notes between the Government of the Republic of Korea and the Government of the Republic of Lebanon
(Signed January 28, 2015), (Entered into force January 28, 2015)

Framework Agreement for Grant Aid between the Government of the Republic of Korea and the Government of Nepal
(Signed October 30, 2014), (Entered into force February 4, 2015)

Framework Arrangement on Grant Aid for the Year 2014 between the Government of the Republic of Korea and the Government of the Kingdom of Morocco
(Signed March 18, 2015), (Entered into force March 18, 2015)

Framework Arrangement on Grant Aid To Be Implemented for the Years 2014 through 2015 between the Government of the Republic of Korea and the Government of the Lao People's Democratic Republic
(Signed July 21, 2015), (Entered into force July 21, 2015)

Framework Arrangement on Grant Aid for the Year 2015 between the Government of the Republic of Korea and the Government of the Republic of Cameroon
(Signed August 18, 2015), (Entered into force August 18, 2015)

Framework Agreement for Grant Aid between the Government of the Republic of Korea and the Government of the Republic of Uzbekistan
(Signed June 17, 2014), (Entered into force September 18, 2015)

Exchange of Notes between the Government of the Republic of Korea and the Government of the Arab Republic of Egypt for the execution of the Feasibility Study of the Integrated Technical Education Cluster in Egypt
(Signed July 26, 2015), (Entered into force October 15, 2015)

2-5. Air Transport

Exchange of Notes for the Amendment to the Agreement between the Government of the Republic of Korea and the Government of the United Kingdom for Air Services
(Signed December 9, 2014), (Entered into force February 4, 2015)

Agreement between the Government of the Republic of Korea and the Government of Canada on Air Transport
(Signed September 22, 2015), (Entered into force February 25, 2015)

Agreement between the Government of the Republic of Korea and the Government of the Hashemite Kingdom of Jordan for Air Services between and beyond Their Respective Territories
(Signed Octover 14, 2015), (Entered into force March 5, 2015)

Air Services Agreement between the Government of the Republic of Korea and the Government of Hungary
(Signed November 28, 2014), (Entered into force May 16, 2015)

Agreement between the Government of the Republic of Korea and the Government of the Republic of Tajikistan for Air Services
(Signed April 12, 2015), (Entered into force August 27, 2015)

Agreement between the Government of the Republic of Korea and the Government of the Republic of Ecuador for Air Services between and beyond Their Respective Territories
(Signed December 17, 2012), (Entered into force November 23, 2015)

2-6. ENVIROMENT / RESOURCES

Agreement for Cooperation on Climate Change between the Government of the Republic of Korea and the Government of the People's Republic of China
(Signed January 29, 2015), (Entered into force February 28, 2015)

Exchange of Notes to Review and Amend the Annex to the Agreement between the Government of the Republic of Korea and the Government of the Australia on the Protection of Migratory Birds
(Signed February 16, 2015/September 3, 2015), (Entered into force December 3, 2015)

2-7. EDUCATION / CULTURE

Agreement between the Government of the Republic of Korea and the Government of the Russian Federation on the Establishment and Operation of Cultural Centres

(Signed November 13, 2013), (Entered into force March 16, 2015)

Arrangement on Cooperation in the Fields of Education and Culture between the Government of the Republic of Korea and the Government of the Republic of Bulgaria for the Years 2015-2018
(Signed May 14, 2015), (Entered into force August 25, 2015)

2-8. ECONOMY / SCIENCE / TECHNOLOGY

Agreement on Economic and Technical Cooperation between the Government of the Republic of Korea and the Government of the Republic of Zambia
(Signed May 8, 1992), (Entered into force April 2, 2015)

Agreement between the Government of the Republic of Korea and the Government of Turkmenistan on Scientific and Technological Cooperation
(Signed April 13, 2015), (Entered into force June 30, 2015)

Agreement between the Government of the Republic of Korea and the Council of Ministers of the Republic of Albania on Economic Cooperation
(Signed September 29, 2015), (Entered into force December 22, 2015)

2-9. INTERNATIONAL ORGANIZATION

Supplementing Agreement between the Government of the Republic of Korea and the United Nations Development Program Regarding the Expanded Scope of the Agreement between the Government of the Republic of Korea and United Nations Development Programme relating to the Establishment of the UNDP Seoul Policy Center for Global Development Partnerships
(Signed October 31, 2014), (Entered into force April 10, 2015)

Partnership Framework Agreement between the Government of the Republic of Korea and the World Food Programme
(Signed February 11, 2015), (Entered into force August 11, 2015)

Agreement on the Extension and Amendment of the Agreement between the Government of the Republic of Korea and the United Nations Regarding the Establishment of the UNISDR Office in Incheon for Northeast Asia and the Global Education and Training Institute for Disaster Risk Reduction

(Signed November 13, 2015), (Entered into force November 13, 2015)

Agreement between the Government of the Republic of Korea and the United Nations Educational, Scientific and Cultural Organization (UNESCO) regarding the International Centre of Martial Arts for Youth Development and Engagement Under the Auspices of UNESCO (Category 2)
(Signed December 1, 2015), (Entered into force December 1, 2015)

2-10. VISA

Agreement between the Government of the Republic of Korea and the Government of the Sultanate of Oman on the Mutual Waiver of VISA Requirements for Holders of Diplomatic, Official, Special and Service Passports
(Signed December 24, 2014), (Entered into force April 11, 2015)

Agreement between the Government of the Republic of Korea and the Government of the State of Kuwait on the Mutual Waiver of VISA Requirements for Holders of Diplomatic and Official/Special Passports
(Signed March 2, 2015), (Entered into force June 24, 2015)

Agreement between the Government of the Republic of Korea and the Government of the Republic of Cape Verde on the Mutual Waiver of VISA Requirements for Holders of Diplomatic, Official and Service Passports
(Signed May 15, 2015), (Entered into force October 14, 2015)

2-11. CONSULAR RELATION

Consular Agreement between the Republic of Korea and the People's Republic of China
(Signed July 3, 2014), (Entered into force April 12, 2015)

2-12. EXTRADITION

Treaty between the Government of the Republic of Korea and the Government of Malaysia on Extradition
(Signed January 17, 2013), (Entered into force April 15, 2015)

2-13. SOCIAL SECURITY

Agreement on Social Security between the Republic of Korea and the Swiss Confederation
(Signed January 20, 2014), (Entered into force June 1, 2015)

Agreement on Social Security between the Government of the Republic of Korea and
the Government of the Kingdom of Sweden
(Signed September 9, 2013), (Entered into force June 1, 2015)

Agreement on Social Security between the Government of the Republic of Korea and
the Government of the Republic of Turkey
(Signed August 1, 2012), (Entered into force June 1, 2015)

Agreement on Social Security between the Government of the Republic of Korea and
the Government of the Federative Republic of Brazil
(Signed Novemebr 22, 2012), (Entered into force November 1, 2015)

2-14. TAX

Agreement between the Government of the Republic of Korea and the Government
of Bermuda on the Exchange of Information relating to Tax Matters
(Signed January 23, 2012), (Entered into force February 13, 2015)

Exchange of Notes between the Government of the Republic of Korea and the Office
of the High Commissioner for Human Rights Permitting the Operation of the Field-
Based Structure of the Office of the High Commissioner for Human Rights in the
Republic of Korea
(Signed May 22, 2015), (Entered into force May 22, 2015)

Protocol Amending the Convention between the Republic of Korea and the Kingdom
of Belgium for the Avoidance of Double Taxation and the Prevention of Fiscal Evasion
with Respect to Taxes on Income, Signed at Brussels on 29 August 1977, as Amended
by the Supplementary Convention Signed at Brussels on 20 April 1994
(Signed March 8, 2010), (Entered into force December 1, 2015)

Convention between the Republic of Korea and the Republic of Gabon for the
Avoidance of Double Taxation and the Prevention of Fiscal Evasion with respect to
Taxes on Income

(Signed October 25, 2010), (Entered into force December 2, 2015)

2-15. BROADCASTING / COMMUNICATION

Agreement between the Government of the Republic of Korea and the Government of the Republic of India on Cooperation in Audio-Visual Co-Production
(Signed May 18, 2015), (Entered into force September 16, 2015)

2-16. TRANSFER OF SENTENCED PERSONS

Treaty between the Government of the Republic of Korea and the Government of the State of Kuwait for the Transfer of Sentenced Persons
(Signed March 16, 2011), (Entered into force October 22, 2015)

2-17. CUSTOMS

Agreement between the Government of the Republic of Korea and the Government of the United Arab Emirates on Cooperation and Mutual Assistance in Customs Matters
(Signed March 5, 2015), (Entered into force December 16, 2015)

2-18. MILITARY / SECURITY

Agreement between the Government of the Republic of Korea and the Government of Romania on the Protection of Classified Military Information
(Signed March 26, 2015), (Entered into force December 10, 2015)

2-19. NUCLEAR ENERGY

Agreement for Cooperation between the Government of the Republic of Korea and the Government of the United States of America Concerning Peaceful Uses of Nuclear Energy
(Signed June 15, 2015), (Entered into force November 25, 2015)

INDEX

TABLE OF TREATIES AND OTHER INSTRUMENTS

AUTHOR GUIDELINES AND STYLE SHEET

I. SUBMISSION

Manuscripts should be submitted in Microsoft Word and electronically sent to ilakoreanbranch@gmail.com.

II. GENERAL TERMS AND PEER-REVIEW SYSTEM OF PUBLICATION

All manuscripts are subject to initial evaluation by the KYIL Editorial Board and subsequently sent out to independent reviewers for a peer review. The Editorial Board accepts manuscripts on a rolling basis and will consider requests for an expedited review in appropriate cases.

III. FORMATING

1. ABSTRACT

Please include an abstract (no more than 150 words) at the beginning of an article.

2. TEXT

Main Text: Times New Roman, font size 12, 1.5 spacing
Endnotes: Times New Roman, font size 10, single spacing

3. Citing Reference

The KYIL requires endnotes with subsequent numbering; the initial endnote should be indicated with '*,' if it is necessary to provide explanatory information about the manuscript.

Please include a reference list for all works that are cited at the end of the manuscript.

IV. NOTES

1. Books

P. Malanczuk, *Akehurst's Modern Introduction to International Law*, 7th ed. (New York: Eoutledge, 1997), p. 1.

2. Articles

Chao Wang, *China's Preferential Trade Remedy Approaches: A New Haven School Perspective*, Vol.21 No.1, Asia Pacific Law Review, (2013), p. 103.

3. Articles in collections

J. Paulsson & Z. Douglas, *Indirect Expropriation in Investment Treaty Arbitrations, in* Arbitrating Foreign Investment Disputes 148 (N. Horn & S. Kroll eds., Kluwer Law International, 2004).

4. Articles in newspaper

YI Whan-Woo, *Korea, New Zealand embrace free trade pact*, Korea Times, November 14, 2014.

5. UNPUBLISHED MATERIALS

PARK Jung-Won, *Minority Rights Constraints on a State's Power to Regulate Citizenship under International Law*, Ph.D thesis (2006), on file with author.

6. WORKING PAPERS AND REPORTS

OECD, *'Indirect Expropriation' and the 'Right to Regulate' in International Investment Law*, OECD Working Paper, 2014/09.

7. INTERNET SOURCES

C. Schreuer, *The Concept of Expropriation under the ETC and Other Investment Protection Treaties* (2005), http://www.univie,ac,at/intlaw/pdf/csunpuybl paper_3pdf. [Accessed on September 22, 2015]

V. GUIDELINE FOR AUTHORS

1. ARTICLE

Manuscripts must be in the form of a regular paper including endnotes and references. The length for an article should not exceed 10,000 words in English excluding notes and/or a full length should be within 15 pages in A4- sized paper. (Letter Size: 8.5 x 11 inch).

2. SPECIAL REPORT

Manuscripts for Special Report must be in the form of a descriptive report which covers the International law issues related to Korea in the past 5 years. Special Report must include author's comments with less than 10 endnotes and 5 references. The length for an special report should be no more than 5,000 words or within 7 pages in A4-sized paper. (Letter Size, 8.5 x 11 inch).

3. RECENT DEVELOPMENT

Manuscripts must cover the trends in international law related to Korea in the preceding year. Recent Development must be in the form of a short report, including less than 5 endnotes. The length for Recent Development should be no more than 2,000 words or within 4 pages in A4-sized paper. (Letter Size: 8.5 x 11 inch).